The Reformation of War

J.F C Fuller

Copyright © BiblioLife, LLC

This book represents a historical reproduction of a work originally published before 1923 that is part of a unique project which provides opportunities for readers, educators and researchers by bringing hard-to-find original publications back into print at reasonable prices. Because this and other works are culturally important, we have made them available as part of our commitment to protecting, preserving and promoting the world's literature. These books are in the "public domain" and were digitized and made available in cooperation with libraries, archives, and open source initiatives around the world dedicated to this important mission.

We believe that when we undertake the difficult task of re-creating these works as attractive, readable and affordable books, we further the goal of sharing these works with a global audience, and preserving a vanishing wealth of human knowledge.

Many historical books were originally published in small fonts, which can make them very difficult to read. Accordingly, in order to improve the reading experience of these books, we have created "enlarged print" versions of our books. Because of font size variation in the original books, some of these may not technically qualify as "large print" books, as that term is generally defined; however, we believe these versions provide an overall improved reading experience for many.

THE REFORMATION OF WAR.

By Col. J. F. C. Fuller, D.S.O.

Author of "Tanks in the Great War," "Training Soldiers for War," etc.

The Spirit of Progress. "Halt! Who goes there?"
The Spirit of Mankind. "War!"
The Spirit of Progress. "Pass, War, all's well!"

LONDON: HUTCHINSON & CO.
PATERNOSTER ROW, E.C. :: 1923

DEDICATE THIS BOOK
TO THE
Unknown Warrior
IN WHOSE BROKEN BODY
LIVES THE MEMORY OF A MILLION BRITISH DEAD
WHO FEAR NOT FORGETFULNESS
IF THROUGH THEIR SACRIFICE
WAR MAY BE ENNOBLED AND REFORMED

PREFACE

> " Big Mars seems bankrupt in their beggar'd host,
> And faintly through a rusty beaver peeps:
> The horsemen sit like fixed candlesticks,
> With torch-staves in their hand . . ."
> King Henry V., IV. ii. 43.

> " O! now doth Death line his dead chaps with steel;
> The swords of soldiers are his teeth, his fangs;
> And now he feasts, mousing the flesh of man."
> King John, II. 1. 351.

ALAS! that I should have been born in the last quarter of the nineteenth century, for, had this event taken place a hundred years earlier, I should have been spared many troubles, including the writing of this book. In those days warfare was so simple, and, by education, I ought to be a follower of Major Gahagan—seeing that I am an admirer of his " tremendous adventures."

> " On they came; my guns and men were ready for them. You will ask how my pieces were loaded? I answer, that though my garrison were without food, I knew my duty as an officer, and *had put the two Dutch cheeses into the two guns, and had crammed the contents of a bottle of olives into each swivel*
>
> " They advanced—whish went one of the Dutch cheeses, bang went the other! Alas, they did little execution. In their first contact with an opposing body, they certainly floored it, but they became at once like so much Welsh rabbit, and did no execution beyond the man whom they struck down.
>
> "'Hogree, pogree, wongree-fum! (praise to Allah and the forty-nine Imaums!) shouted out the ferocious Loll Mahommed when he saw the failure of my shot. ' Onward, sons of the Prophet! The infidel has no more ammunition. A hundred thousand lakhs of rupees to the man who brings me Gahagan's head!'
>
> " I gave one thought to my blessed, my beautiful Belinda, and then, stepping into the front, took down one of the swivels. A

Preface

shower of matchlock balls came whizzing round my head. I did not heed them

"I took the swivel and aimed coolly. Loll Mahommed, his palanquin and his men, were now not above two hundred yards from the fort Loll was straight before me, gesticulating and shouting to his men I fired—bang ! ! !

"I aimed so true that *one hundred and seventeen best Spanish olives were lodged in a lump in the face of the unhappy Loll Mahommed* The wretch, uttering a yell the most hideous and unearthly I ever heard, fell back dead. The frightened bearers flung down the palanquin and ran. The whole host ran as one man, their screams might be heard for leagues. '*Tomasha, tomasha,*' they cried, 'it is enchantment' Away they fled, and the victory a third time was ours Soon as the fight was done, I flew back to my Belinda . ."

In his heart of hearts, who would not be a traditional soldier, a Gahagan with his fair Belinda ? And yet, through some trick in my nature, I intend to inquire into the probabilities of future warfare in place of examining the tactics of the Ahmednuggar Irregulars. I admit it is a surprising thing to do, seeing that I have successfully passed all my military examinations and some even with distinction ; but the ways of man are inscrutable, so I will say no more

I intend inquiring into the nature of future warfare, not because I love war or hate war, but because I believe that war is of the inevitable, and that the greatest of all heresies and delusions concerning it is to suppose that the Great War of 1914-1918 is the last of all wars. That it may be the last of its kind I full-heartedly agree to, so much so that I believe the nature of the next great war will be totally different from the last ; so different that, even if great nations go to war in 1950, the recent war will appear to those not far distant fighters as a struggle between barbaric hordes, a saurian contest, not mediæval but primæval, archaic, a turmoil, which in the history of the evolution of warfare is more distant from that day than the Marne was from Marathon.

If, after meditating on the views set forth in this book, the reader believes that I am right, even if only partially so, then this book is worth supporting ; if he believes, however, that I am

Preface

wrong, even if totally so, then this book is worth refuting ; for war is a serious problem, and the next war the most serious of all problems : this at least the last war should have taught us. To meditate is not only to think and think again, but to think rightly, logically according to facts, to discover the soul of thought ; and this can never be done if our minds are shackled by our sentiments or stamped by our emotions. To anathematize war is to gibber like a fool, and to declare it to be unreasonable, is to twaddle like a pedant. Love is unreasonable and so is madness. All things divine and diabolical are unreasonable, and mixed with clay from out these two unreasoning opposites emerges man, a vibrating mass of unreasoning instincts which will out, and demoniacally so when they are imprisoned. As well attempt to damp down Erebus with a duster as to attempt to control the primitive instincts of man by oath, syllogism, or agreement.

To some, the one unforgivable sin in man is that he is human —a thinking beast, a discontented animal ; these believe in original sin. I do not ; I believe in original thought and spew out that nauseous mental drug called imitation. I may be a heretic, a military Luther, yet nevertheless I try to accept man as God made him, and not as Mr. Smith would like him to be. Tell me, studious reader, which of us two blasphemes, Smith or I ?

Frankly I am critical, not only because I refuse to be led by a halter, but because, in my heart, I have a very warm place for Mr. Smith, who, as Private, Sergeant, Subaltern and General, has been for many years my friend and companion. I have watched him in two long wars struggling against odds, and I have learnt to appreciate his virtues, and his failings, and his indomitable courage. He is a man who possesses such natural pride of birth that, through sheer contempt for others, he refuses to learn or to be defeated. He divides humanity into two classes Englishmen and niggers, and of the second class some happen to be black and others white. He only condescends to differentiate between these sub-classes by calling the latter dagoes. To him, all white folk, outside his own little islands, are such. From these he has nothing to learn, yet he is tolerant, tolerant as he would be to his

Preface

dog ; he has, in fact, raised the vice of contempt to a high virtue and on this virtue is the British Empire founded.

Having nothing to learn, through sheer power of domination, he has become the prince of rulers, and through sheer refusal to be defeated by niggers the master of improvisation. He is always there, for the sun never sets on his Empire, but he is never ready. For readiness would presuppose fear, and what has he, as an Englishman, to be afraid of ? He is an incarnation of King Henry V , and every battle he fights is an Agincourt.

Surely, then, it is but folly to disturb his confidence ? It would be so if the world were what it was, but the world has changed and with it has changed the art of war. The jar of science has been fished up from out the deep, and its seal has been broken, and no English contempt for others will coax the Jinn back into his bottle. We must face facts Courage is still a great virtue, but the power of knowledge is equally great, and because the Englishman lacks this power, through his sheer contempt to learn, and because I, as an Englishman, love my countrymen, therefore I intend to flog Mr. Smith with criticism. Whether I shall succeed in waking him from his self-pride I cannot tell, for his skin is thick, and he sleeps soundly ; but if I can persuade him to turn over in his bed and for a moment look the other way—future-wards, then I shall not be disappointed. He will accuse me of producing a nightmare, and then, through sheer contempt for such things, he will either fall to sleep again, or perhaps he will rise from his couch.

For many years now have I attempted to wake him, and I have written much on war, so much that this book is but a compilation of past writings brought up to date.* Much that I have written I have already scrapped, and much that I write now I shall scrap if I write more, for knowledge is an ever changing power. The man who never changes his mind, has mineralized his intellect. He is but a walking stone ; he may be shale or Aberdeen granite, it matters not, for dynamite will shatter him,

---

* In the Appendix will be found a list of these I have not quoted them in the text as in most cases the wording has been changed

Preface

and it is with dynamite I intend to work. Yet this does not prohibit the discovery of a still more powerful explosive, and, if any of my readers can present me with one, I will accept it, for knowledge to be strong, must be free. To shackle it is, in my humble opinion, to sin against God, for His highest gift to us is intellect.

In this book I do not intend to enter deeply into the biology of war, but in Chapter I. I will briefly examine this subject, for there is such a condition as this, and so little is it understood that even to-day, in this age of scientific thought, there are still many among us who fondly delude themselves into believing that disarmament and words can abolish war. " Take away our weapons and we still have our fists, our teeth and our nails," shriek human instincts; " and as for words. . . ." the answer is all but lost in a derisive laugh, " we will force you to eat them and then we will eat you. . . . Think you that we can be measured by foot rule and square ? Out fool, our road is freedom; the direction of our energy you may control, but the onrush of our flight you will never stay."

To those who thus believe, this book may assist them to prepare for war and so lessen, if only for themselves, its catastrophies. To those who do not, then may this book assist them to attack war. I write for both, for those whom I believe to be wise and for those whom I believe to be foolish, for my object is to induce all conditions of men not only to talk of war but to think of war. Thus and thus only shall we learn how to understand war, especially the nature of the next war ; thus shall we learn how to enhance the virtues of war and how to lessen its vices, and, above all, how to fend war off until mankind has recovered from the recent turmoil, and not only recovered but has replaced the civilization then shattered by a nobler human edifice. Without war there would be no driving out of the money-lenders from the temple of human existence. Without it, customs, interests and prejudices would rot and putrefy, and mankind would be slowly asphyxiated by the stench of his own corruption. The Great War, economically, may have been a disaster, yet the sufferings caused by it were the birth-pangs of a new dispensation. Every gain demands a sacrifice, not even a child can be born into this world without the agony of one poor soul, the least offending of all—its mother.

That the ideas set forth in this book will be generally accepted by soldiers I more than doubt. As a soldier I am a heretic. I am a heretic because I have torn up the Old Testament of War and in this book have attempted to replace it by the first pages of a new one. Novelty is a mental laxative which is not tolerated by the military monk. Reader, if you doubt me, then turn to history. Every military invention of note has either been opposed or attributed to the Devil—gunpowder, cannon, naval armour, rams, rifles, breech-loading guns, gas and tanks have all been opposed by the military hierarchy of their day. But they *are* devilish say you, then I answer: " Fool, hold your tongue," for you who are not soldiers are mentally just as constipated. Was it not a civilian who brought a bill before the British Parliament " to prevent the effeminacy of men riding in coaches " at the time when coaches were struggling into existence, and yet others who decried the steamship, locomotive and motor-car. Nearly every great discovery has been opposed—chloroform, vaccination, the law of evolution, salvarsan, auto-suggestion, and so might be added example to example. Yet opposition has had its value, it has forced the new idea to struggle for its existence, and in this struggle has the new idea grown strong, and as it gains strength so does the old idea compromise, knuckle under and, eventually, disappear. Every pioneer is somewhat of a martyr, and every martyr somewhat of a firebrand who kills with ridicule as well as with reason.

I have not written this book for military monks, but for civilians, who pay for their alchemy and mysteries. In war there is nothing mysterious, for it is the most common-sense of all the sciences, and this I will show in Chapter II. If it possess a mystery, then that mystery is unprogressiveness, for it is a mystery that, in a profession which may, at any moment, demand the risk of danger and death, men are to be found willing to base

Preface

their work on the campaigns of Waterloo and Sedan when the only possible war which confronts them is the next one.

In Chapter III. I will examine the ethical side of war, for without a full understanding of this side can there be no debrutalization of the art. In Chapter IV. I will show what price the nations of Europe paid for copying the past, and then in Chapter V. how out of folly blossomed wisdom ; how it was discovered that science was the backbone of victory, science which since 1870 had advanced like a giant in seven-league boots while soldiers were forming fours and practising the goose-step.

In Chapters VI., VII., VIII. and IX., I will deal with future warfare from a general standpoint, setting before the reader a series of possible pictures rather than a mass of probable detail, so that, from the general panorama, he may carry away with him an idea of the tendencies of war.

I will show that gas can be made the most humane of weapons ; that the aeroplane will create a new line of attack ; that the tank is as superior to present-day troops as modern battleships are to galleys and galleons. I will examine the purposes of fleets and speculate on their strategy and tactics in the future, and show that though the principles of war do not change, their correct application is subject to circumstances.

In writing this book it was first my intention only to deal with the question of future great wars, but, in thinking this matter over, I have considered it as well to add a chapter, Chapter X., on small wars and internal security, as these problems are those which immediately concern us in our great problem of Imperial defence. As this question is one which is ever latent and from which we are never free, I have dealt more with present than with future possibilities, but have again attempted to avoid much detail.

In the remaining three Chapters—XI , XII. and XIII , I have sketched the groundwork of reformation. Taking the body of man as my prototype, I have outlined the machinery of reorganization. In Chapter XI. I have attempted to create a military brain, an organ which can control the entire defence forces of the nation. In Chapter XII. I have attempted to fashion a mould in which a new army can be cast, and in Chapter XIII. I have attempted to show that beyond the mind and body of man stands society, and so also with the defence forces, beyond these lies the nation, and that between these two must there be harmony; consequently without national reform can there be no true military reform, for the reform of both is interdependent.

Now that it is written and I can look back on this book, it appears to me that I have not so much set out to discover a new world as to uncover an old one: " The thing that hath been, it is that which shall be; and that which is done is that which shall be done: and there is no new thing under the sun."

For the student, let him visit the London Museum and on the top storey he will find in a small room a model of St. James's as it was in 1814. On it he will see rising out of the Green Park a temple. It is called the "Temple of Concord," and on the wall he will see a picture of this "pious hope" which resembles a painted wedding cake surrounded by smoke and fire, and from the inscription on this picture the student will learn that, at midnight of August 1, 1814, London witnessed the celebration of the Great Peace.

The booming of those maroons and the star showers of those rockets have long passed into oblivion, and so has that Temple of Concord. A hundred years later, almost to the minute, Europe was once again flaming with war. What a lesson! Indeed " there is no new thing under the sun."

In this book I shall omit much which, were books less expensive to produce, I should have included. Some points I shall repeat again and again, and with a purpose—to drive them home. Traditionalism is the dragon I am out to slay, that servile monster which breathes forth wars of bloodshed and destruction. I will show that the true purpose of war is to create and not to destroy, and that, still to-day, all armies and fleets are spell-bound by the past, and that the nations

Preface

which support them and pay vast sums for their maintenance, are paying for either cut-throats or for phantoms.

Human intuition is nearly always right, but human tuition is nearly always wrong, and in this book I will examine the meaning of these two forces, how instinct is true and how learning is so frequently false. It is the next war which vitally concerns us and not the last, and this next war I believe will be very different from the last, and here is my first repetition. Quite possibly, when Europe is once again aflame, those already enlisted may find the army a safer habitation than an office in Lombard Street. Then, in place of witnessing the Israelites fleeing to Brighton, shall we behold them flocking to Great Scotland Yard !

J. F. C. F.

Café des Aveugles,
November 20, 1922.

CONTENTS

CHAPTER	PAGE
Prologue	1
I.—The Origins of War	6
II.—The Science and Art of War	24
III.—The Ethics of War	56
IV.—The Last Lap of the Physical Epoch	75
V.—The First Lap of the Moral Epoch	102
VI.—The Weapon of the Future	120
VII.—The Future of Air Warfare	136
VIII.—The Future of Land Warfare	152
IX.—The Future of Sea Warfare	170
X.—The Problem of Imperial Defence	189
XI.—The Meaning of Grand Strategy	211
XII.—The Reformation of the Army	229
XIII.—The Peace which Passeth Understanding	256
Epilogue	279
Appendix. Bibliography	285

The Reformation of War

PROLOGUE

COMMON-SENSE

PHILOSOPHY is a love of wisdom, and wisdom is the power of forming the fittest judgments from whatever premises are under consideration. Philosophy is, therefore, an evolutionary system of thought which has as its objective the survival of the fittest thoughts. While animals progress through the struggles of body, humankind, as distinct from animals, progresses through the struggles of mind, but with this difference: that, while in animal life every unit must struggle in order to survive, in human life the struggles of one great brain will, on occasion, remould an epoch. We find, therefore, that human beings may be divided into two categories—the masters (supermen) and the slaves (super-monkeys); in fact, into creators and imitators. This has always been so, and is likely to remain so, for without the second there can be no opposition to the first, and opposition is the manure of progress, and progress, seemingly, is of the will of God.

If the aim of wisdom is to arrive at the fittest judgments, then, indeed, is common-sense the true philosophy of life. To do the most appropriate thing at any moment is what is generally known as a common-sense act, in other words, common-sense may be defined as: " thought and action adapted to circumstances."

Common-sense is the secret of the masters, but to the slaves it is the greatest of all heresies, for to doubt that "thought and action are adapted to conventions" is to them the one unforgivable sin. In the great masters common-sense is not only spontaneous but prescient, for not only are actions adapted to circumstances, but the circumstances themselves are seen in advance of their happening. In this form common-sense is known as "genius," which, in nature, is creative and not formative; that is to say it produces wholes and does not merely set together parts. Genius may be classed, therefore, as masculine in character, for it produces the seed of a new life, while labour, the work of the slaves, is feminine, for it takes many months, many years, to build the finished article, and, then, it frequently spoils it in the process.

In the philosophy of common-sense there is no absolute truth, and, whether the absolute exists or not, it does not fall within its purview; metaphysics have but a very subordinate place in the realms of common-sense, the normal sphere of which is the existing and the evolution of the actual.

The absolute, especially under the conception of the absolute truth, is the undying cause of mental warfare. Millions of brains have thought upon this subject, hundreds of thousands of books have been written to explain it, and, worst of all, millions of lives have been sacrificed in the wrangles, quarrels and disputes which have arisen through its questing. To the multitude, this search after the incomprehensible has worked like some deadly drug. To them it has invoked false dawns to still-born days. To them, for a moment, it has shattered darkness, it has tantalized them with unreachable things—fraternity and the death of strife; it has shown them the squalor and sordidness of their surroundings, and then it has left them, dazzled and squinting, with the meanness of their thoughts, the smallness of their hearts, and the impotence of their souls, to scramble back into the night which knows no dawn, breathing profane words and groping after moonbeams and shadows.

The absolute may be "The Pearl of Great Price" . . . The Stone of the Wise" . . . or "The Lamp of Illimitable

Light." For the great it may be the "Universal Solvent," but for the multitude, and the world is made up of multitudes, it is with the rush-light of common-sense that we must seek to guide humankind, lest they be utterly blinded. For them, progress is not to be sought for in the solution of some infinite equation, but in the banishing of phantoms and the pricking of many-coloured bubbles; for each man carries about with him a book of lies—his preconceived thoughts, and lives in a world shackled by Euclidian lines—his fears and prejudices. Each word must be rewritten, each line dissolved, and he who can replace "length without breadth" by a cobweb, frees humanity until the web be broken. Slavery is the self-damnation of the credulous, and it must ever be remembered that most men are mental malingerers.

In the philosophy of common-sense, the goal is contentment, and, to the multitude, this goal is symbolized by health and happiness. Hitherto, so I feel, the great peace and war thinkers have given to the crowd speculations and uncertainties, vociferations and the ululation of words, full of meaning to themselves, possibly, but unintelligible to their servants: sterile words, words which cannot sprout or wax, inert words without blood or sap, cold words without warmth or fire. Words which, being either not understood or misinterpreted, cause wrangles, arguments and quarrelling—truly unbalanced things and, therefore, contrary to common-sense which aims at an equilibrium of reason and action

To the masses of humankind there are three happinesses in this world—sex, food and freedom. " Kiss, eat and do as we like." Thus, towards the abbey of Theleme do they wend their way, bickering about things spiritual and material, their very longings being filled with the itch of war. They pluck dead fruit and in anger they turn on one another, one saying: " What profiteth a man if he gain the whole world and yet lose his soul," and another with blasphemy replying : " A pair of boots is more important than all your Madonnas."* Thus

* " Memoirs of a Revolutionary," Krapotkin, vol. 11. 86.

are the masses rent, one side seeking some infinite desire, and the other some finite balsam. Thus, between the absolutism of both is the grist and chaff of life ground into war. Proportion is lost ; there is no give or take , life grows rigid, laughter ceases, one side cries " vice " and the other " virtue " The veil of the temple of peace is rent, and behind it grins the god of war—that panic mystery of progress.

Common-sense merely shifts these points of view, bringing them within one focus. Vice is the salt which gives life its savour —true ! Like a patch on a girl's cheek, it accentuates a beauty which is not its own. Vice, in fact, is the spur which sets virtue in motion.* The savour of life is its virtue, and yet this savour is far from being the mere salt, which, of itself, leads to unquenchable desire. The common-sense man does not inveigh against vice or exalt virtue ; when contentment does not exist, and discontent is war, he harmonizes these two. He does not seek a universal balsam, but a human anointment by an integration and agreement ; not an absolute truth, but an equation of circumstances which will be true—that is, will be righteous as long as these circumstances exist. He seeks the best at any given moment and not the best for ever. He is the arbitrator, and, like a good judge, he is so rare a being that, once he has harmonized one set of differences, he should not be allowed to take root , he has his circuit and should journey from one discontent to another, so that his energies may never slacken and ever find new worlds to conquer.

In war common-sense plays a similar part If peace be called virtuous and war vicious, then it is in the harmonization of their differences and not in the permanent state of either that a solution to righteousness must be sought. To understand this righteousness we must understand what peace and war entail.

* " Vice, crime, disease, decay and death are just as natural and necessary events as virtue, health, growth and life , ever present processes that are kept in check while evolution is in full vigour, they will increase when it has reached and passed its height : their presence and functions now are the augury of a larger presence and function some day "—" The Pathology of Mind," Henry Maudsley, p 192

Prologue

We must understand man as man, and the contentedness and discontentedness of man as human and not as metaphysical problems. To-day we stand at the parting of the ways, behind us lingers an old-world conception rooted in the events symbolized by " 1815." In front of us is cast the shadow of a new era which, in its time, will be symbolized by " 1918." Both were conceived in peace, both were born in war. Nations must either move or perish, they dare not wait for miracles to reincarnate them, for to wait is to paralyse the will to act. This will is the true wand of the magician, that sceptre of common-sense which rules the orb of human reason.

Thoughtful reader, common-sense has been my rush-light, it has lit my path through the chaos of past wars and, by the glimmer of its flickering flame, I have attempted to peer down the rugged track of future warfare, that track which at some uncertain day to come will once again loom into a great highway of strife along which will tramp those legions yet unborn. How wends the trail, what of the country it traverses ? Is it mountainous or rocky, wooded or a region of swamps ? And what of those yet distant warriors, are they armed as to-day, are they of the past or for the future ? Have they common-sense emblazoned on their standards, or do they advance under the faded banners of tradition ? Are their actions adapted to the circumstances which will then confront them ? Do they aspire after miracles, or drunken are they on the valour of ignorance, or are they equipped with that unshakable confidence begotten of imagination and nurtured by foresight ? These, in all modesty, for learning has made me doubtful, are some of the questions I shall attempt to answer. The book now opens : fare thee well !

I

THE ORIGINS OF WAR

THE philosophy of war and the philosophy of life are but synonyms for that system of knowledge which resolves human phenomena into their causes by an analysis of the struggle for existence. This struggle, though science differentiates between organic and inorganic, eventually finds its source in the molecular and atomic energies of matter and in the energy of the ether itself. Beyond these, human understanding, at present, is unable to penetrate.

We start with the known, the world as we think it to be, as it has seemed to us and is likely to continue to seem ; we travel into the unknown, yet ever before us and behind us hang the curtains of the unknowable, distant in places, close touching here and there. Through these we cannot see, even with the eyes of uttermost imagination. Though war and the struggle for existence may cease, could we but penetrate this veil, all our inferences so far go to prove that, on this side of it, war is an ultimate factor in Nature as she reveals herself to us through the limitations of the human mind.

We think we can, symbolically, picture to ourselves a state of complete inertia, just as we think we can picture to ourselves the shape of a fourth dimensional figure, but, in reality, such a state is incomprehensible, though in some form or another it is innate in every human heart. The religiously minded seek the life eternal, where there is no marriage or giving in marriage ; in other words, no duality ; likewise the city clerk he also seeks, even if an inadequate, yet a fixed wage so that he may be relieved

The Origins of War

from the horror of plus and minus quantities. Thus, throughout life itself, do we see on the one side a desire for rest, and on the other a desire for activity in order that rest may some day be accomplished.

I will postulate that we do start with inertia, the unknowable ; then, let us picture to ourselves, how we cannot say, that an activity is begotten within it · this activity then is war, whatever may be its complexion, for it will produce within inertia, a vibration, a disruption, a tearing and rending asunder. Henceforth, we have a duality—tendencies towards rest and tendencies towards activity, stability and mobility, a clash between these two in the ether, in matter and in life. Thus has the roar of war deafened the uttermost limits of eternity before the stars twinkled or the sun shone, and, as far as the human mind can fathom, is likely to resound through these abysmal depths until the universal blankness of inaction covers the infinite with its pall of perfect peace.

This desire for peace, and for the peace which passeth understanding, is innate in the heart of man : " anything for a quiet life," is the cry of the millions which surround us. It forms their spiritual goal, which is quite unattainable since Eve ate of the apple—henceforth " in the sweat of thy face shalt thou eat bread, till thou return unto the ground." Allegory though this may be, Eden is not of this life, for, though the lion may be brought to lie down with the lamb, the struggle for existence will still continue. Lambs will go on nibbling the young grass, and lions will die of indigestion, and the world will be peopled with gambolling foolish folk who, eventually, will find their normal level through the horrors of over-production. Thus does Nature instil the battle in one form or another in order, presumably, to improve the stock, so that the curse of Eden may be accomplished.

Though the desire of man is peace, the law of life is war ; the fittest, mentally or bodily, survive, and the less fit supply them with food, labour and service. Life lives on life ; look around and see if this be not true, and though the majority of human kind has given up cannibalism, many are still meat eaters ;

nevertheless, quite possibly the flesh of animals may also, some day, become revolting to the palate, and men may even gasp with horror at the idea of boiling a turnip. The advent of synthetic food will, however, in no way alter the law of life, though it may change the convolutions of the intestines ; for operate this law must, in the pulsations of the amœba and in the vibrations of the highest mind of that super-race with whom, for nearly three thousand years, we have been persistently threatened by revolutionaries—yet we remain human, ever and always human, and this is the keystone in the arch of our philosophy.

Thus it will be seen that the pendulum of life swings between two extremes—fear and love, and though man desires rest, the hand which holds the balance has ordained that he must seek it through activity. Man possesses no right to live, but solely might to kill and so to preserve life ; this is his one great birthright which holds good not only for primitive man but for human society as it is organized to-day ; for do not we find that, in most countries, in order to curb this might, the penalty is death, that is the very exercise of it, or imprisonment for life, which is but a delayed execution at the public expense ?

True, man desires life, for it is sweet to live ; he desires life, and though there can be no right in this desire, it is the strongest of his instincts, the instinct of self-preservation—the ultimate source of all human sorrow and of all human joy. This instinct urges him to protect his life, to preserve it, to link his life with that of woman, to duplicate their lives in the lives of their children and to protect this duplication. In the family, primæval or of to-day, there is a human right—protection, which in its turn, like an arch, rests on the abutments of physical strength and mental cunning. The stronger survive through brute strength, and the more cunning through craft ; thus begins that interminable struggle between muscle and mind which is the mainspring of all progress.

In the primitive family man is the hunter, he has but one object in life—to kill ; to kill for food, to kill for warmth and to kill for protection ; his impulse is purely an active one. With

The Origins of War

woman it is otherwise, her desires are not active but restful. In place of killing, her will is to preserve life. She prepares the food supplied to her by her husband, the hunter; she suckles her children, she fashions the home. Habit teaches her order, from order emerge customs and laws. In her long lonely vigils, while her man is on his bloody quest, she dreams, and from her dreams are born the gods, and from the contemplation of her children, as they roll in the grass at her feet, is conceived the stupendous vision of immortality.

In the family is born the spirit of co-operation, that working together for the common good through an integration of ideas and by a division of labour. Then families struggle with families, conquer and coalesce, and tribes emerge and are welded into nations. And, when history opens her gloomy portals, there stands War—the god of creative destruction, that grim synthetic iconoclast.

I will now examine this struggle, not from the point of view of the so-called " Realities of War," so frequently described by shell-shocked war correspondents, but from that pivotal point— the human instincts.

All human activities are ultimately girt by a mysticism unfathomable to the reason, which may only be sensed by a vague irrational intuition. The mentality of the great captain is difficult to analyse; frequently, he is a student, but study alone will not create him, frequently, he is inordinately brave, but neither will courage alone differentiate him from the herd. Possibly he is but the focal-point of his epoch, fashioned by the very circumstances which he eventually controls by fusing with them his own creative power. Identifying his power with that of his age, he concentrates it and wields the new creation like a weapon; conjuring forth the primal instincts always latent in man, he leashes and unleashes them, and men follow his touch, harnessed as they are to his will and he to theirs. This awakening of the primitive instincts is one of the most mysterious forces in war, a force which, if understood, will show that either wars are inevitable, or that the excitement which goes to engender them must, during peace time, find a healthy outlet if they are to be kept in leash.

The dormant instincts in man, once let loose, normally crystallize round a leader, who, in the eyes of his followers, becomes a super-man, a power to be venerated. During life his creative mind controls them, but, when dead, his spirit petrifies, and what was once the focal-point of individual energy becomes the static tombstone of collective idolatry. An image is raised; though called by his name it is soulless, it breathes no new word, neither can it move, for it is lifeless, it is but a make-belief.

Round this image congregate the priests of the cult of war; their words are his words, but his words are dead words, words of the past, which now bear little relationship to truth, who never stays her onward step. Doctrines grow into idolatrous dogmas, so that the worship of idols replaces the belief in living things. It is thus that nations are destroyed through the crystallization of ideas in traditions and stagnation of effort due to lethargy of thought.

From the military aspect, such idolatry as this does not only mean unprogressiveness in the science and art of war, but also aggressiveness towards indulging in war, this aggressiveness being due to two main causes

(i) The valour of ignorance of the nation.

(ii) The barbaric stimulus of the army.

The first is due to a lack of power to control policy. Nations are always competitors, especially great civilized nations, and, consequently, the weaker is forced to accept the will of the stronger, and, when the weaker happens to be a prosperous and wealthy nation, this acceptance of the will of the stronger, and sometimes less prosperous, is irritating. So much so is this the case that the weaker, not being able to adjust by force the balance to its favour, resorts to craft. Craft leads to secrecy, and secrecy to suspicion and discontent, which frequently lead to an open quarrel between the parties concerned, the one not knowing the intention of the other.

The Origins of War

If we now examine modern history, we shall find that, though military might has sometimes detonated wars, the most prevalent detonator has been diplomacy; craftiness and especially diplomacy which attempts to make good a deficiency of power by an excess of duplicity, for this type of craftiness ends in contempt. Diplomacy in its turn is spurred on by national ambitions which, in a wealthy nation, are many and complex. These, even though unsupported by power, breed among the ignorant masses a valour based on the ignorance of the requirements of war and, frequently, force diplomacy to offer veiled or open threats, though the diplomatists themselves fully realize that this process can only succeed through bluff, and if their opponent pays to see the hand, seeing it he will laugh and most certainly take the pool. A nation, even more so than an individual, is sensitive to ridicule, for the masses possess little wit, and it is ridicule, in its various simple and complex forms, which is a sure irritant of war.

As the first is due to a lack in the equilibration of power between two or more nations, so is the second due to the existence of a hiatus between the mentalities of the nation and its army. National progress seldom can be stayed even by the will of the majority, because, on account of competition, an evolution of the old hunting spirit, the minority, by compulsion the thinking (more crafty) section of the community, can seldom be brought to concentrate wilfully on its own destruction. Its tendency, anyhow, is to live and not to die. It frequently arises, however, especially in prosperous nations, that the national will to hunt for wealth is so great that it monopolizes all their efforts, and, consequently, that little thought is given to the maintenance and protection of their wealth through military action. In these circumstances, an army, which should be *of* the nation, becomes separated from it. It develops into a caste, and, being neither looked upon with affection nor cared for, it loses pace in the race of national progress and becomes barbaric by growing out of date. Then, when diplomacy fails, and the national equilibrium is upset by insult or ridicule, the nation, which is ever a heterogeneous crowd swayed by its primitive instincts, receives its impulse from its army and its military leaders; this impulse being mainly subconscious. Reacting by suggestion on the crowd mind, it detonates war even before the nation is prepared to accept it, and the result is, frequently, a disaster.

A barbaric army, that is, one separated in intellect from the nation to which it belongs, is an incentive to war without being an efficient weapon wherewith to wage it. Civilization cannot safely progress under the protection of such a force; consequently, all that goes to build up the mentality of a nation must go to build up the mentality of its army. These two must be one in mind, one in soul and one in body, though this does not necessarily mean that the whole nation must consist of drilled soldiers, but that the soldiers and civilians, in thought and progress, are living in one camp.

The pathology of war may be traced to a decay in or retardation of the mystic impulses which, springing from the instinct of self-preservation, control the destinies of nations The true might of a nation is to be sought for not so much in the strength or perfection of its army, which is but the means of materializing this might, but in the health of its spirit, that is its will to preserve itself from dangers internal and external. This spirit or vitality, so necessary to its existence, finds its outlet through the two primitive instincts of hunting and breeding. Hunting evolves into the pursuit of commerce, which, when stabilized in a civilized State, becomes labour without excitement. The natural pleasures of life are denied, cramped and crushed, day in and day out, by a monotonous routine. The stimulus of the hunt being absent, the body becomes lethargic and the mind dulled by a grim monotony. When such a state eclipses the soul of a nation, the primitive instincts gather in stormy clouds Then man's mind broods and is filled with the gloom of discontent; he becomes nomadic in spirit, the old desire of the forests and the jungle is awakened in his soul, it flames forth like some subtle lightning, and there is war. The pent-up instincts have flashed forth, man is once again the healthy heathen, the roamer

The Origins of War

over the mountains and the reveller in the mists. The intoxication of the chase is upon him, the instincts of millions of years are unleashed. He is freed for a space from the fear of death. Now for the nation is there glory in death, in self-sacrifice and renunciation, as there was once glory for man in risking his life in the winning of his mate and in the protection of his family and his lair.

To reduce life to a geometric figure, with its Euclidian laws, its parallels which never meet and its mathematical lines and points, is not only to suppose that life is an inert substance, but that humanity is governed by reason, which it most certainly is not. For, if it be the exception rather than the rule for any two rational individuals to agree on any one argument, how much more so is not this the case when opinions are being discussed collectively ? Reason is indeed a potent faculty of the mind, but it is only one of a number of potent faculties, all of which ultimately are swayed by the primitive instincts. Further, it is the first to volatilize directly the stimulus of fear is applied to the sympathetic minds of a crowd of persons.

The more geometric the life of a nation becomes, the more are its instincts and desires pent up, and the more do they attempt to find some outlet for their vigour. During the Middle Ages the greater part of Europe was shrouded under a religious pall, and the horror of the static state rested on the Western World like a huge coffin lid. Had not crime and cruelty given an outlet to man's natural appetites, the world would have gone mad; as it was, it was half insane ; and only war and brutality prevented it becoming totally so. To-day, we possess religious freedom, yet democracy, the new cult, is fast foisting on to us a static organization. The State is replacing the Church, and State domination must end in geometricity of thought and action, the enslavement of the individual and the charging of the Leyden cells of war. There can be nothing more appalling to the philosopher than to watch the doctrines of those with universal brotherhood on their lips, percolating through society like water through a rock, when it is apparent, by universal inference, that

14   The Reformation of War

these doctrines will one day solidify and break the nations saturated with them into a thousand fragments.

To restrict the ravages of the worst of all wars, namely, civil war, which is a crime against Nature, since in place of preserving national existence it destroys it, there is implanted in the heart of man an impulse which directs the energies of all progressive nations externally against those which surround them. This impulse is the first cause of organized wars; it is the instinct of self-preservation seeking security by establishing unattackable frontiers. In primitive times a tribe could only feel secure when the tribes surrounding it were less powerful than itself; if equally powerful, then warfare was incessant until the strongest gained inter-tribal supremacy. To-day it is much the same, strong nations cannot tolerate strong nations as neighbours, and are only deterred from attacking them if the balance of international power is against them. Their impulse of self-preservation bids them extend their frontiers to impassable or easily defensible obstacles, or else to nations so inferior in military strength to their own, that they have nothing to fear. In the case of England, in spite of her secure frontiers—the sea, this impulse is constantly active. Her history is free from serious revolutions, because the hunting spirit of her people expended itself in adventure, such as that which led Drake around the globe. Cromwell, though the child of revolution, in his wisdom so completely directed this spirit externally that no revolution of a serious character has since his day occurred in England. For self-preservation, England's frontiers are the sea coasts of other nations, and, when land frontiers are impossible to avoid, she has nearly always attempted to protect them by the creation or maintenance of weak buffer States.

The second great cause of war is in nature economic. In primitive times, pillage, or the killing of one man by another for personal gain was a common act. As civilization advances, this personal act is replaced by a tribal or racial act of war. A tribe is killed off and its belongings taken, and, if its land be

The Origins of War

annexed or occupied, in nature, such a war becomes organized, since permanent garrisons are created. Thus far the natural history of the primitive form of war, evolving into the organized, is simple. Not so, however, its evolution through the psychological channels. To steal a man's meat undoubtedly calls, in a primitive people, for vengeance ; so also does any detraction from a man's prowess, for it lowers him in the eyes of his family and so attacks him psychologically by wounding his vanity. To degrade a neighbouring tribe to serfdom or slavery is to attack it psychologically on wholesale lines. If the tribe be effete, it will probably die out ; if virile, it will probably rebel and attempt to purge itself of its masters and so regain its former freedom The same applies to the enslavement of nations, and in order to obviate such a catastrophe, nations raise armies to protect them against so oppressive a fate.

As a war of vengeance generally originates from a war of pillage, so does a war of purgation normally arise from an act of conquest, and conquest, in its modern sense, may be viewed under three economic headings.

(i) The conquest of land in order to obtain raw material.
(ii) The conquest of man-power in order to manufacture commodities.
(iii.) The conquest of free markets in order to sell commodities.

All three of these types of conquest may be accomplished without the clash of steel, just as the enslavement of a weak tribe by a strong may be accomplished by fear or by a moral threat. But, if the original owners of the land, the man-power enslaved, or the possessors of the markets, are virile, bloodless though these conquests may be, they frequently lead to the most bloody of wars of purgation, because conquest generally carries with it a restriction of the primitive hunting instinct in the conquered.

From the national standpoint, a war of conquest has nothing whatever to do with right or wrong, for Nature knows nothing of morality, unless morality be defined as race survival. Efficient races conquer and enjoy their conquests, just as efficient hunters kill and enjoy their prey. So also are effete races conquered, and, should they be eaten up, they deserve their fate. If they can, however, overthrow their conquerers then equally do they deserve their liberation. A race which submits to slavery is a race the virility of which has grown sterile. Nature abhors a mental eunuch as fervently as she abhors a physical vacuum.

Great nations are born in war, because war is the focal-point of national concentration ; great nations decay in peace, because peace is the circumference of the circle the centre of which is this focal-point—the greater the diameter or time the greater the danger resulting.

From the material aspect of war, chiefly through the sexual instinct, is evolved a nebulous and later on a fixed psychological character. Man has to win his mate by being the strongest of his sex, should his strength fail him, he must resort to craft, which is synonymous to insulting the strength or abilities of his opponent by taking what might to-day be called a mean advantage of him. He lurks in the bushes or in the shadows of night and assassinates, rather than fights his competitor. Such a type of attack, from the physiological standpoint of the survival of the fittest, is revolting to the strong, and it must be remembered that it is the physiological aspect of war which is always the most prominent in man's mind. Such an act as this is " unsportsmanlike," it is comparable to shooting a fox in a hunting county, or attacking a lion with a machine-gun in a game preserve. It cries for vengeance, for, if it succeed, there will be scant protection for the offspring of even the strongest. From the wars of muscle against muscle is thus evolved the war of brain against brain, in the form of personal vengeance. The antagonist is not killed for his belongings, but in order to get rid of him as an individual and later on as a public nuisance. Vengeance grows into morality, which may be defined as : that state of existence which best enables the individuals composing society to live peacefully together. Morality is not an instinct but a compromise ; from it evolves legislation, which metes out punishment to those who injure

The Origins of War

peaceful race survival. As politics are dependent on the will of the majority, a will which is never for long stable, to endeavour to establish an international code of laws on a footing similar to that of national legal codes is to attempt the impossible, for without political power the legislation of politically irresponsible courts is valueless ; for political power is based on the will of the majority of a nation, which, in its turn, is governed by the instinct of national preservation.

The evolution of wars of vengeance is exceedingly intricate. First, they are pursued to avenge personal injury, the theft of another man's belongings—his flint arrow-heads or his wife Secondly, to avenge the theft of his sentiments—slander against his person or the deprivation of the affection of some woman. As such, wars of vengeance are as common to-day as 50,000 years ago. Thirdly, they develop into protecting the race from insult and depredation, and, when races depend for their existence upon commerce, they direct their efforts against dishonest and underhand practices. Fourthly, they develop into avenging insults directed against the political and religious systems of nations, and here we find vengeance based on a multitude of capricious ideas. The Arian schism hinged on the word " Homoousios," and a war between England and Spain, in 1739, on the severance of an ear. These pretexts cannot be considered as real causes of war, but rather as the detonators of the pent-up hunting instinct in man which has been tamped down by artifice. Society may be likened to a permanent powder magazine formed of innumerable sentiments. When these are scattered and far spaced, the danger of explosion is small, but when concentrated one spark may lift the roof off a generation.

In all these phases of war, whether slow and internal or rapid and external, whether directed against individuals or nations, whether military or commercial, the sum total of horror is purely relative to the state of the sentiments of the day—they are dynamite or crude black powder ! Thus a war, to-day, between the Americans and Japanese, waged in order to obtain human flesh for food, would freeze the blood in the heart of every

European outside Russia, even if it resulted in only a few dozen people being eaten. After prolonged periods of absence from a certain condition, its occurrence becomes a novelty, a new creation which appals the inert mind. Such minds can find no comparison wherewith to measure the cataclysm, though, if these minds were by nature introspective, they would realize that, as science has ameliorated the conditions of peace, so equally can science ameliorate the manners of war.

In war, novelties of an atavistic nature are generally horrible; nevertheless, in the public mind, their novelty is their crime; consequently, when novelties of a progressive character are introduced on the battlefield, the public mind immediately anathematizes them, not necessarily because they are horrible but because they are new. Nothing insults a human being more than an idea his brains are incapable of creating Such ideas detract from his dignity for they belittle his understanding. In April, 1915, a few hundred British and French soldiers were gassed to death; gas being a novelty, Europe was transfixed with horror. In the winter of 1918-1919, the influenza scourge accounted for over 10,000,000 deaths, more than the total casualties in killed throughout the whole of the Great War; yet the world scarcely twitched an eyelid, though a few people went so far as to sniff eucalyptus.

One of the main arguments against armies is their futility; but, if this be true, this argument can with equal force be directed against peaceful organizations; for surely it is just as futile to keep vast numbers of a nation on the brink of starvation and prostitution, as happens in nearly all civilized countries to-day, as it is to keep an insignificant minority of this same nation on the brink of war.

Human nature, fortunately, is not changed by wild illogical statements or even by logical comparisons. Petronius Arbiter, eighteen hundred years ago, wrote in his Satyricon :

> " As for Trimalchio, he has as much land as a kite can fly over, he has heaps upon heaps of money. There is more silver lying in his porter's lodge than another man's whole estate is worth. And,

The Origins of War

as for slaves, wheugh ! by Hercules, I do not believe one tenth of them know their own master."

Substitute factory hands for slaves, and the Rome of Nero is not very different from the England of Tennyson :

" Peace sitting under her olive, and slurring the days gone by,
When the poor are hovell'd and hustled together each sex, like swine :
When only the ledger lives, and when only not all men lie ;
Peace in her vineyard—yes ! but a company forges the wine."

This, say you, has all been changed, democracy has to-day unhovelled the multitudes, and Socialism is offering to the world a new and beautiful future. This future is, however, nothing more than a mirage of the past—material gain and greed, eagerly grasped at by the hungry. I will quote again :

' Why do we prate of the blessings of Peace ? We have made them a curse ;
Pick pockets, each hand lusting for all that is not its own ;
And lust of gain, in the spirit of Cain, is it better or worse
Than the heart of the citizen hissing in war on his own hearthstone ?
But these are the days of advance, the works of the men of mind,
When who but a fool would have faith in a tradesman's ware or his word ?
Is it peace or war ? Civil war, as I think, and that of a kind
The viler, as underhand, not openly bearing the sword "

In spite of the shrieking peace-mongers, the fact is that the state of peace is the state of war, and the horror of peace is the horror of war ; this may not be rational, but it is, nevertheless, true, true even if history be only but an indifferent witness. It is here that we merge into the purgative character of wars of vengeance—fevers begotten by communistic social rule, which restricts the outlet of man's natural appetites. Wars of revolution are caused by despotism, the worst form of which is communism, not only the communism of the gutter but the communism of bureaucratic government. All men are proclaimed or treated as equal, the law of the survival of the fittest is abrogated in a mist of words and in a flow of ink ; the struggle for existence is abolished, and the immediate result is that it asserts itself in its most brutal forms. Sentiments group themselves and concentrate, and the magazine of society becomes sensitive to combustion at the slightest moral shock.

Philosophically, there can be no end to war as long as there is life or motion, for the very elements struggle in ceaseless combinations and, as far as we can at present judge, will continue to struggle until the crack of doom. The greatest world-war which our globe ever experienced was a bloodless one ; it occurred millions of centuries ago, when the earth, then an incandescent cloud of gas, tore itself away from the sun its mother and with flaming caul proclaimed its identity. From this great war all others have originated and will continue to evolve progressively, ever tending towards some unknown goal.

Modern wars are, in the main, progressive in nature, for they sweep aside obsolete laws and customs which have lost their meaning and spur men awake to the realities of life, so that they may cease for awhile dreaming of life's little troubles. To prohibit wars of conquest, if such a prohibition were possible, and to permit wars of purgation would end in a universal catastrophe. If rigidly adhered to, such a policy would lead to complete isolation of each separate nation, to an end of commerce and an end to the exchange of ideas Such a state is inconceivable, and human wars, it is thought, as the Buddhists proclaim of sorrow, can only cease with a cessation of desire.

Henry Maudsley, the eminent psychologist, accentuates this very clearly in this book " The Pathology of Mind," when he writes :

> " Have not nations owed their formation as much to brotherly hate as to brotherly love—more perhaps to the welding consolidation enforced by the pressure of hostile peoples than to the attractive forces of their components ? And what is the spur of commerce but competition ? War in one shape or another, open or disguised, has plainly been the divinely appointed instrument of human progress, carnage the immoral-seeming means by which the slow incarnation of morality in mankind has been effected.
>
> When we look at facts sincerely as they are, not satisfied to rest in a void of speculative idealism and insincerity, we perceive that in every department of life the superior person uses his superior powers to the inevitable detriment of the inferior person, even

The Origins of War

though he may afterwards dispense benevolently out of his superfluity to some of those who fall by the wayside. The moral law only works successfully as a mean between two extremes, excess of either being alike fatal. He who aspires to love his neighbour as himself must at the same time take care to love himself as his neighbour, making himself his neighbour while he makes his neighbour himself; his right duty being to cultivate not a suicidal self-sacrifice which would be a crime against self, but just that self-sacrifice which is the wisest self-interest and just that self-interest which is the wisest self-sacrifice. So he obtains the utmost development of self within the limits of the good of the whole. He will not go very far in morality if he compound for lack of self-renunciation on his part by a special indulgence of his own self-love in dictating sacrifices to other people. Were men to carry the moral law of self-sacrifice into rigorous and extreme effect they would perish by the practice of their virtues. When they had succeeded in eradicating competition, in making an equal distribution of wealth, in prolonging the feeblest life to its utmost tether, in banishing strife and war from the earth, in bringing all people on it to so sheep-like a placidity of nature that they would no more hurt and destroy, and to such an ant-like uniformity of industrious well-doing that no one would work for himself but every one for all, they would have robbed human nature of its springs of enterprise and reduced it to a stagnant state of decadence. A millennium of blessed bees or industrious ants! For it is the progress of desire and the struggle to attain which keeps the current of human life moving and wholesome alike in individuals, in societies, and in nations. Not to go forward is to go back, and not to move at all is death."

If progress be rendered impossible, only two other courses are open to humanity: stagnation or retrogression. The first means war, as we know it to-day, and the second, war as it was known in the past. Retrogression can only lead to one goal, the goal we started from, a sliding back into the brute, in which process of retirement we shall have to pass through all past phases of human warfare until, naked and unarmed, we tear each other to pieces with our nails.

To weep and gnash our teeth over preparations for war, because they cost so much, is but a symptom of decadence. "How can we afford these ships or these armies?" This is the whine of a small householder and not the cry of a virile nation. Neolithic man wept similar tears, no doubt, over his arrow-heads. "How can I afford all these days chipping this wretched flint, my body aches for food and my brood is starving?" He did afford those days, and had he not done so, his race would have been exterminated. Nature cares nothing for the sweat of man's brow or the leanness of his purse; nations must, therefore, not only afford to survive but must *will* to do so. If some war commodity be beyond the national means or the national powers of labour, nations must not cease in their efforts or rely on second-rate weapons, but, instead, they must either increase their powers of labour or substitute for these costly weapons cheaper and more effective ones. The nations which can accomplish this survive; those which cannot—perish. Nature tolerates no unearned rest: "In the sweat of thy face shall thou eat bread," this is her irrevocable dictum. There is no permanent rest for humanity. Forwards lie the pains of growth, backwards the agony of decomposition. To stand still is to rot. The Saurians are dead and gone, yet the little ant survives and multiplies.

As to the functions of the State, the State should remain inert, that is to say it should so govern a nation that equal opportunity for the evolution of all creative and receptive brains is rendered possible. This is not communism, which aims at assisting the weak, but race survival, which aims at assisting the strongest to forge ahead through the agency of a virile competition. It has little to do with the distribution of wealth, but everything to do with the catholicism of health. Some will continue to be born rich and some poor; nevertheless, it should be a national point of honour that no stone be left unturned which will enable all to be born strong, and to be provided with equal opportunities of education, of marriage and of law. The function of the State is to level the social tilting ground for the national tourney between thought and action; to see that for either side it is free from pitfalls, and that there is no hitting below the belt. As long as the State does not produce this condition of impartial inertia, so long will wars of purgation arise and lead to wars of conquest. When

The Origins of War

all States do produce it, as unsentimentally as a judge administers justice, then indeed may collective acts of brigandage become as infrequent as their individual counterparts. Bellona will not have ceased to be, but she will have changed her complexion from a tawny red to a leprous grey. Battlefields will become bloodless, and the agony of muscle will be replaced by the agony of mind. To drive a nation mad may then quite possibly be considered a superb victory. Thus does civilization stride forward on the stepping stones of death and madness towards life and the fullness of life, until her path is lost in the gloom of an inscrutable future.

Be this as it may, " the will to live " is the ultimate horizon of her philosophy. Far distant may this circumference grow in ever increasing circles, but, in the centre of these, squats their originator, a shadowy form, all but indiscernible to the philosopher, totally unseen by those filled with windy words : the form of primitive man, gorged on the flesh of his prey and basking in the sun.

II

THE SCIENCE AND ART OF WAR

HAVING now analysed the soul of war and, rightly or wrongly, having assumed that wars in one form or another are inevitable, in this Chapter I will examine the science and art of the mind and body of this subject. I do so because, when we come to consider the future tendencies of war, not only is it important to realize that future warfare must be an evolution of present and past warfare, but that all forms of warfare are founded on a common science

From a cursory study of military history, a student might well be deluded into believing that war is so closely related to the roulette table as to be classed as a veritable game of chance. What does he see ? The efforts of many noted generals who have been either gamblers pure and simple, or else keen but inept dabblers in dark sciences. These, he soon finds, have worked much like the alchemists of the Middle Ages, who sought for perpetual motion, the universal solvent, the philosopher's stone and the elixir of life, in mixtures compounded of dragon's blood, grated unicorn's horn and the marrow of consecrated cats.

Even in the Great War of 1914-1918 we can discover few scientific reasons for the innumerable actions fought, no firmer basis than Marshal Saxe could discover in his day when he wrote :

"War is a science so obscure and imperfect that, in general, no rules of conduct can be given in it which are reducible to absolute certainties , custom and prejudice, confirmed by ignorance, are its sole foundations and support."

The Science and Art of War

The armies of 1914 were imitators of past methods of warfare, for they had been fed on past battles. Science does not imitate, for science unravels and creates.

What is science? Science is co-ordinated knowledge, facts arranged according to their values, or to put it more briefly still and to quote Thomas Huxley, science is "organized common sense . . . the rarest of all the senses."

War is as much a science as all other human activities, and, like all other sciences, it is built upon facts, of which there are an innumerable quantity. From these facts may we extract the elements of war and the principles of war and the conditions of war—the circumstances in which the principles must be brought to govern the elements.

What is the simplest possible type of human warfare? A fight between two unarmed men. What is their object? To impose their wills upon each other. How do they accomplish this? By giving blows without receiving them or the fewest possible number. In these words have we completely laid bare the essential nature of the fight, in fact we have discovered the pivotal problem in the science of war—the destruction of the enemy's strength (physical or moral), which not only embraces his army but the whole of his nation, and which constitutes the crucial problem in the art of war: "how to kill, disable, or capture without being killed, disabled, or captured."*

In war we start with man, the author of all human strife. To defeat his adversary he must will to do so, he must move towards him, he must hit him and he must prevent himself from being hit, or, otherwise, he may fail to impose his will, which is enforced and protected by his actions.

Man, in himself, may be compared to the ether, out of which the other elements are evolved. In war the physical elements arising out of the body of man are: movement, weapons and protection.

* This is the traditional problem. Later on I will show that for body should be substituted mind.

26   The Reformation of War

Examining movement first, we find that, tactically, there are two types: protective movements and offensive movements; the first I will denote by the term " approaches " and the second by that of " attacks." In the former the one thought of the soldier is " to prevent himself from being hit," and, in the latter, " to hit his enemy." The more he can hit the less he will be hit, consequently, indirectly though it may be, not only is the whole action protective in character, but it becomes more and more so as the offensive succeeds. From this it will be at once seen that any idea of thinking of the offensive and the defensive phases of war, battle or duel, as things in themselves apart, is absurd ; for these two acts form the halves of the diameter of the tactical circle, the circumference of which is the fight. They are, in fact, the positive and negative poles of the tactical magnet called battle.

Of weapons there are two types—hitting and hurling weapons. The first I will call " shock weapons," such as the bayonet, lance and sword, and the second " missile weapons," such as arrows, bullets, and gas. As the tactical object of physical battle is to destroy the enemy, which is best accomplished by clinching with him, the infantryman's offensive weapon is the bayonet and his bullet is his defensive weapon, on account of its ability to protect the advance of the bayonet. Thus, we see that, whenever two weapons of unequal range of action are employed, the one of longer range is always the defensive weapon and the one of shorter range the offensive one, and even if three or more weapons be used, this holds equally good for all. From this appreciation may be deduced a tactical rule of the highest importance : In all circumstances missile weapons must be employed to facilitate or ward off the shock.

Protection, or the defensive, has little to do with holding positions or beating back attacks, for it is just as much part and parcel of every forward movement as of every holding or retrograde one. I have already pointed out how the bullet defends the bayonet and how the approach secures the attack by lessening casualties when the soldier is advancing and not

The Science and Art of War

actually using his weapons. Both these forms of protection are indirect, that is to say, they do not ward off blows but impede blows from being delivered. Besides these indirect means of protection, which include the use of camouflage and smoke clouds, several direct means have frequently been employed, such as armour, earthworks and fortifications. Under this heading, to-day, must also be placed the anti-gas respirator. Direct protection is such as will nullify the effect of blows. Mobile direct protection is generally the most effective, for any change in location necessitates a change in the enemy's tactical organization, and consequently a loss of time for destructive effect. When, as in a tank or battleship, mobile direct and indirect protection can be combined, the highest form of security is obtained ; this fact was all but unrealized in the last great war, though a study of the art of war in the Middle Ages will show that it formed the tactical backbone of the combat between armoured knights.

I have already made mention of the fact that to imitate is not necessarily to work scientifically. Science extracts knowledge from the unknown by applying to it certain laws which universal inference has established. Thus we have the laws of gravitation, of causation and of evolution War has also its laws or principles, and they are to be found in the duel as in the battle. As regards these principles of war there has been much discussion of an unscientific nature. Before the Great War of 1914-1918, every Field Service Regulations made mention of principles of war and pointed out their importance, but did not name them. The British Field Service Regulations of 1914 stated : " The fundamental principles of war are neither very numerous nor in themselves very abstruse," and then left the readers in complete doubt as to what they were. Some twenty years ago Marshal, then Lieut.-Colonel, Foch wrote a learned book on " The Principles of War," in which he mentioned four, and then, apparently in doubt as regards the remainder, placed " etc." at the end of this list.

There are eight principles of war, and they constitute the

28 The Reformation of War

laws of every scientifically fought boxing match as of every battle. These principles are:

    1st Principle.—The principle of the objective.
    2nd Principle.—The principle of the offensive.
    3rd Principle.—The principle of security.
    4th Principle.—The principle of concentration.
    5th Principle.—The principle of economy of force.
    6th Principle.—The principle of movement.
    7th Principle —The principle of surprise.
    8th Principle —The principle of co-operation.

No one of the above eight principles is of greater value than the other. No plan of action can be considered perfect unless all are in harmony, and none can be considered in harmony unless weighed against the conditions which govern their application. Seldom can a perfect plan be arrived at because the fog of war seldom, if ever, completely rises. It is, however, an undoubted fact that the general who places his trust in the principles of war, and who trusts in them the more strongly the fog of war thickens, almost inevitably beats the general who does not.

These principles are, in my opinion, of such importance, being in fact the governors of war, that, as far as space will permit, I will consider them in detail. First, then, what is the objective in war?

(1) *The Principle of the Objective.* The object of a nation is national preservation, which, in a civilized race, may be defined as honourable, profitable and secure existence. Here we find three sub-objectives, an ethical objective, an economic objective and a military objective. These three combined I will call the political objective or policy of the nation, the stability of which depends on the will of the people.

In modern warfare it does not pay to outrage the sentiments of the day, neither does it pay to destroy the economic resources of the enemy. Consequently, when all peaceful methods of settlement have broken down and a nation is reduced to military

The Science and Art of War

action in order to maintain or enforce its policy, its object should be to impose its will with the least possible ethical and economic loss not only to itself but to its enemies and to the world at large. A nation which wins a war through foul play degrades itself in the eyes of other nations and loses the trust of the world. A nation which destroys the economic resources of its enemy, destroys its eventual markets, and thus wounds itself.* War must entail some loss, but the less this loss is the greater will be the victory; consequently, the military object of a nation is not to kill and destroy, but to enforce the policy of its government with the least possible loss of honour, life and property. If the enemy can be compelled to accept the hostile policy without battle, so much the better. If he opposes it by military force, then it should never be forgotten that the strength of this force rests on the will of the government which employs it, and that, in its turn, this will rests on the will of the nation which this government represents. If the will of the nation cannot directly be attacked, then must the will of the army protecting it be broken. In the past this will has been attacked by attacking the flesh of soldiers, and, so consistent has this been, that the idea has arisen that the military object of war is to kill and to destroy. Thus, in the popular and military imaginations, the means have obscured the end; consequently, the prevailing idea of all parties in the recent war was destruction, to destroy each other, and so blinded were they by the means that they could not see that in the very act they were destroying themselves, not only during the war but in the peace which must some day follow the war.

I believe that the world is slowly learning this lesson, and that, as in my opinion wars are inevitable, the old idea of warfare based on destruction will be replaced by a new military ideal, the imposition of will at the least possible general loss. If this be

* It is true that a self-supporting nation does not suffer in proportion to one not self-contained, but it must be realized that ecomomics and ethics are closely related, and, even if destruction does not economically affect the destroyer, the ethical repercussion resulting through the bankruptcy of the victim is very likely to wound him morally.

so, then the means of warfare must be changed, for the present means are means of killing, means of blood ; they must be replaced by terrifying means, means of mind. The present implements of war must be scrapped and these bloody tools must be replaced by weapons the moral effect of which is so terrific that a nation attacked by them will lose its mental balance and will compel its government to accept the hostile policy without further demur. In this book I will show the probable nature of the first stage in this new evolution of war ; meanwhile, I will examine war from the present military aspect

In organized warfare, if the objective cannot be gained by political action, recourse is made to force, the military objective being the defeat of the enemy's military strength so that his national policy may be transmuted. This objective is attained by a harmonious employment of the remaining seven principles of war. Without a definite objective there can be no definite military policy or plan, and without a policy or plan, actions cannot be co-ordinated ; consequently, the principle of the objective may also be considered as the principle of co-ordination, for, as Napoleon once said : " There are many good generals in Europe, but they see too many things at once. I see the enemy's masses and I destroy them." By this appreciation of the objective all his movements were controlled.

According to the objective depends the direction taken by an army, and on its direction depends its supply. The enemy is at A, we are at B. Does the line joining these two points give us our direction ? Yes and no ! Yes, if the seven remaining principles are not adversely affected by our moving in this direction, and if the conditions permit of us doing so. No, if otherwise. We should not, however, discard this direction offhand, even if we find that some of the principles are difficult to apply ; instead we should test each possible line of advance until we arrive at the line of least resistance, bearing in mind that the principle of the objective aims at creating such a situation as will force the enemy to accept the policy he is fighting against.

The Science and Art of War

(ii.) *The Principle of the Offensive.* Will the objective that we have selected enable us to apply the principle of the offensive ? If it will not, then the objective selected must be discarded, for the offensive in war is the surest road to success. If it will, then in which direction should the offensive be made ? The answer to this question depends on the conditions of war (existing and probable circumstances), which should be looked upon as the correctors of all military movements.

Thus, if time be against us, time in which an enemy can mass his reserves to meet our offensive and so outwit us, the offensive becomes futile or dangerous ; unless, possessing more men than brains, our object is simply to kill as many of the enemy as we can, regardless of cost, which is not only a violation of the principle of economy of force, but the poorest of poor generalship. A private soldier thinks in terms of killing men, but a general should think in terms of disorganizing and demoralizing, that is of defeating armies. " Push of pikes " is a simple game compared to defeating an army, which requires an acuter intellect than that of a lusty halberdier.

Seldom will it be possible to march straight towards the enemy's main force in order to defeat it. Its whereabouts may be unknown, but, even so, the ultimate objective—disorganization and demoralization, remains constant. Consequently, though many acts may be required before the curtain of victory is finally rung down, each act must be a distinct progression towards the transformation scene of peace. If this be not the case, then an infringement of the principle of the objective will take place. This must be guarded against, for each blow must form a definite link in an offensive chain of blows, in which moves, as in chess, are seen ahead.

A general will seldom win without attacking, and he will seldom attack correctly unless he has chosen his objective with reference to the principles of war, and unless his attack is based on these principles. Imagination is a great detective, but imagination which is not based on the sound foundation of reason is at best but a capricious leader. Even genius itself, unless it be stiffened by powerful weapons, a high moral, discipline and training, can only be likened to a marksman armed with a blunderbuss—ability wasted through insufficiency of means. Conversely, an efficient army led by an antiquated soldier may be compared to a machine gun in the hands of an arbalister.

(iii.) *The Principle of Security.* The objective in battle being to destroy or paralyse the enemy's fighting strength, consequently the side which can best secure itself against the action of its antagonist will stand the best chance of winning, for by saving its men and weapons, its organization and moral, it will augment its offensive power. Security is, therefore, a shield and not a lethal weapon, consequently the defensive is not the strongest form of war, but merely a prelude to the accomplishment of the objective—the defeat of the enemy by means of the offensive invigorated by defensive measures. The offensive being essential to success, it stands to reason that security without reference to the offensive is no security at all, but merely delayed suicide.

As danger and the fear of danger are the chief moral obstacles of the battlefield, it follows that the imbuing of troops with a sense of security is one of the chief duties of a commander, for, if weapons be of equal power, battles are won by a superiority of nerve rather than by a superiority of numbers. This sense of security, though it may be supplemented by artifice, is chiefly based on the feeling of moral ascendance due to fighting efficiency and confidence in command. Given the skilled soldier, the moral ascendancy resulting from his efficiency will rapidly evaporate unless it be skilfully directed and employed. Ultimately, as in all undertakings, civil or military, we come back to the impulse of the moment, that is to the brains which control each individual nerve which runs through the military body. To give skilled troops to an unskilled leader is tantamount to throwing snow on hot bricks. Skill in command is, therefore, the foundation of security, for a clumsy craftsman will soon take the edge off his tools.

The basis of strategical security is the soundness of the

The Science and Art of War

general plan of action, the infrequency of the change of objective or of direction, and of the absence of unnecessary movement Strategical security is also arrived at by placing an army in a good position to hit at the communications and headquarters of the enemy while protecting its own : by so disposing a force that it may live at ease and fight efficiently.

Grand tactical security may be defined as the choosing of a vulnerable target or the refusal to offer one. Here the factors are mainly those of time and space—the rapid massing of weapons at the decisive point whether for attack or defence, and the general organization of the battle itself. Minor tactical security embraces the entire gamut of a soldier's actions : his individual moral and efficiency, the quickness and audacity of his leader, the judgment and determination of his commander and the confidence of his comrades, as well as the superiority of his weapons, means of movement and protection.

(iv.) *The Principle of Concentration.* Concentration, or the bringing of things or ideas to a point of union, presupposes movement ; movement of ideas, especially in an army, is a far more difficult operation than the movement of men. Nevertheless, unless ideas, strategical, tactical and administrative, be concentrated, cohesion of effort will not result , and in proportion as unity of action is lacking, so will an army's strength, moral and physical, be squandered in detail until a period be arrived at in which the smallest result will be obtained from every effort. The central idea of an army is known as its " doctrine," which, to be sound, must be based on the principles of war, and which, to be effective, must be elastic enough to admit of mutation in accordance with change of circumstances. In its ultimate relationship to human understanding, this central idea or doctrine is nothing else than common-sense, namely, action adapted to circumstances. The danger of a doctrine *per se* is that it is apt to ossify into a dogma and to be seized upon by mental emasculates who lack the power of analytic criticism and synthetic thought, and who are only too grateful to rest assured that their actions, however inept, find justification in a book which, if they think at all, is, in their opinion, written in order to exonerate them from doing so. In the past, many armies have been destroyed by internal discord, and some have been destroyed by the weapons of their antagonists, but the majority have perished through adhering to dogmas springing from their past successes, that is self-destruction, or suicide, through inertia of mind.

Though an army should operate according to the idea which, through concentration, has become part of its nature, the brain of its commander must in no way be hampered by preconceived or fixed opinions, for, while it is right that the soldier should consider himself invincible, it is never right that the commander should consider himself undefeatable. Contempt for an enemy, however badly led, has frequently led to disaster ; therefore it is the first duty of the commander to concentrate on common-sense, and to maintain his doctrine in solution so that it may easily take the mould of whatever circumstances it may have to be cast in. Strategy should be based on this doctrine of action adapted to circumstances, and, consequently, concentration in strategy may be defined as making the most of opportunity and also of forecasting and foreseeing the possibility of opportunity before it arises.

As strategical actions chiefly depend on means of movement, so equally does the concentration of the forces engaged in them depend on communications; consequently, from the network formed by the lines of supply is evolved grand tactical concentration, the object of which is to overcome resistance by breaking it down or turning it to advantage.

From the point of view of the battle itself, concentration has for centuries been based on the maxim of " superiority of numbers at the decisive point," because numbers were the coefficient of weapons, each man normally being a one-weapon mounting. This maxim no longer holds good as a general rule, and in its place must be substituted · " superiority of moral, weapons, means of movement and protection." Men, in themselves, are an encumbrance on the battlefield, and the fewer men we employ,

The Science and Art of War

without detracting from sufficiency of weapon-power, the greater will be our concentration of strength, for the aim of concentration is as much concerned with securing an army against blows as it is with enabling an army to deliver them

(v.) *The Principle of Economy of Force* Economy of force may be defined as the efficient use of all means : physical, moral and material, towards winning a war. Of all the principles of war it is the most difficult to apply, because of its close interdependence on the ever changing conditions of war. In order to economize the moral energy of his men, a commander must not only be in spirit one of them, but must ever have his fingers on the pulse of the fighters What they feel he must feel, and what they think he must think ; but while they feel fear, experience discomfort and think in terms of easy victory or disaster, though he must understand what all these mean to the men themselves, he must in no way be obsessed by them. To him economy of force first means planning a battle which his men *can* fight, and secondly, adjusting this plan according to the psychological changes which the enemy's resistance is producing on their endurance without forgoing his objective. This does not only entail his possessing judgment, but also foresight and imagination. His plan must never crystallize, for the energy of the battle front is always fluid. He must realize that a fog, or shower of rain, a cold night or unexpected resistance may force him to adjust his plan, and, in order to enable him to do so, the grand tactical economy of force rests with his reserves, which form the staying power of the battle and the fuel of all tactical movement.

On the battlefield, to economize his own strength and by means of feints and surprisals to force the enemy to dissipate his, is the first step towards victory. Every weapon which he can compel the enemy to withdraw from the point of attack is an obstacle removed from the eventual path of progress. Every subsidiary operation should be based on the objective and effect a concentration of weapon-power on the day of decisive action. Every subsidiary action should add, therefore, an increasing value to victory, that is the power of producing a remunerative tactical dividend. " Is the game worth the candle ? " This is the question every commander must ask himself before playing at war.

By this I do not mean that risks must never be taken, far from it, for it is by taking risks which are worth taking that, more often than not, the greatest economies are effected and the highest interest secured. In war, audacity is nearly always right and gambling is nearly always wrong, and the worst form of gambling in war is gambling with small stakes ; for by this process an army is eventually bled white.

Economy of force is also closely related to economy of movement. Many generals have attempted to win a military Marathon in sprinting time. They have thrown in all their reserves at once, and so have lost their wind within a few hours of the battle opening. Such operations as these are doomed to failure long before the first shot is ever fired.

(vi.) *The Principle of Movement.* If concentration of weapon-power be compared to a projectile and economy of force to its line of fire, then movement may be looked upon as the propellant and as a propellant is not always in a state of explosive energy, so neither is movement. Movement is the power of endowing mass with momentum ; it depends, therefore, largely on security, which, when coupled with offensive power, results in liberty of action. Movement, consequently, may be potential as well as dynamic, and, if an army be compared to a machine the power of which is supplied to it by a series of accumulators, should the object of its commander be to maintain movement, he can only accomplish this by refilling one set of accumulators while the other is in process of being exhausted. The shorter the time available to do this the more difficult will the commander's task be ; consequently, one of his most important duties, throughout war, is to increase the motive power of his troops, which depends on two main factors—moral and physical endurance.

In war, the power to move must first be considered in the form of the general will to move. In battle the forward impulse

The Science and Art of War

comes from the leaders and the troops themselves. They are, in fact, self-propelled projectiles and are not impelled forward by the explosive energy of command. Such energy scarcely if ever exists; what does exist is direction to its impulse, and the reinforcing or recharging of this impulse with more power by means of reserves. These reserves not only endow the combatants with physical energy but with a moral sense of power and security which impels them forward.

Even with an army of high moral, that is to say an army which possesses the will to move towards danger, or, inversely, the will to refuse to move away from danger, it must ultimately be the physical factor, the muscular endurance of the men themselves, which sets a limit to their power of movement. In order to increase muscular movement, by conserving it as long as possible, mechanical means of movement have for some time been employed for the strategical and administrative movements of an army; so much so that the approach movements to-day are based on locomotives and lorries. The result of this is that, while strategical mobility, namely movement at a distance from the enemy, has enormously increased, tactical movement, through increase of impedimenta, has decreased in inverse proportion, until battles founded on muscular movement have become more often than not static engagements based on broadside fire from fixed positions. In order to overcome this immobility, mechanical cross-country movement has been forced on armies, and, whatever may be the prejudice shown to its introduction, the complete replacement of muscular movement by it is as near a certainty as can be foreseen.

(vii.) *The Principle of Surprise.* Lack of security, or a false interpretation of the principle of security, leads directly to being surprised. The principle of surprise, like a double-edged tool, is an exceedingly dangerous one in unskilled hands; for, being mainly controlled by psychological factors, its nature is less stable and the conditions affecting it are more difficult to gauge.

Surprise, in its direct meaning, presupposes the unexpected, which, throughout history, may be considered under five general headings :

(i.) Surprise effected by superiority of courage.
(ii.) Surprise effected by superiority of movement.
(iii.) Suprise effected by superiority of protection.
(iv) Surprise effected by superiority of weapons.
(v.) Surprise effected by superiority of tactics.

To gain superiority in anything or any quality takes time, consequently we find that, although minor surprisals may be gained by seizing upon the right opportunities, the possibility of effecting major surprisals is based extensively on forecasts and preparations made during days of peace, especially as regards the nature and requirements of the next war, for the surest foundation of being surprised is to suppose that the next war will be like the last one. In modern times, similarity between wars has seldom occurred, as the most casual retrospect into military history will prove ; consequently, when a commander attempts to copy former battles, we find that an army is frequently surprised with its eyes open. It sees things coming, but, blinded by prejudice and shackled by tradition, it does not perceive their consequences, which are only realized when their causes have taken or are actually taking effect.

On the battlefield itself a general is frequently surprised by his own stupidity, his lack of being able to understand conditions or to apply to them the principles of war. His stupidity sometimes takes the acute form of completely misunderstanding the endurance of his men ; not realizing what they can do, he orders them to do something which they cannot do, and the result is chaos and loss of life. Surprise among troops, as among individuals, is largely a matter of nerves. The nerves of an army are not only to be found in the individual temperaments and collective suggestibility of the officers and men, but also in its staff organization. The trunk nerves of an army are its general staff, whose one great duty is to convey the impressions felt by the rank and file to the brains of their commander. If this be

The Science and Art of War

neglected the best laid plan will fail and paralysis of action will result in being surprised.

(viii) *The Principle of Co-operation*. Co-operation is a cementing principle ; it is closely related to economy of force, and therefore to concentration, but it differs from both of these principles, for while mass is the concentrated strength of the organism and economy of force the dispersed strength which renders the former stable, co-operation may be likened to the muscular tension which knits all the parts into one whole. Without co-operation an army falls to pieces. In national wars, the value of co-operation is enormously enhanced, fusing, as it does, the body and soul of a nation into one intricate self-supporting organism. All must pull together, for such wars are the wars of entire nations, and, whatever may be the size of the armies operating, these should be looked upon as national weapons, and not as fractions of nations whose duty is to fight while the civil population turns thumbs up or thumbs down. Gladiatorial wars are dead and gone.

We find, therefore, that for us co-operation in war embraces the whole gamut of our Imperial existence, which means that during war one master mind must control the whole national machinery, in order to reduce the friction which its adjustment by many hands inevitably creates. Take, for instance, the government of a nation at war. If there be friction in the government, there is friction not only throughout the nation but throughout the army. No man can efficiently serve two masters, neither can two masters lead and direct the same man. If in a cabinet of six members each strives to conduct a war departmentally, according to his own particular degree of ignorance in strategy, in place of one objective there will be six objectives, or, worse still, six phases of one objective. When such a state of affairs arises it is time to declare a dictatorship, for dispersion of force in war is to commit suicide while temporarily insane. There can be but one main objective ; consequently, all subsidiary ones must be reduced to their utmost limit to enable the concentration of all requisite battle-power at the decisive point. One objective requires one master-mind to formulate the general plan, and not half a dozen jacks of all trades to dissipate it. One master mind must control the war, and all other minds must accept or be compelled to accept his ruling.

Tactically, co-operation is based on battle organization, weapons, protection and movement, skill, confidence, discipline and determination : it is moral, physical and mechanical. This means that all must work for the attainment of the objective and not for themselves. The weeding out of fools and knaves is, therefore, the first step to be accomplished. The second is the scrapping of bureaucratic processes and shibboleths, and the bringing of ability to the top. Senility of thought is the antithesis of co-operative action. A vintage of new ideas is always produced in war, and the vats must be sufficient and the bottles strong enough to hold it ; for new ideas, like new wine, go through a process of fermentation, which in an army commanded by a weak-headed general can only lead to tactical intoxication. Co-operation in its widest sense spells not only military efficiency but national and Imperial efficiency, which centred round one line of direction impels all the life and fighting strength of the nation towards victory. Without such an axis an army fights floundering.

Principles in themselves are not worth the paper they are written on, for they are but mere words strung together in a certain order. Their value lies in their application, and this application depends on the thousand and one conditions which surround the elements of war during operations. What are these conditions, for without knowing them it is manifestly impossible to apply the principles ? Conditions are innumerable and ever changing, but the following are some of the most important : Time, space, ground, weather, numbers, training, communications, supply, armament, formations, obstacles and observation.

Each of these conditions may be considered as possessing a dual nature—a power of increasing the strength of the offensive and a power of increasing the strength of the defensive ; each,

The Science and Art of War

therefore, may be looked upon as possessing power to enhance offensive and defensive action in war.

A commander has three means at his disposal to deal with a condition :

(i.) He may avoid it.
(ii.) He may break it down.
(iii.) He may turn it to his own advantage.

The third course, which masters the difficulty, is manifestly the best, and it is the one which even a superficial study of military history will show was employed by the great Captains of war, it was in fact the secret of their success.

At the beginning of this Chapter I stated that, when two men fought their object was to impose their will upon each other. Up to the present I have mainly considered the means employed in order to accomplish this, and the principles governing these means. I will now turn to the psychological side of war, and show that it also has its elements, principles and conditions.

I will examine once again the primitive duel between two unarmed men, and from it will extract certain facts which may be classed as psychological elements. We first find the primordial material—man, but this time represented not by muscle but by mind. As the physiological object of the fighter is " to kill without being killed," so is his psychological object " to will without being willed." In these five words is presented the pivotal psychological problem in the science of war—the destruction of the enemy's will, which not only cements together his army but the whole of his nation in a vast living mosaic.

In war, as in all other phases of human activity, we find that the elemental psychological power is mind. In the case of our two unarmed fighters, both fear the other, there is no courage in the normal meaning of the word ; both desire to kill the other, and both instinctively take advantage of any opportunity to do so, especially, if by so doing, little risk be run. We here obtain three elements :

(i.) Will—desire to kill.

The Reformation of War

(ii.) Cunning—opportunity to kill at the smallest risk.
(iii.) Fear—desire to live.

The first is the mobile element, the second and third the offensive and the defensive elements respectively.

In primitive man, the first is awakened through threats to self- and family-preservation; in civilized man, though these bear equal sway, to them must be added the more recently acquired instincts of race- and national-preservation with all their ramifications—social, political and commercial. From the second, the making good of opportunity, we get a most complex evolution · cunning evolving into knowledge, education, science and art. From a tactical standpoint, natural cunning, as it presents itself in the primitive duel, evolves into the skill of the scientific fighter. Skill, reacting on the will, is a great incentive to moral, or confidence. The greater the skill of the soldier, the greater will this confidence become, and, as confidence in the weapons used plays as important a part in the growth of moral as skill in the use of the weapons themselves, we find that every improvement in weapons carries with it a psychological impulse Thus, a man, who unarmed, will tremble before a footpad, feels no fear when covering him with a revolver. This is so important a point that it forms one of the main problems of this book. Weapons being material means of accomplishing mental impulses, not only do they stimulate the will by instilling confidence (moral), but skill in their use depends on this stimulation. Therefore, we find that, in order to control the third element, the mental powers of the soldier, as aggregated in his will, must never become slack, lazy or paralysed. They must be held in a state of attention on the " desire to win." This state of attention may be symbolized by the quality called " courage," which, in war, simply means a state of less fear than that in which the enemy is in, and not necessarily a sense of personal superiority such as might be felt by a poet or artist over a clodhopper or successful grocer. This state of courage, it will be seen, is equally dependent on skill in movement, weapons and protection, and the superiority of these

The Science and Art of War

elements themselves over those of the enemy. Thus, from will, through the reaction of cunning, which I will now call moral, and fear, is scientific fighting evolved.

Though the principles of war are equally applicable to the psychological aspects of this science, there are certain definite psychological principles which may be abstracted alike from the primitive duel and the scientific battle. There is, first of all, a desire or " determination " to fight, either on one side or both The contest opens, therefore, with two wills in opposition. The giving and aiming of blows is made in order to enforce the will, and the avoiding of them to prevent the will being enforced. This enforcement I will call " demoralization," and the avoidance of it " endurance " From these we can extract three great principles ·

(i.) The principle of determination.

(ii.) The principle of demoralization.

(iii.) The principle of endurance.

These psychological principles constitute a definite link between the physical and mental sides of the science of war, which may be depicted as follows :

MAN

Muscle $\begin{cases} \text{Movement..(Principle of Determination)..Will} \\ \text{Weapons ..(Principle of Endurance)....Moral} \\ \text{Protection..(Principle of Demoralization)..Fear} \end{cases}$ Mind.

We start with man physical and man mental, he must possess the will to fight and the power to move, the connecting link is the principle of determination or the will to win. He must possess the moral to hit and the power to hit, here the connecting link is the principle of endurance. He must endow his adversary with a fear which will force him to protect himself or seek protection, which is acknowledgment of lack of endurance (temporary or permanent), and inferiority of determination ; here the connecting link is the principle of demoralization. Thus, we see that, in war, the " will to win " is the power of being able to endure and to demoralize, and that the three psychological elements are not " things in themselves " but coefficients of the elements of war—movement, weapons and protection.

As I have dealt at some length with the principles of war, it is only fitting that I should now examine these psychological principles, for they are no less important. Briefly, the following are my views.

(1.) *The Principle of Determination.* The limits of the principle of determination are first defined by the national objective of war, and secondly by its military objective. Between these two boundaries this principle operates.

From the national point of view, there is the will to impose upon the enemy's government a policy distasteful to it; this policy must be clean cut, for on its stability rests the military objective, which psychologically is the " will to win." Subjectively, this will is concentrated in the mind of the commander, whose plan of action is the means of enforcing the national policy; this plan must also be clean cut, that is to say it must be so simple that its very nature will give rise to the fewest possible complexities. As the stability of this plan will depend on the stability of the policy, the commander-in-chief must not only be acquainted with the nature of this policy, but with any changes rendered necessary through fluctuations in national conditions. Inversely, any changes in plan will entail modifications in policy; consequently, we find that both the plan and the policy are correlatives, that is they are dependent on each other's stability. Now, as every policy must be plastic enough to admit of fluctuations in national conditions, so must each plan be plastic enough to receive the impressions of war, that is power to change its shape without changing or cracking its substance. This plasticity is determined psychologically by the condition of mentality in the two opposing forces. There is the determination between the two commanders-in-chief, and between them and their men, and, ultimately, between the two forces themselves. The " will to win " is, therefore, first of all a duel between two brains each controlling a weapon called an army; and secondly, a struggle between two armies

The Science and Art of War

each equipped with various types of weapons. If all these various weapons, each influencing in its own degree the mentality of its wielder and that of his opponent, can be reduced in number, the principle of determination becomes more simple in application If, again, similarity of protection becomes possible, simplicity is increased ; and if, finally, similarity of movement can be added, physically the simplest form of army is evolved.

I will now examine the psychological side. If the will and moral of each individual can be brought to a high but equal level and his fear to a low and equal level, the commander-in-chief will possess known qualities out of which to construct his plan. It will be seen, therefore, that, in its broadest sense, the principle of determination is the simplification of the means so that the will of both the chief and his men may become operative.

(ii) *The Principle of Endurance.* Springing directly from the principle of determination is the great principle of endurance. The will of the commander-in-chief and the will of his men must endure, that is they must continue in the same state It is the local conditions, mental and material, which continually weaken this state and in war often threaten to submerge it. To the commander endurance consists, therefore, in power of overcoming conditions—by foresight, judgment and skill. These qualities cannot be cultivated at a moment's notice, and the worst place to seek their cultivation is on the battlefield itself. The commander-in-chief must be, therefore, a mental athlete, his dumbbells, clubs and bars being the elements of war and his exercises the application of the principles of war to the conditions of innumerable problems.

Collectively, in an army, endurance is intimately connected with numbers, and, paradoxical as it may seem, the greater the size of an army the less is its psychological endurance The reason for this is a simple one : one man has one mind , two men have three minds—each his own and a crowd mind shared between them ; a million men have millions and millions and millions of minds. If a task which normally requires a million men can be carried out by one man, this one man possesses

46 The Reformation of War

psychologically an all but infinitely higher endurance than any single man out of the million. Man, I will again repeat, is an encumbrance on the battlefield, psychologically as well as physically; consequently, endurance should not be sought in numbers, for one Achilles is worth a hundred hoplites.

(iii) *The Principle of Demoralization.* As the principle of endurance has, as its primary object, the security of the minds of men by shielding their moral against the shock of battle, inversely the principle of demoralization has as its object the destruction of this moral first, in the moral attack against the spirit and nerves of the enemy's nation and government; secondly against this nation's policy; thirdly against the plan of its commander-in-chief, and fourthly against the moral of the soldiers commanded by him. Hitherto the fourth, the least important of these objectives, has been considered by the traditionally-minded soldier as the sole psychological objective of this great principle. In the last great war the result of this was, as I shall show presently, that the attack on the remaining three only slowly evolved during days of stress and because of a faulty appreciation of this principle during peace time

I will now turn to the psychological conditions of war.

In considering these it must first be realized that all conditions are, in part at least, psychological That is to say they stimulate the brain in a greater or lesser degree; but while hundreds affect war materially, such as roads for supply and the influence of gravity on the flight of projectiles, thousands more directly affect the mind of the soldier, and through his mind his body, and through his body his actions. Psychologically, we may divide these conditions into three general categories: those which are common to men either individually or collectively; those which affect the soldier as an individual, and those which affect a mass of soldiers as a homogeneous crowd. The following are examples of these categories

(i.) *General Conditions:* Safety, comfort, fatigue, catchwords, loyalty, honour, faith, hatred and cheerfulness.

The Science and Art of War

(ii.) *Individual Conditions :* Knowledge, skill, determination, endurance, courage, imagination, confidence, talent and sense of duty.

(iii.) *Collective Conditions.* Suggestion, intuition, superstition, esprit de corps, tradition, moral, education, patriotism and comradeship.

I do not propose to analyse these conditions as it would take a long time to do so, nevertheless it should be remembered that the psychological principles in war cannot be applied correctly unless the conditions which go to build up soldiership have been stabilized, long prior to war, in days of peace.

The process whereby this stability is effected is called training. Training forms the true foundation of battle, which should be a continuation of the soldier's education, just as war itself should be a continuation of peace policy. For this to be possible it will be at once seen that training should not be based solely on the known conditions of past wars, but above all on the probable conditions of the next war. That, consequently, these conditions must be foreseen ; therefore, on the correctness of their forecasting will, to a great extent, depend the continuity of peace training in the form of battle tactics when war breaks out. Once we have diagnosed the conditions of the next war, then, by applying to them the psychological principles, we shall build up a scientific system of training. In fact, we shall start winning our battles from to-day onwards on the barrack square and in the class-room. Training, such as this, may well be called the art of war, the foundations of which I will now inquire into.

In analysing tactics, or the art of fighting, the military student usually visualizes the battle as a " thing in itself." The correct appreciation is diametrically opposite, for battles consist of a complex series of individual fights, each compounded of the elements of war operating concentrically round the problem of how to give blows without receiving them. This problem may be divided into four sub-problems, which every commander should consider prior to an operation taking place.

The Reformation of War

These four problems are :

(i) How to keep men alive ?

(ii.) How to keep movement alive ?

(iii) How to keep weapons alive ?

(iv.) How to keep moral alive ?

As the commander has four problems to solve so also has the soldier. He has :

(i.) To hit his enemy while at a distance from him.

(ii) To move towards him.

(iii) To hit him at close quarters.

(iv.) To avoid being hit throughout this engagement

The whole of these eight problems are in nature protective, and they form the foundations of offensive power, which endow it with stability of action as well as security during action and after defeat.

I cannot here do more than glance at this fundamental problem of battle organization : how to organize an army so that it possesses power of stability and mobility. Briefly it may be explained as follows As the bones of man's body give stability to his muscular movement, so must every force of soldiers possess within their organization certain troops which can resist attack and certain others which can develop their mobility out of this resistance. The battle of Crecy was virtually won by the English archers, the mobile element. They could not, however, have accomplished what they did had not the men-at-arms and dismounted knights formed a stable base from which they were able to develop the full power of their bows. A scientifically organized army is one which possesses a brain and a body, both of which possess a positive and a negative pole, stability and mobility The stability of the brain is its faculty of reason based on knowledge, and its mobility the faculty of imagination based on the products of reason. The military body is divided into two main forces: those which disorganize the enemy's brain and body—that is, break down its stability, and those which annihilate the broken fragments. Each fraction of this body must possess power to

The Science and Art of War

resist movement and power to develop movement. Its mobility depends on a combination of weapons and movement, and its stability upon that of weapons and protection From these two— its stability and mobility, are its offensive and protective powers reciprocally developed. Thus, in the hands of man, do we see a harmonious inter-relation between the three physical elements of war, and, according to the degree of harmony attained, do the plans of man succeed or fail. This brings us to the problem of grand tactics or battle planning

In every plan the first question is to decide on the objective. In physical warfare the military objective is the defeat of the enemy's army, so that the will of his government may be attacked. Where, then, is the decisive point, the point at which the enemy may most economically be defeated ? The schoolmen answer " The decisive point depends on circumstances," and some suggest a flank and others a central objective The schoolmen, if they only thought in simpler terms than they are wont to do, could have long ago given a better answer to this question, which I will examine from a very simple point of view.

Every organization has one great prototype—the body of man. When a boxer fights another he tries to get a left or right on the side of his opponent's jaw. Why ? Not to break the jaw, the external body, but to derange the brain, the internal organ, because more than any other organ the brain controls the body.

The brain of an army is its command, and the command of an army is its decisive point, and no blow should be delivered without reference to this point Though the brains of an army control its whole body, nevertheless the prevailing idea in tactics is one of brute force applied by weapons to the enemy's battle body Batter the enemy's muscles blue and black and get battered black and blue in return, is the traditional method, and then only, when one side is rendered physically impotent, attack the brains !

I fully agree that more often than not it is impossible to strike straight to the jaw because our opponent carefully protects his chin. This does not, however, vitiate the fact that the decisive point is the command of the opposing army, and that the more

The Reformation of War

the enemy is forced to protect it, the less will he be able to hit out.

The elements of grand tactics are in essence very simple, once the decisive point has been agreed upon. The object is either to paralyse or disintegrate the enemy's command, which may be carried out by four acts, separate or combined. These four acts are:

(i.) *Surprise*. An enemy may be surprised, which implies that he is thrown off his balance. This is the best method of defeating him, for it is so economical, one man taking on to himself the strength of many. Surprise may be considered under two main headings: surprise effected by doing something that the enemy does not expect, and surprise effected by doing something that the enemy cannot counter. The first may be denoted as moral surprise, the second as material.

(ii.) *Envelopment*. An enemy may be enveloped and so placed at a severe disadvantage. Envelopment, whether accomplished by converging or overlapping, presupposes a flank, a flank which may be tactically rolled up, or, if turned, will expose the command and lines of communications behind it. The attack by envelopment is a very common action in war, which more often than not has led to victory.

(iii.) *Penetration*. An enemy's front may be penetrated in order directly to threaten his lines of communications behind it, or to hit at his command, or to create a flank or flanks to be enveloped. Normally, when once a hostile front is broken, the two sections are rolled up in opposite directions to each other, or one is held while the other is hammered; an operation which, if carried out successfully, usually leads to a total disintegration of the enemy's strength.

(iv.) *Attrition*. An enemy may be worn out by physical and moral action; this, though the usual method of defeating him, is also, frequently, the most uneconomical method, for the process of disintegration is mutually destructive.

Outside these four grand tactical acts of battle there is little to be learnt in grand tactics.

The Science and Art of War

Once the direction of the decisive attack is fixed, the grand tactical plan is arrived at by applying the principles of war to the conditions under which war has to be waged; in other words, liberty of movement has to be gained. Free movement, which is the object of all strategy, is conditioned not only by impulse but by the form of the object moved. In war, the will of the commander is the impulse, and the strategical distribution of his army the form of the military projectile, which should normally, like an arrow-head, be triangular, the main force in rear of it operating like the shaft behind the head. Generally this head consists of an advanced guard and two wings. The secret of all economical military formations is that they must possess a harmony of offensive and defensive power through movement, movement in its broadest sense being "locomobility," that is freedom of movement in all directions.

Liberty of movement is the basis of liberty of action, which is a compound formed out of superiority in the elements of war. It is the foundation of minor tactics and consists of the following values:

(i) Man.
- Superiority of will.
- Superiority of endurance.
- Continuity of co-operation.

(ii.) Movement
- Superiority of speed.
- Continuity of movement.
- Superiority of manœuvre.

(iii.) Weapon.
- Superiority of weapons.
- Superiority of clinching.
- Superiority of fire.

(iv.) Protection
- Inferiority of target.
- Continuity of supply.
- Superiority of mobile protection.

These must not only be mixed but amalgamated if liberty of action is to possess a practical value. Thus, continuity of ammunition supply is useless if superiority of weapons does not exist; and superiority of fire is useless if it does not produce continuity of co-operation. Liberty of action does not mean moving anywhere, but moving according to plan. It does not mean acting anyhow, either wholly or in part, but acting harmoniously towards the attainment of the objective. The relation of each of its components to the whole of its components, as represented by liberty of action itself, must be dynamic. Liberty of action is not the free will of the commander as a thing in itself, but the harmonious application of the principles of war to the conditions of the moment. The conditions formulating the lines of least resistance, and the will of the commander progressing, by means of the elements, along these lines according to the dictates of the principles. Liberty of action is the perfect correlationship between the elements and conditions by means of the principles. It is not so much the domination of one will over another as the adjustment of one will according to the other. Liberty of action is, therefore, the offspring of two wills rather than the force engendered by one; it is the analogy of two opposites.

In an army, as a whole, liberty of action is expressed in the soul of the team. Each separate action is identified with the whole action of the army and not as a part of the whole; it is a psychic power and not an organic act. It is manifested through a general will, a general endurance, and a general co-operation. It seeks action through a general mobility, a continuity of this mobility and the power of harmonizing it within itself. It attains result through the superiority of weapons, the superiority of fire, and the power of clinching, which it protects by the inferiority of the target offered to the enemy, the continuity of supply of ammunition, weapons, means of movement and men, and by the various forms of protection, the most important of which are of a mobile nature. Finally, liberty of action is based on harmony of movement, mental, physical and mechanical, which harmony, in itself, constitutes the energy of the compound.

If the nature of the elements of war is understood, and if we realize what is meant by liberty of action, it must, conse-

The Science and Art of War

quently, follow that there are both correct and incorrect offensive and defensive formations for weapons within units and for units themselves. I have already pointed out that the organization of every unit should possess stable and mobile qualities. I will now carry this analysis one step further.

In an attack, the first question to ask ourselves is : how to advance ? The second · what will prevent an economical advance ? Here again the old problem, of how to give blows without receiving them, confronts us. The clearance of obstacles to movement is essential; consequently, we arrive at a very common-sense answer, namely, that—few attacks except normal attacks are likely to succeed ; in fact a normal attack should be what its name implies—an attack according to principles governed by conditions, i e , economical.

Once resistance has been reduced to a normal condition ; it logically follows that a normal formation can be devised which will suit this condition, and that, until this condition is arrived at, no formation will prove economical.

I have already explained that movement has two forms— the approach and the attack; consequently, there are two main formations in battle :

(i.) The approach formation : The fundamental formation for the approach is one which will combine mobility and security with potentiality of offensive power.

(ii.) The attack formation: The fundamental formation for the attack is one which will enable the maximum number of weapons to be used with fullest effect.

The normal approach formation is the column,* and the normal attack formation is the line.

Whether an offensive be carried out over open field land or against a strongly fortified position, its foundations are to be sought for in the base of operations from which the attack

---

* The smallest column is the infantry section in single file It was used by Cyrus and Alexander, it was revived by Sir John Moore, forgotten, and once again to-day finds its place in infantry tactics See " The Procedure of the Infantry Attack," by the writer, R U S I. Journal, January, 1914.

54   The Reformation of War

is launched. In the past this base has been considered as the original starting line, and, if battles can be won in a single onslaught, this assumption is correct. As this can seldom be done, and as battles normally are won by relays of attacks, each relay must start from a stable base ; consequently there must be a base of operations to each objective requiring a fresh echelon of troops. Each echelon and each wave of each echelon must be sufficiently self-contained not only to be in a position to capture an objective, or line of resistance, but to hold it, and so form a base of operations for the echelon or wave following it. Further, each wave must be protected by the one in front of it as well as those behind it and on its flanks, and, as the first wave cannot be so protected and the last is frequently similarly situated, it is essential that the leading troops and those which will form the ultimate battle front should be drawn from a *corps d'élite*, the former setting the example and the latter instilling confidence.

Having now explained what I mean by a progressive base of operations, I will examine the action developed from this base. First, we have got to assemble the troops ; secondly, these troops have got to approach towards the enemy ; thirdly, they have got to attack him, and fourthly, destroy him physically or morally. Here we obtain four minor tactical acts :

(i.) The assembly.

(ii.) The approach.

(iii.) The attack.

(iv.) The pursuit.

The first is preparatory to the second, the second to the third and the third to the fourth.

The attack may be divided into two stages according to whether missile or shock weapons are used. These are .

(i.) The act of demoralization (fire fight).

(ii) The act of decision (shock).

The act of annihilation or pursuit is virtually a new attack requiring fresh troops and troops of a more mobile nature to those pursued. To summarize

The Science and Art of War

A battle is an enormously complex action consisting of a number of simple parts. First, we must grasp the conditions, and, by so doing, ride the course. We then must take all the conditions which we know and weigh out their values in terms of assistance and resistance. Those we do not know but suspect we must consider even more carefully than those we know, allowing for a considerable margin of error, and always giving the benefit of doubt to the enemy.

Having collected and codified these conditions, we must next apply to them the principles of war. We must decide upon our objective, applying the offensive to those conditions which will assist us and security to those which will not ; thus shall we master conditions and harness them to our will. We then think in terms of concentration, of economy of force, of movement and surprise ; finally, we weave the whole together in a close co-operation.

By now our battle plan will have evolved almost unconsciously, and our plan is our grand tactics.

From this point we think purely in terms of fighting, the skeleton is complete, all that now remains to be done is to clothe it with flesh and muscle—the elements of war. We think in terms of men, movement, weapons and protection. What are they all going to do ? Then human and animal endurance and communications, protection by armour, earth, fire and formation. All these give us our battle tactics. Then, there is the battle itself, in which the moral and physical powers of man come into play. The approach merges into the attack, and the offensive and defensive powers of weapons, shielded by direct and indirect protection, carry the man forward. Such is battle and such is war—a science and an art based on sure foundations, rooted fast in the past, with its boughs and leaves moving this way and that above and around us according to the conditions of the moment, but governed by the laws of existence—action and inertia.

III

THE ETHICS OF WAR

THE ethics of war is a subject which in the past has not been very carefully considered, and yet, without a just comprehension of it, it is quite impossible to sift the virtues of war from its vices. Hitherto, and from time immemorial, there have existed two opposite ethical schools of military thought—the peace-mongers and the war-mongers. To the first, war appears as the greatest of calamities and to the second, a beneficial necessity. Both, in the main, dislike war, but while the first seek its abolition through concord and disarmament, the second aim at its restriction through threat and preparation. In my own opinion there is right and wrong on both sides, for nothing in this world is absolutely good or absolutely evil, and the mere fact that in war an enormous energy is expended should lead every thinking man to suppose that, even if in the past this energy has been chiefly made use of for purposes of destruction, there may be some hidden path along which, should it be directed, prosperity in place of calamity will result. With this idea before me, it is my intention in this Chapter not so much to seek this path as to examine the values of war, for when once these are discovered the path itself should in the main become apparent.

Starting with an assumption that wars are an inevitable constituent of human progress, an assumption I have examined in Chapter I., I will first inquire into the ethical objective of nationality, for on this objective must the true military ethical aim be founded, because military might is but a means of enforcing national policy.

The Ethics of War

The science of ethics is the science of duty collective and individual. The duty of a nation is to survive; first, with profit to itself, and secondly, with profit to humankind; by which is meant that each succeeding generation should intellectually, morally and physically be superior to the generation which begat it. Ethics teach men their duties not only towards each other but towards themselves, and it is upon these duties that national stability is founded.

Race survival, or the struggle for existence between the weaker and the stronger, breeds cunning and co-operation, without which a nation must retrogress. Either the weaker in body must become more cunning (mentally able) in mind, or else they must unite co-operatively in order to survive. Consequently, weakness, as well as strength, possesses qualities of virtue and vice. Virtue, ethically, being defined as: those conditions which enable a race to survive, and vice as: those which accelerate its decline and hasten its extinction. Virtue and vice are, therefore, purely relative qualities, they are in no wise, in the Kantian sense, "categorical imperatives," but, in place, improvised factors conditioned according to local requirements. What is virtuous to-day may be vicious to-morrow, and what is vicious in the Antipodes may simultaneously be virtuous in the land of the Hyperborians.

Opposition, which presupposes weakness, is the incentive of mental progress both in the individual and in the race, for it constitutes the inhospitable region in which intellect *must strive* to live and either dominate or succumb. Mind fights muscle (superiority of human strength or numbers) with weapons of cunning which frequently turn conditions to the favour of the physically weak or outnumbered. Ethics have, therefore, little to do with moral customs established by majorities but much with the psychology of mind.

I have shown in Chapter I., how cunning threatens the existence of the strong—the cunning savage of primeval days lures his adversary away from security and kills him unawares. I also pointed out that this cunning, as a mean effort to survive, becomes repellant to the strong. It is stamped as ignoble, for a scrofulous cripple may kill an athlete. The idea of the human louse arises, an individual living on the mental deficiency of his neighbours, and the growth of this organism is restricted by laws and ethical codes. Inversely, prowess is endowed with a nobility of character, for upon prowess is the physical health of the family or race founded, progeneration being a physical and not a mental act.

From prowess, especially the prowess of the male as he finds favour in the eyes of the female, is born the instinct of self-distinction, the personal ethical factor, which evolves into the collective ethical factor when it merges into race-distinction, and, eventually, into race-pride and patriotism.

If we inquire into the nature of these factors we shall find many components, some transient and some permanent. Of the latter, the bulk may be placed under one common heading: the greatest ethical virtue or factor of either the individual or the nation being " common-sense."

The means of attaining the ethical objective of a nation is therefore common-sense. Honesty is common-sense; truthfulness is common-sense; courage is common-sense, because all these qualities assist in the survival of individuals and the race, and not only in survival but survival with profit through co-operation based on mutual confidence, trust and respect.

The reverse of common-sense is common-nonsense, a factor far too little appreciated. Thus a society in which every man lies is a nonsensical society; so equally is one in which every man steals or every man cohabits with his neighbour's wife. Nonsensical periods, at times, sweep over a nation just as they do over an individual, especially during the periods of youth and decay (change). A spirit of comic opera, tragic enough to the actors but laughable to the onlookers, will sometimes possess an entire nation. They stamp out their intellect in a social delirium tremens, the product of imbibing strong doctrines to excess. They conscript their labour, socialise their women, and then, after an ebullition of liberty, equality and fraternity, whatever

The Ethics of War

these intoxicants may mean, grab from each other whatever is left of their past prosperity and revert to honesty, truthfulness and moral conduct, because without these ethical factors it would be impossible for them to survive. They must either succumb to common-sense or perish nonsensically; this is the ethical law of survival.

If ethics be defined as " the science of duty," and duty, from its national aspect be defined as " the obligation to survive with profit," then ethics may be considered as the psychological aspect of biology, that is the science of life. Life never ceases to change, and, if ethics be a branch of this science, it, consequently, must be dynamic in nature, that is it must ceaselessly change coincidently with changes in man and in the society to which man belongs.

A moment's consideration will reveal to us that the motive powers in man are either instinctive or acquired, the former being far more stable than the latter; so also in ethics do we find a similar division. Psychologically, the instinctive qualities originate from the instinct of self-preservation and the acquired from innumerable artificial conceits springing mainly from that of self-distinction—the outer manifestation of the preservative qualities in the individual or race. The strong man advertises his strength brutally, he breaks the neck of a bull; the weak man's cunning slays the brute with a sharp flint or bullet. By openly demonstrating what each can do, they mutually teach the other their respective deficiencies and so exaggerate their intrinsic ability by swelling it with the admiration or envy of those who watch them, and, consequently, add moral power to their physical or mental strength.

In ethics, the process is very similar. We start with foundational or stable ethics, those based on the instinct of self-preservation; we progress through these codes to those of collective or social health, and through these to the codes of dynamic ethics, or the ethical comments arising through the mobility of changefulness in ratiocination and local circumstances. These, originating as unwritten rules of procedure, crystallize

60 The Reformation of War

into customs and become petrified. Thence arise the internecine conflicts between instincts and acquirements—the social skeleton tries to shake off the withered flesh

Thus, ethics may grow from a duty into a compulsion and evolve into a series of penal codes by which society is imprisoned and against which creative thought within society is ever striving, until, like a bodily fever, it sloughs the no longer sentient skin in a war of purgation. Ethics in the form of copy-book virtues are, therefore, a cause of war—wars of liberation which racially are endemic in character, that is contagious. One nation catching the psychological bacillus of liberty from another, is cast into a delirium in which the ossified ethical codes become mere " scraps of paper," social scabs, things to be torn up and scratched at by the instincts which are again freed from restriction. As restrictions no longer exist, they, like wild-fire, flow out athwart civilization and, on occasion, do not stay their fury until they have utterly consumed it.

Ethics, as customs, manners, conventional morals and fashions, are, when in a healthy state, mobile in nature. To discover whether any of these transient virtues are growing vicious simply requires the application of common-sense. That is, a comparison should be made between the effects of the doubtful virtue and the ethical objective—survival with moral profit, any deficiency being made good by action adapted to circumstances. Unfortunately, as common-sense is the rarest of all the senses, this simple process of gauging the temperature of the social body by this ethical thermometer is, more often than not, attempted by legal casuistry and a reshuffling of letters and words : an action which would do credit to an Assyrian sorcerer yelling barbarous names at the moon.

Besides those codes of morals which stimulate or restrict the evolution of the race, innumerable traditions exist both as stimulants and as narcotics. The power of tradition is immense, both as a beneficial influence and as a malevolent one, according to its relationship to circumstances.

Normally the origin of **a** tradition is to be sought for in

The Ethics of War

some successful individual action which has resulted in a betterment—intellectual, moral or material. Success depends, to a very great extent, on creative brain power and opportunity, which is nothing less than the exploitation of existing circumstances by existing means. This cause, as far as the individual is concerned, is temporary in nature. With a man's death his creative energy ceases, circumstances change and his theories of success lose their applicability.

In the individual, common-sense usually succeeds in pruning out dead personal traditions, because the individual nearly always possesses creative power of thought. The individual has to live on his own ability and energy, and, as an individual, he generally refuses to commit suicide by adhering to the obsolete traditions of his family; besides this, these traditions, being for the most part unrecorded, die with their begetters. This is, however, far from being the case when traditions spring from collective acts or are absorbed by congeries of men. To the crowd the novel is, more frequently than not, the heterodox, because the crowd possesses little or no power of reason, and acts of individual ability irritate and insult it by diverging from what it accepts unthinkingly as established truths. These collective traditions grow into static and, frequently, meaningless shibboleths, which the receptively-minded accept without criticism, because they do not possess the ability to formulate it. They grow into vested interests and prejudices which clog all progress. He who has does not wish to part with what he has, even if it be but an irrational idea, and the more he is induced to part with it, the more prejudicial does he become. He fights the new idea, he slanders it, he anathematizes it, for progress is unpalatable to his static taste. He wishes to be left alone and do what his father and grandfather did before him, for what he has inherited, however rotten it may be, is a personal and treasured possession, it is part of himself, for acquisitiveness is an instinct in man.

When, in place of the individual, the crowd is considered, these vested interests and prejudices become deeply rooted in its

The Reformation of War

nature, and in no assemblies is this more apparent than in those which represent religious orders, political denominations and military castes. Leaving the first out of account, I will examine the remaining two because they are closely related, every civilized army being managed by a political department of the government of the nation to which it belongs.

State departmental rule, I will assert before I prove it, is a system of management normally founded on common-nonsense, or upon action adapted to traditions in their static forms of interests and prejudices. What do we see ?

A body of men precipitated into office from the test tubes of examinations which, at best, only prove the blotting-paper nature of their brains—their power of absorbing ink visually. Once deposited alembic-like on an office stool, the official process of mental distillation begins. A fixed salary sterilizes their creative powers ; promotion by seniority demonstrates to them the uselessness of ability and the value of senility, and the prospects of a pension and the possibility of losing it, should they court disfavour, shackle and gag them—mind, nerve and jaw. They become monks in a monastic institution and repeat rituals which have lost their meaning, magical *mantras* which render their thoughts comatose to all reality beyond their files. They grow in strength and breed families called sub-departments ; fill these with branch memoranda, which are revolved in never ceasing revolution like the prayer-wheels of the Mahayana Buddhists It is so easy, so soothing, so absolutely safe—thus time, the controlling factor in life, is drowned in a sea of ink.

Then one day, these Trappists, fat on mental indolence, are awakened into the reality of a common-sense life outside them by seditions among those on whom they have successfully eked out their anæmic existence. War is in men's minds ; creative thought is stalking through the land ; the race instincts are once again abroad. But the monks cannot see them in their true form In place they see devils, and horrified they return to their files, splash ink and rotate their wheels with as unchaste a frenzy as tame mice in a rotary cage. Thus are great nations periodically

The Ethics of War

inflicted with a fever by the insanitary mental conditions of their government departments, their political incantations, their prayer-wheels, their files, their ink and their lack of human-touch.

In the armies of most modern States, we find the same cramping influence of tradition at work and due to the same causes: fixed pay, promotion by seniority and mental emasculation by pensions. There is little or no incentive to creative thought and every incentive to remain static. The whole atmosphere is unethical, that is unprogressive; consequently, soldiers become monastic in mind; they think in meaningless shibboleths, perform unintelligible rituals, and base their duties on established rules and the dotting of an "i" elaborately legislated for in some obscure and rigid regulation. They are Homoiousians or Homoousians in thought. The result of this is that it is not age which renders them impotent to the realities of war, but the gelding-knife of fixed ideas. Their thinking power is rendered sterile by the darkness of unreality. Like weeds growing in a cellar, so do armies become lank and lean in mind and colourless in intellect by gazing at the walls of the mental dungeons in which they are imprisoned.

Common-sense is again the remedy, common-sense which replaces common-nonsense and which asks: "What is the object of war?" And which answers: "The security of existence, prosperity and honour by the fullest exploitation of the people and their resources." As long as this common-sense question is not asked by the nation and the answer demanded of its army, so long will this army remain an immoral association, that is one which does not fulfil or guarantee the ethical needs of the people. Salvation is through common-sense, which should be the supreme canon and law of the military hierarchy.

During periods of stress, such as war, the character of a nation reveals itself. If the war be unimportant, its loss may not materially affect the nation, yet, nevertheless, it will be a blow registered against its prestige, its moral capital upon the stability of which so much of its material prosperity is founded. Its credit will be lowered in the eyes of others, and a series of such blows may exhaust the national moral to such an extent that the prestige of the nation is laid bare to a knock-out blow. If the war be important, victory becomes vital, and the nation subconsciously realizing this, sets to work to divest itself of the formalities of everyday life. Traditions one by one are discarded and replaced by common-sense actions, and, as this process grows, the great stable and foundational race ethics reveal themselves, and the nation stands or falls on its character, to which is intimately related the justice of its cause.

Thus are the ethics of race progress frequently refined by war by being liberated from the jargon of meaningless shibboleths, the small-talk of politics and the strangling customs of bygone ages. War sweeps these aside like a storm of rain cleansing the foul streets of a dirty city. The process is uncomfortable, especially for those who are caught in the storm, but the result is the reinvigoration of the race through the self-revelation of its character. It finds that it possesses something more precious than conventions, grades, rules and regulations. It finds that, though these under certain conditions are inevitable, they are not essential, and to be purged from them, even but for a time, is a stimulus to the national health. It finds that it *has* a will to accept self-sacrifice and a soul above the pettiness of peace.

War is a great physician, a great medicine, a great purge. As the body of man, unless his body be exceptionally well regulated, requires an occasional aperient—a dose of calomel, so does a nation require an occasional war to free it from the costiveness of traditions; and, if foreign wars be rendered impossible, then Nature will simply replace them by internal revolutions. Thus we see that war may sometimes become an ethical factor of great value. This being so, I will now consider the nature of the ethical object of war.

As the military object of war is to defeat the enemy, and as the economic object is to add to the prosperity of the nation, so is the ethical object to enhance the national character, that is

The Ethics of War

to increase its respect in the eyes not only of the enemy but of neutral nations. A man who fights cleanly is always applauded even if he lose ; consequently, under certain circumstances, it is even more important to win the ethical objective than the military one ; these circumstances depending almost entirely on the mentality of the combatants If their ideals be of a material nature then the military objective becomes the most important ; if of a moral, then the ethical objective is paramount.

In most cases the endurance of a war is based on the ethical nature of its cause If race survival be this cause, then the war is founded on justice, and, as justice is a common-sense virtue, whether the artificial laws and customs of civilization prohibit wars or not, wars will continue, for the greatest of all laws is the unwritten and unwritable law of self and racial preservation. A man steals another man's wife : this is a definite common-sense injustice in a community where the men and women are numerically equal. Should, however, the number of women fall, I will suppose, to half that of the number of men, it is manifestly unjust to the race, whatever it may be to the individuals, that one man should have two wives or even that one man should possess one wife Consequently wife-stealing ceases to be an act of injustice and becomes *of necessity* a natural virtue ; for the strongest and most cunning will come into possession of the women, and, consequently, the race will prosper through an act which may be classed by the weaker party as one of the grossest injustice and immorality.

So also in war is the ethical process very similar , justice depending on the instincts which underlie civilization and the conditions which surround it, and not on the conventions which veneer it. If a war be waged for the personal benefit of individuals, it normally will prove a vicious war, but if for the benefit of the race, a virtuous one If, further, this war be fought not only for the benefit but for the self-preservation of the race fighting it, it will then become a common-sense war of necessity, that is a righteous war, which means, to refuse to wage it would be the grossest act of national immorality.

Great wars directed towards an ethical objective may consequently be looked upon as a new dispensation which breaks up the atheism of peace begotten by long periods of personal indulgence in place of racial improvement. Peace solidifies customs, and customs and traditions strangle the national will. Then comes war and sweeps these aside; it ploughs through accepted dogmas and roots up the weeds of civilization, preparing the ground for the next and better crop. War proves a nation not only capable of mastering its enemies, but of mastering itself; of sacrificing interests and prejudices for the common good, and of emerging from wrack and ruin, sorrow and woe, cleaner mentally and socially than before the sword was drawn.

Wars between great nations seem terrible to mean little men, men meanly brought up and meanly educated, men who can only see great things in a mean little way. But indeed such wars are grand and glorious when compared to the hideous strife of mediæval man, of unorganized mobs, of murderous bullies, and of that great degenerate scum which bubbles up upon the surface of a nation at every crisis. War may be ghastly or sublime; it is both, but Nature cares neither for the one nor for the other; she orders evolution, and evolve we must, on her lines and not on those expectorated by some decayed pedagogue. On the lines of war, in which a nation accumulates the wealth of the weak, thus are the strong rewarded; of peace, in which the strong develop their spoil, thus are the cunning recompensed; of commercial war, in which the workers accumulate the riches of the masters; of commercial peace, in which wealth is developed and diffused throughout the world. Peace in decay is more terrible than even a war of wantonness and destruction, as Carlyle so dramatically exclaims:

> "Call ye that a Society, cries he again, where there is no longer any Social Idea extant; not so much as the Idea of a common Home, but only of a common overcrowded Lodging-house? Where each, isolated, regardless of his neighbours, clutches what he can get, and cries 'Mine!' and calls it Peace, because in the cut-purse and cut-throat scramble, no steel knives, but only a far cunninger sort, can be employed?"

The Ethics of War

When this type of peace begins to asphyxiate a nation, it is time to press our swords, however rusty, upon the grindstones of war and cut the throat of the wanton who has deceived us.

As the ethical object of a nation is to gain a moral or commonsense superiority over its neighbours, that is a reputation for honesty and fearlessness in all their many forms, it stands to reason that this objective must be maintained when peace gives way to war, unless ethics are to be cast overboard. Normally, in a healthy nation there should be no break in policy; consequently, in war the policy of rightfulness must be continued without interruption if an ethical profit is to be secured

In the past, and to a very considerable extent at present, the traditional methods of peace have not been based on a policy of rightfulness but on one of compromise between what nationally is considered good and evil. Most civilized governments have attempted through diplomacy (the object of which should be to guarantee and safeguard peaceful prosperity and honour) to divide the nations which surround them into two categories—future friends and future foes (the good and evil). These categories have then been subjected to a diplomatic bombardment, the former with moralizing impressions and the latter with demoralizing ones. In this bloodless contest the main weapons have been the newspapers of prospective friends and foes, over which frequently controlling interests are obtained. If this unethical process of waging war continues, then, at a near date, we may find that one nation will become the actual owner or hidden controller of another nation's press, and that the words which express the policy of an enemy are thrust down the throats of ignorant people like home-made jam. Words, much more so than thoughts, are omnipotent among crowds, but they must be intelligible, and if the difference originating with Babel can be overcome by an international press, the nation which can control its interests will be in a powerful position to poison the minds of its selected foes. Such action as this I believe to be grossly immoral, and that, in place of its reducing the incidence of war, it will greatly increase it, especially war in its most disastrous form, namely, civil war.

If this unethical form of diplomacy continue, then it will follow that the grand strategy of the nation, that is the utilization of the national energies for purposes of war, will follow suit. Thus, if it be discovered that a nation's mentality is represented by $10x - 7y$, x representing his possible assets and y his probable deficits, in peace time a prospective adversary might so direct his grand strategy as to reduce x and to increase y. Thus, if one of the x's represents political stability, an unscrupulous nation might attempt to reduce this power for war by sowing seeds of political discord in its competitor's government. If one of the y's be social unrest, it might decide to increase its disruptive influence by stimulating its strength. The first of the means whereby to accomplish this is, as I have already stated, the control of the victim's press, the second the control of the victim's banks. The former constitutes the surest means of disruption and the latter the surest of obtaining information, for, of all records, a nation's pass-books will furnish the most accurate source of information regarding the lives of the leaders of the victim nation, who may, consequently, be blackmailed into declaring war or maintaining peace.

The above processes of corrupting a nation's " will to win " by depriving him of the " power to will " during days of peace are, I affirm, both immoral and Machiavellian, and, worse still, they are foolish, because, in place of enhancing the virtues of a nation which so acts, they render visible its own vices. No man of worth will trust a cheat, a bully, or a cad, however skilful and successful he may be. For a time he may knuckle under, but only to await his chance ; then he will turn on the trickster and rend him, and rightly he will show no mercy Rightfulness begets mercy in the heart even of a ferocious enemy, and every nation should remember that, in war, it may be defeated, and that, if defeated, according to its past deeds it will be judged and punished.

In spite of the above opinion, war, it must be realized, is not a tourney but a life struggle for existence in which there is no belt

The Ethics of War 69

which may not be hit under, and, as long as traditional diplomacy exists, this belt will be hit under, for, as I have shown, the ethical objective of war finds its origin in the ethical objective of the nation during the peace which preceded the war. In type, it will follow type, though the tune is played in a higher octave

Should the ethical outlook of the nation be material and barbarous, so will its actions in war be material and barbarous ; consequently, to blame its soldiers for acting materially or brutally is illogical, for they are but the instruments of the policy which has been established by the nation during peace time. The immoralities of war are normally but a continuation of the immoralities of peace. Like an individual soldier or an army, war, as a whole, possesses its moral side, which is the spiritual expression of the accumulated impressions that each individual member of the nation has received during peace time. Consequently, if wars are to be made less barbarous, it is useless restricting the bodily and mechanical activities of the soldier, for these are not ends in themselves. Instead, the spiritual and ethical outlook of the nation must be improved If war is to be made less brutal, then indeed must philanthropists watch the cradles and the nursery in place of the arsenals and the barrack-room.

Besides the ethical object of the war, viewed as a great national benefit, since time immemorial war has had its traditions and customs which accelerate or retard victory according as their values may be equated in terms of common-sense. Thus, to assassinate prisoners is not so much an immoral act as an uneconomical one. If prisoners are killed off, it will mean that the enemy will fight to the death ; that his men will retaliate by killing the prisoners they capture ; that the use of prisoners as labourers or hostages will be lost, and that the moral effect of the savagery resulting will upset that cool, deliberate determination which is so necessary in order to control the actions of soldiers on the battlefield. Assassination is, therefore, quite as much a vice in war as in peace. Thus again, the sacking of towns and the killing of civilian inhabitants is wrong, unless these acts can find a commensurate compensation of real military value ; not so much because they entail the loss of property and life, but because they lead to the moral disintegration of an army and sow seeds of hatred which will survive the war.

It must not, however, be forgotten that, while a few years ago, armies alone went forth to battle, to-day entire nations go to war, not only as soldiers but as the moral and material suppliers of soldiers. This being so, we find that, while a short time back, it was clearly possible to differentiate between the military and ethical objectives of nations at war, to-day this differentiation is becoming more and more complex ; so much so, that both these objectives are likely to coincide, and, when this takes place, to attack the civilian workers of a nation will then be as justifiable an act of war as to attack its soldiers.

The ethical traditions of war have little to do with the paper customs and usages manufacturered by elderly and talkative busy-bodies in the quietude of philanthropic debate, but much with unwritten acts of chivalry which refine the brutality of the art. Many of these acts survive to grow into shibboleths which become astringents to victory. Others, more stable in nature, prove true solvents of future difficulties, and these, as might be expected, are based on common-sense. Chivalry, in the broadest meaning of the word, is the cultivation of respect in an enemy for or by his opponent. Outstanding acts of courage, of courtesy, of humanity, give birth to a feeling of superiority or inferiority according as one side excels or falls short of the other. This feeling of superiority, of *noblesse oblige*, is purely ethical, yet it forms the basis of the physical superiority which victory demands. The side which, in war, first attains a superiority in chivalry is the side which attains a spiritual victory over its enemy, a victory which normally not only precedes a material success but which wins the ethical objective of war, which is the true foundation of the peace which follows it.

These acts of chivalry are to a great extent individual acts based on the individual culture of the race. An army of gaol-birds, however well disciplined it may be, will, on the battlefield

The Ethics of War

revert to type directly restraint is released ; so also will an army of cultured men ; but the difference between these two types is, that while in the former case the soldier reverts to a criminal, in the latter he usually continues as an honourable man, for honour is part of his permanent status. On individual acts of honour is chivalry founded.

In many respects war may be compared to a game. It has its rules, which are elastic enough to be of general application ; but there is this difference. While in a game the referee is represented by a third party, a disinterested judge, in war there is no third party, the referee being replaced by the conscience of the combatants themselves. As I have already remarked, there is no belt which may not be hit under ; nevertheless, though this be the case, a wise fighter will think twice before hitting below a certain moral line, because the tactical advantage accruing may be cancelled out by the ethical loss resulting. If in a game of football, however, the referee abscond, and one side, arming itself with sticks, assails the other, it would be ethically and competitively wrong if the side so attacked did not protect itself. Ethically so because brutality would usually triumph ; competitively, because the unarmed side would inevitably be driven from the field. In such circumstances common-sense again holds final judgment, as it always must ; and when, in its accepted forms of chivalry, it can no longer be applied, then application must be sought for through any and every means which will wipe out the insult of a dishonourable opposition. Men who take on the nature of vermin must be exterminated, and in their extermination is the entire moral progress of mankind moved one step nearer its final and unknown goal. To refuse to use base means against a base foe is to set a premium on crime, and in war there are crimes as well as honours. To tolerate crime is neither to act chivalrously towards a criminal or chivalrously towards oneself ; it is the act of a fool, that is of a man who values his self-preservation at the price of a custom which ceasing to be marketable has become counterfeit.

Ultimately, from acts of chivalry on the battlefield do we soar

72   The Reformation of War

to those acts which form the ethics of grand strategy, the fuller meaning of which I will discuss in Chapter XI. To damage a nation morally during days of peace is not good enough ; it is but a poor endeavour, which normally must bring but little profit. Ethically, during war, as I will show, grand strategy does aim at demoralizing the enemy, yet also does it consist in the enhancement of a nation's worth in the eyes of its actual or potential enemies. Integrity, honour, justice and courage are the weapons of the grand strategist, which not only demonstrate a nation's moral worth but its martial power. The cultivation of these in peace time forms the backbone of success in war.

As long as war is looked upon as a calamity, a kind of international influenza, so long will the true ethics of war be obscured. Up to the present it has been of necessity calamitous, for the means of waging war have been means of destruction, though these means have shown a steady improvement since the days when primitive man wielded the flint axe. I will show, I hope quite clearly, that modern science has now placed at the disposal of the soldier means which it was totally impossible to make use of a few years ago, and that these means will humanize war and raise it from its present barbarous footing to a higher ethical position. While, in the past, because in war men had to be killed, no civilized soldier has suggested that, consequently, nations through their peace policy should aim at secret assassination ; so I believe that, in the future, when it is realized that the most humane method of waging war is the moral attack on the enemy's nerves, no civilized soldier will suggest that the peace policy of war should be based on international terror. This may be the method of atavistic revolutionaries, social throwbacks to the days of Nero, but I fervently hope that they will not be countenanced by soldiers or sane politicians.

For these views to be accepted by armies, there must be a radical change in their political and military mentality. New ideas must be considered freely, criticized freely and judged publicly, and if found more profitable than existing ones—accepted When in a normally healthy family a child is born, the

The Ethics of War

parents are not only congratulated but are proud and pleased at the event. When, however, in an army some unfortunate individual gives birth to a new idea, he is execrated, and why? Because any new idea is apt to disturb the vested interests and prejudices which bulk so large in military organization It is the old question of creative thought, the irresistible force, seeking for a niche in the stable opinions which surround it. It is again the old question of the selection of the fittest by means of a struggle between fit and unfit.

The idea is the child of circumstances; it does not spring fully armed from a single head, but is engendered in this head by the rottenness of its surroundings. It is by observing rottenness that purity, or improvement, arises, consequently, the lustiness of the rottenness is very natural, for rottenness is also striving to endure.

When we glance through military history, we find that most new ideas, which eventually materialize into theories or concrete form, originate in piratical exploits outside the existing military organization, and that only after a period of virulent abuse do they become adjuncts or undesirable foster-children in the military family.

The idea proves its value and its champions exaggerate its powers. Opinion now accepts the idea under the covering fire of an offensive directed against the exaggerations. The idea is attached to the traditional elements and begins to consume them, until from the ashes of the old organization arises a new, which usually proves that the exaggerations fall totally short of the full development of the idea. Everyone is now contented; the originators of the idea because they have actually outstepped their predictions; the old school also, for, after all, were not these predictions incorrect? Circumstances having proved them to have fallen sadly short of the mark. The new idea, consequently, is accepted, and, under the new school, which step by step adopts the mentality of the old school, stabilizes, and in its turn has to be broken up by another volcanic eruption.

It is now my intention in the remaining ten Chapters of this book to place a few new ideas before the reader, so that he may judge whether present-day military, naval and air force organizations are the best in order to maintain or enforce policy, and if not, whether my suggestions are better or worse. If better, then I trust that he will support them, for our present defence forces are costing £150,000,000 a year.

IV

THE LAST LAP OF THE PHYSICAL EPOCH

IN this Chapter I intend examining the nature and character of the Great War of 1914-1918, and to show that, tactically, it was based on a gigantic misconception of the true purpose of war, which is to enforce the policy of a nation *at the least cost to itself and enemy* and, consequently, to the world, for so intricately are the resources of civilized states interwoven that to destroy any one country is simultaneously to wound all other nations.

In August, 1914, it cannot be said that the armies of Europe were unprepared for war ; they were prepared, and to the proverbial last gaiter button. But for what kind of war, this is the crucial question ?

Ever since 1866 and 1870, the eyes of the General Staffs of Europe had been blinded by the brilliance of von Moltke's strategy. Soldiers had gazed on the bayonet points of Sadowa and Sedan until they were hypnotized by these great battles, and, under the influence of this hypnosis, they dreamt of the next war as an immense 1870 operation involving unlimited slaughter.

Their doctrine was founded on two tremendous fallacies. First, that policy is best enforced by destruction ; secondly, that military perfection is based on numbers of soldiers. They did not realize that Sadowa and Sedan were won by the weapons of 1866 and 1870. That these weapons had long been replaced by more effective ones. That during the forty years following the capitulation of Paris, science, industry and means of transport had revolutionized the civilized nations of the world. Not realizing this vast change in the conditions which would surround the next war, and meditating on war as a thing in itself, as an end rather than as a means towards an end, the General Staffs of Europe calculated the respective strengths of their armies in tons of human flesh. Then, in 1914, these armies marched after phantoms which, like will-o'-the-wisps, led them to the slaughter-houses of the Grand Couronné, the Marne, Aisne, and Ypres, and, at length, to a partial realization that war is a living art, a system of knowledge and action which must be fed on the civil sciences and nurtured on the civil industries in order to maintain its strength and purpose—the enforcement of a nation's policy with the least detriment to the peace which must follow final victory.

In their conservatism and lethargy armies are indeed extraordinary organizations. Browsing through peace time, like human cattle they are slaughtered during war So constituted that ability has the greatest difficulty to struggle to the top, the selection of the fittest to command has seldom a refining influence on their constitutions; consequently, when a great Captain does arise, irrespective of the circumstances which surrounded his successes, his system, even if he has no system, is turned into an infallible doctrine, a dogma which becomes a millstone Marshal Saxe, from whose works I have already quoted, realized this full well when he wrote:

"Gustavus Adolphus invented a method which was followed by his scholars and carried into execution with great success; but since his time there has been a gradual decline amongst us, which must be imputed to our having blindly adopted maxims, without any examination of the principles on which they are founded; . from whence it appears that our present practice is nothing more than a passive compliance with customs, the grounds of which we are absolute strangers to."

Such was the military outlook before the Seven Years' War, and such was the military outlook in July, 1914.

From 1870 onwards, a new civilization had arisen in Europe, based on the enormous growth of railways and the facilities

The Last Lap of the Physical Epoch

rendered possible by the motor car and lorry. Soldiers had studied these means, not in order to mechanicalize armies, that is to replace muscular by mechanical power, but from the point of view that these means of movement would enable an enemy's frontier to be submerged under a veritable inundation of flesh. Millions of men would sweep forward and, like immense clouds of locusts, would gain victory by sheer weight of numbers. This doctrine was so simple; moreover the railway appeared to render it possible Hence the horde armies of 1914

The strategist had, however, forgotten the tactician No man could control such vast numbers of men, which, in France, formed two great human stop-butts This was a colossal error, but not the biggest, for the strategist and the tactician both forgot human nature.

The supreme duty of the soldier is to fight and not to die. As, in 1914, armies could not live on the surface of the battlefield, there was no choice but to go under the surface; consequently, trenches five hundred miles long were dug, and armies, like foxes, went to earth; because, since 1870, the magazine rifle, the machine gun and the quick-firing field cannon had replaced the weapons of that day. Consequently, the tactics of Sedan had been rendered quite obsolete—almost as obsolete as the electrical sciences of 1870 would be if compared to those of 1914.

In order to secure these trenches from surprise attack, each side turned itself into an immense spider, and spun around its entrenchments hundreds of thousands of miles of steel web—the common commercial article known as barbed wire, miles of which had been used in South Africa, in 1901, and hundreds of miles of it in the defences of Port Arthur, in 1904. But these wars, especially the latter, though closely studied by soldiers, were examined through 1870 spectacles, and their tactical lessons were blurred through strategical study Yet one man at least, though not a soldier, did clearly see what the influence of modern weapons on the traditional methods would lead to. This man was Mr. I. S. Bloch, a banker in Warsaw, who, in 1897, published a book in six volumes on " The War of the Future." At the time, soldiers derided Mr. Bloch's ideas and deductions; a wiser procedure would have been to have read his work and to have absorbed a little knowledge. In the English translation of the last volume, which was published in 1899 under the title " Is War Impossible," Mr. Bloch writes:

> "At first there will be an increased slaughter—increased slaughter on so terrible a scale as to render it impossible to get troops to push the battle to a decisive issue. They will try to, thinking that they are fighting under the old conditions, and they will learn such a lesson that they will abandon the attempt for ever. Then, instead of a war fought out to the bitter end in a series of decisive battles, we shall have as a substitute a long period of continually increasing strain upon the resources of the combatants. The war, instead of being a hand-to-hand contest, in which the combatants measure their physical and moral superiority, will become a kind of stalemate, in which, neither army being willing to get at the other, both armies will be maintained in opposition to each other, threatening the other, but never being able to deliver a final and decisive attack. . . That is the future of war—not fighting, but famine, not the slaying of men, but the bankruptcy of nations and the break-up of the whole social organization. . . . Everybody will be entrenched in the next war. It will be a great war of entrenchments. The spade will be as indispensable to a soldier as his rifle. . . . All wars will of necessity partake of the character of siege operations. . . . Your soldiers may fight as they please; the ultimate decision is in the hands of famine. . . ."

The above constitutes an accurate forecast of events in 1914-1917, which were rehearsed ten years previously, on a smaller scale, at Nan Shan, Liao Yang and Mukden. Their deduction was a matter of pure common-sense. Given a magazine rifle firing ten aimed rounds a minute, a machine gun firing five hundred rounds and a field gun firing ten rounds, even in 1904 it was beyond question that the tactics of 1870 were as unsuited to twentieth century weapons as the machine tools of an 1870 workshop would be unsuited to a twentieth century manufactory. In connection with this criticism, which I believe to be sound, though possibly unpalatable, I will hazard to quote two personal experiences. In April, 1914, when a student at the Camberley Staff College, I had occasion to visit an Artillery

The Last Lap of the Physical Epoch

Practice Camp at Larkhill (Salisbury Plain), and so struck was I by the power of the quick-firing field gun that I wrote the following

> "The leading lesson which I learnt whilst at this camp only accentuated what reading had already led me to suppose, namely, that artillery is to-day the superior arm, and that, consequently, battles will become more static, i e., entrenched. That its power is so great that the infantry assault will be chiefly rendered possible by the demoralization of the enemy by means of artillery fire. This logically leads to penetration in place of envelopment as the grand tactical principle of the attack, because freedom of manœuvre will be limited by wire and field works, to an enormous expenditure of ammunition at the decisive point, and to consideration whether a special motor ammunition column should not be formed to supply alone the guns taking part in the decisive artillery attack"

This deduction was not accepted

During the same month I wrote a memoir on the tactics of penetration* in which I considered the tactics of the next war. In it I said.

> "To-day we have, besides the magazine-rifle, the characteristics of which are understood, two, comparatively speaking, new weapons the quick-firing field gun and the machine gun Realizing this, we can predict with absolute certainty that the general who makes the truest use of these weapons, that is so deploys his men that their fullest power is attained, will win, unless he is hopelessly outnumbered. If this general further devise a system of deployment which will not only accentuate the power of these weapons, but also the defects in his opponent's formation, he will win irrespective of numbers, as surely as 1,400 Swiss beat 15,000 Austrians at Mortgarten, and as surely as 90,000 Austrians were beaten by 33,000 Prussians at Leuthen. This is a certainty.
>
> "From 1840 to the close of the nineteenth century, improvements steadily forced the rifle to the fore A similar progress did not take place in the manufacture of cannon, breech-loading guns not being finally adopted by the British Army until 1886. By the beginning of the present century we find the rifle master of all it surveyed, machine guns were being still used experimentally, trajectories were slightly more curved than to-day, indirect laying was only exceptionally employed ; but of all the changes intro-

---

* Published in November, 1914, in the Journal of the Royal United Service Institution under the title "The Tactics of Penetration A Counterblast to German Numerical Superiority."

duced since the Russo-Japanese war, the general adoption of quick-firing artillery by civilized armies is out and out the greatest. This gun, if correctly employed, will, I feel, revolutionize the present theory of war by substituting as the leading grand tactical principle penetration for that of envelopment.

* * * * * * * *

"To-day, on account of the rapidity of fire of the modern field gun, there will be no necessity either to hold back guns in reserve, or to withdraw them from their positions, for all that will be necessary will be to mass ammunition opposite a definite point, or a topographically weak point, or a point which has become or is likely to become a decisive point, so that the guns commanding this point, few or many in number, may pour a continuous and terrific deluge of shells on this point, and so enable the decisive attack to proceed against it. Admitting that this is feasible, then the problem resolves itself into one of supplying these breaching batteries with sufficient ammunition ; this problem should not be a difficult one to solve now that motor transport is in general use

"If I am right in this deduction, then I am right in adding : that that side which can first throw its adversary on the defensive, and, by so doing, can select at will the decisive point of attack—or which can, through a careful study of the ground, foresee this decisive point, or any moderately weak point—has all to gain by so doing. The defence cannot gauge, or will have the greatest difficulty in gauging, even by means of aerial reconnaissance, the point against which the decisive attack is going to be launched if the assailants' preparatory attack be violently offensive. All it can do is to attempt to take the attack, or assault, in flank, just as the 52nd Regiment took the Old Guard of Napoleon in flank at the close of the Battle of Waterloo, or as Colonel Daubeney, in his astonishing charge at Inkerman, cut the great Russian trunk column in two as it neared the Home Ridge."

I then examined the dangers of the above proposals and suggested the use of the machine gun in order to lessen them. I wrote :

"There is as much difference between machine-gun and infantry fire to-day as there was between light infantry and heavy infantry fire a hundred years ago. So great is this difference that we might almost say that the light infantry of the future will be evolved from the machine gunners of the present. That is that the assaulting column of the future will be flanked by these terror-spreading weapons, and that these new light infantrymen, like the old, will not

The Last Lap of the Physical Epoch

only precede the assaulting column by working up close to the line of the holding attack, but will flank it on both sides, producing a somewhat similar effect on the hostile line as grape, canister and case shot did during the first fifty years of the last century "

I concluded this memoir by saying

" I have no doctrine to preach, for I believe in none Every concrete case demands its own particular solution, and for this solution all that we require is skill and knowledge, skill in the use of our weapons, knowledge of our enemy's formations

" A physician who is slave to a doctrine, as was the famous Doctor Sangrado in ' Gil Blas,' ends by killing his patients ; a general who is under the spell of some such shibboleth as the oblique-order, envelopment, penetration, or the *offensive à outrance*, ends by destroying his army There is no difference. If there is a doctrine at all, then it is common-sense, that is, action adapted to circumstances.

" I do not lay down that I am right in basing my proposed deployment for penetration principally on the power of quick-firing artillery ; but all I can say is this . that a careful study of past and present history has led me to the following conclusions :

(1) " That weapons when correctly handled seldom fail to gain victory.

(2) " That armies are more often ruined by dogmas springing from their former successes than by the skill of their opponents . . ."

The criticism on this memoir was " Lacking in sound military judgment."

I must offer the reader an apology for the introduction of so much personal matter, and I must ask him to believe me when I say that I have not done this in order to pat my prevision on the back, but to show that it is possible for a soldier, possessing a normal standard of intelligence, to be wise *before* the event. So frequently have I been told how easy is it to be wise *after* the event (which is surely better than never being wise at all), that I have quoted the above extracts from my writings, extracts containing military opinons which, though imperfect, were not lacking in sound military judgment, as the history of the war testifies, in order that such of my readers who are not altogether blinded by tradition may have some confidence in the new ideas contained in this book I do not ask them to swallow

82   The Reformation of War

these ideas whole, but I do ask them not to proclaim them indigestible before mentally they have tasted them. I will now return to the magical year—1866.

From the battle of Sadowa onwards, tactical envelopment became a shibboleth, and any idea of defensive warfare a heresy. Not that envelopment in itself is not an admirable manœuvre, but that its effectiveness depends on circumstances, the conditions of the moment under which the principles of war have to be applied. So also is the offensive a military virtue, but this in no way means that the defensive is a military vice.

In August, 1914, the German armies were drawn up in phalangial formation from Aachen to Basle. Their right was to wheel through Belgium, round Paris, and then advance eastwards, sweeping the armies of France into Germany and Switzerland. This plan was extraordinarily simple and the railways appeared to render it possible. It was so simple that the German General Staff were apparently of the opinion, as their system of promotion did not guarantee their possessing a skilled leader when war broke out, that genius could be replaced by mechanical movement ; in other words, that the goose step could replace intellect ! The unexpected was expunged ; consequently, a reserve to meet it was unnecessary. They violated the principles of concentration and economy of force, and sealed their fate by so doing.

The French General Staff must have realized the extreme likelihood of the German right wing marching through Belgium. Bearing this in mind, where then should their reserve army have been ? At Paris, because Paris is the biggest railway centre in north-eastern France. Where were their reserves ? Near Verdun ! Even if the Germans had restricted their front of attack to the line Thionville-Basle, the best position of the French reserves was Paris ; even if they had proceeded by sea and disembarked their armies at Cherbourg, Brest or Bordeaux ; even if they had landed them at Toulon or marched through Italy or Switzerland, the *only* strategic position for the reserves was Paris ! Why were the reserves near Verdun ? Because, after the crushing defeats sustained by the French armies in 1870, this staff had

The Last Lap of the Physical Epoch

turned to that oracle of modern warfare—Napoleon, and in his wars had sought an answer to the problem of future victory. In his many campaigns, they discovered that he frequently made use of a lozenge formation—an advanced guard, two strong wings and a central reserve. Here then was the secret of success. So they drew up their plan accordingly, forgetting that, in the days of Napoleon, railways did not exist, and that, consequently, his reserves were so placed as to be within easy marching distance of the other forces. Had the French General Staff done what Napoleon, in the strategical circumstances which railways had created, could scarcely have failed to do—concentrate every available man at Paris, wait, see and spring, instead of the French Armies being swept into Switzerland, the whole of the German right wing would have been annihilated and, quite possibly, the war would have been won in six weeks.

"It is the MAN, not men who count in war," once said Napoleon. I will add to this aphorism: such a man does not turn his brain into a museum for past battles—for the only war for him is the next war!

Once the first great operation of the war—the German envelopment of the French armies, had been frustrated by the counter-attack of the Allies during the latter stages of that series of battles known as the battle of the Marne, equilibrium was established on the slopes of the river Aisne. This condition was followed by a race to the coast and culminated in the defeat of the Germans at the first battle of Ypres, at which battle traditional warfare on the Western Front terminated. Henceforth for several years the war on this front was destined to become a war of entrenchments, a siege, and the main weapon in the armoury of the besieger is famine.

Meanwhile, at sea another war was in progress, a war but distantly connected with the land operations except for one incident which in fact constituted the most astonishing naval operation of the war.

On August 4, 1914, two German warships, the *Goeben* and *Breslau*, were busily engaged in taking in supplies at Messina

The Reformation of War

They could not escape through the Straits of Gibraltar nor through the Suez Canal. They could either seek refuge in Pola or in the Sea of Marmora. Of these two lines of retreat, the first was objectless, the second full of possibilities; consequently, Admiral Souchon adopted the second line and sailed for the Dardanelles, through which he steamed on August 10. In England this astute move was derided, because the greatest naval power in the world could only think traditionally of naval warfare. Ships as fighting machines were understood, but as political instruments —no ' such use was beyond the traditional ken. Out of the *Goeben* sprouted the Gallipoli campaign, and out of its failure the Middle East Problem. What a move : for the West, the most decisive since Trafalgar.

While, prior to the war, in the great armies of the world, we find man-power obliterating tactics, so in the great navies do we find machine-power doing exactly the same thing. Men and more men, battleships and more battleships, but how these men or battleships should fight or be fought, and what influence the inventions of the last forty years would have on tactics was not even imagined. On land, soldiers were expected to fight much as they fought in 1870, and at sea sailors would fight much as they fought in 1805. Such was the position in 1914. Well might Admiral Mahan write :

" The student will observe that changes in tactics have not only taken place *after* changes in weapons, which necessarily is the case, but that the interval between such changes has been unduly long. This doubtless arises from the fact that an improvement of weapons is due to the energy of one or two men, while changes in tactics have to overcome the inertia of a conservative class ; but it is a great evil. It can be remedied only by a candid recognition of each change."

So conservative had the naval mind become that, in 1914, it had not fully realized the greatest of all modern influences on sea fighting—the replacement of wind by steam as a means of fleet propulsion. The doctrine of fleet tactics, as held in July, 1914, was in brief : " parallel actions with a hope of envelopment." These actions to be fought at what to-day would appear to be ridiculously short ranges.

The moral influence of the unknown factors of modern naval warfare—the realization of the conditions under which the objective had to be gained, the power of weapons the nature of which was not fully understood, and lack of knowledge in tactics, consequent on this ignorance, were due not so much to inefficiency as to the fact that mechanical progress had outstepped tactical thought and training. Time, in fact, had been insufficient wherein to digest science, and the result was that, while the grand tactical purpose of the opposing fleets had been based on decisive action during peace time, directly war was declared the unknown quantities, the resultants of science, materialized, and the war at sea, like the war on land, assumed a deadlock, attrition replacing the offensive as the grand tactics of the opposing sides.

Thus we see that, when we examine the opening phases of the Great War, traditionally educated and trained armies and navies have but one chance of success, that is the initial operation they undertake. Success being based on the fact that as their opponents may also be tradition-bound, their own tradition may triumph over that of their adversaries. Also we see that, if the initial clash of arms does not result in victory, at once the influence of weapons, means of movement and protection, which have been designed since these traditions became stabilized in blind custom and routine, exert their sway and bring traditional warfare to an end, and out of the knowledge gained from these weapons slowly evolves a new doctrine which replaces the old dogma.

Throughout the Great War, we watch this struggle between the new and the old. The old cannot imagine that its dogma is wrong : was not it successful in 1870, and has not it been laid down in every manual and text book since ? The new scoffs and exaggerates ; it is carried away by its own novelty, which gains an unnatural brilliance by being contrasted with the opaque substance of dead thought. When we examine

86   The Reformation of War

the military history of the late Middle Ages, it astonishes us to watch the Chivalry of France being, for the space of a century, mown down by arrows and still not grasping the tactical value of the bow. In years to come, some future historian may possibly contrast, with this suicidal adherence to custom, the fact that, though in 1904 the machine gun had proved itself to be the most deadly of small-arm weapons, ten years later the great armies of Europe had to learn this lesson again. In fact it would appear that both soldier and sailor possess no power of absorbing tactical knowledge except through personal experience. In 1899 a British Division was equipped with twenty-four machine guns; in 1914 it was still equipped with twenty-four ; yet, in 1918, fearful cost in life had compelled the number of automatic weapons to be increased to over five hundred. Accepting this number as necessary, why was the 1914 equipment the same as that of 1899 ? The answer is, it had become a tradition that the number of machine guns in a battalion should be two ; just as in the fourteenth century it was a tradition that no gentleman could fight save on horseback.

The objective in war may, as the text books declare, be the imposition of the will of one army on the other, yet history shows that the purpose of an army or navy has, in peace time, little to do with war, its object being not freely to evolve but in place to maintain its traditions. Some are vital to its existence, others full of the germs of decay. Both are, however, holy, and to attack either is military blasphemy. I will now turn to the next period of the Great War — the attack by matériel.

After a few weeks of *real* warfare, the *offensive à outrance*, that high gospel of the pre-war manuals, was reduced to a wallowing defensive among mud holes and barbed wire. Armies, through their own lack of foresight, were reduced to the position of human cattle. They browsed behind their fences, and on occasion snorted and bellowed at each other. The one problem which now confronted them was : how to re-establish movement, for until one or both sides could move there was no possibility

The Last Lap of the Physical Epoch

of a decision by arms, and famine alone must become the arbiter of peace. Some there were who actually recommended this course, but their voices were drowned by shouts for shells. Shells were to be the panacea of all difficulties, more shells and still more shells, and then by steel a road could be blasted to Paris or Berlin. A veritable blood and iron lust swept over the armies of Europe.

As the entire arsenals of the civilized world could not possibly meet the demand, the General Staffs turned to the industries of their respective nations, and a new battle was begun. Which nation would produce the largest output ? For on this output, so it was thought, would victory depend. Of all great industrial countries, Great Britain was the least well prepared for this engagement, because the true meaning of the quick-firing gun had not been grasped. Nevertheless, the astonishing ability for improvisation possessed by Englishmen enabled them so well to cope with the supply, that the General Staff literally became intoxicated on T N.T. We now lose sight of strategy and tactics in a storm of shells and roaring high explosives; our very tympanums are rent !

For the preliminary bombardments of the battle of Hooge, we fired 18,000 shells; for those at the battle of the Somme, 2,000,000 shells, for those at Arras, in 1917, 2,000,000 shells, and for those at Ypres the same year, 4,300,000 shells. At the last-mentioned battle the tonnage of shells fired during the preliminary bombardments alone amounted to 107,000 tons, the cost of which has been estimated at £22,000,000, a figure very nearly equal to the total yearly cost of the pre-war British Home Army. If this enormous expenditure had resulted in victory, to the traditional soldier it would have been cheap at the price. But it did not result in victory, and it could not result in victory, and for the following very simple reason. In the process of digging up trenches by means of shell fire, everything in the neighbourhood of the trenches was dug up. Roads vanished, tracks vanished, railways vanished and the surface of the ground vanished under the influence of the material earthquake to which

The Reformation of War

all things were subjected. The enemy was killed, his wire entanglements were cut to pieces and his trenches were blown in. Yet in these very acts of destruction was an impassable crater area formed, and, when surface water abounded, as at Ypres, or when rain fell in torrents, as at Beaumont Hamel, none save water-fowl could have crossed the morass of mud, and then these birds would have done better to fly. In place of accelerating infantry movement, every shell that fell impeded this all necessary act of winning the war by force of arms.

There was another reason, and a more visible one still, why this monstrous attack by shells was doomed to failure when directed against a well-organized antagonist, namely, that bombardments lasting from seven to twenty-one days in duration rendered any form of surprise impossible. When a big game hunter visits East Africa to shoot lions, he does not equip himself with a bassoon, and then, when a lion is met with, walk round the beast for a fortnight playing on this instrument. He does not thus comport himself, since all idea of surprise would vanish, and so also would the lion. Unfortunately, a staunch and determined enemy does not behave like a wild animal, in place of bolting from the bassoon, he assembles his forces opposite the spot which is being, like Jericho, trumpeted to earth, and, when the attack is well bogged in the slough created by gun-fire, attacks in his turn. That our great artillery battles killed thousands of Germans is undoubted, they could not help doing so, but equally is it certain that they resulted in terrific casualties to ourselves. The battles on the Somme, in 1916, and at Ypres, in 1917, cost the British Army in killed, wounded and missing, over 800,000 casualties, and as we were the attackers, the probabilities are that our casualties were considerably heavier than those of the Germans. Also is it asserted that these battles were of assistance in beating the enemy, that they used up the enemy's fighting forces and accelerated demoralization : but it may well be asked—at what price ?

In my own opinion, the monopoly of strategy and tactics by shell bludgeoning prolonged the war in place of shortening it. It

The Last Lap of the Physical Epoch

dulled the imagination of the higher command, who became obsessed by two ideas: fill the trenches to hold them, and blow them to pieces to capture them. Consequently, we see during this period, which was a long one, the art of war slipping back to the position it held in the days of the Macedonian phalanx. As the brain power of the opposing armies grew smaller, for all General Staffs fell victims to the shell-plague, the bodies of these same armies grew bigger and bigger, until the administrative organization for the supply of matériel alone absorbed such vast numbers of men that, through shortage of man-power, the fighting troops were nearly strangled by those whose duty it was to administer to their needs—armies had now become pot-bellied and pea-brained.

The completeness of the deadlock, the seemingly impossible task of re-establishing movement in the decisive theatre of the war, resulted, in a marked extent, in a monopolization of the war plan by amateur political strategists. The war had either to be won, lost, or drawn; consequently, as the problem on the Western Front was considered unsolvable, some other front had to be discovered. Already, early in 1915, the Germans had changed their main objective. Their intention was no longer to destroy the French armies but the Russian, because of all the armies contending the Russian army was in tactics the least developed, for their traditionalism was very old and very obsolete, and more hidebound than that of France. The giant said: I have 15,000,000 men classified for mobilization; I have as many infantry divisions as France and Germany put together, and of cavalry beyond number. I will " make up for deficiencies in technique by lavish expenditure of blood; " and before the war was a year old the Russian casualties totalled just under 4,000,000! In 1917, Brusilov's armies lost no less than 375,000 men in twenty-seven days, and about 1,000,000 in four months. All we can do is to gasp at this madness. If war, as it is so often asserted, is a continuation of peace policy, then war is also a link with the policy which will follow victory. During peace, man's policy is to live and not to die: consequently, if war be a continuation of this policy, then soldiers should not be sacrificed like rabbits in an Australian catch.

"The Russians," writes General Knox, "were just big-hearted children who had thought out nothing, and had stumbled half-asleep into a wasps' nest." In nature they were generous, always willing to sacrifice themselves for their allies, in character corrupt, and in disposition childlike. The leadership of their generals was beneath contempt. Just before Tannenberg, General Samsonov sent back for his sword, remarking "that he was now in an enemy's country, and must go armed." His "all prevailing idea was to try and see the battle with his own eyes," *à la* Cossack. Rennenkampf was just as bad; on one occasion when the Germans withdrew, he said to another officer: "You can take off your clothes now; the Germans are retiring," quite failing to see that it was the very moment to attack and not to go to bed. Cavalry charged trenches; the Guards refused to promote ensigns from the ranks, "as men so promoted might remain with them after the war!" A minister was entitled to draw horse hire per verst for twenty-four horses when, *by rail*, he visited Vladivostock! And when General Gulevich received a telegram appointing him to an active command, as he at first thought, he was much upset, for it was his custom to rest in bed between two and five p.m. daily. But when he discovered that the appointment was *only* that of Chief of the Staff of the North-West Front he was greatly relieved, and at once gave orders for a thanksgiving service to be held. "Few officers attended this service, for they had all rushed off to scribble memoranda for the General's guidance of the honours and rewards they wished to receive."*

I have made this digression into the internal state of Russian military traditionalism not only to show to what a parlous state of inefficiency stagnation may bring an army, but because it had a pronounced influence on the economic phase of the war. Not only did the deficiencies of the Russian army demand an

* "With the Russian Armies, 1914-1917," Major-General Sir Alfred Knox, K.C.B., C.M.G.

The Last Lap of the Physical Epoch

enormous provision of munitions, but they dragged the war eastwards. For the Germans this change of front was comparatively easy; for us and the French it would have been impossible had we not possessed command of the sea. Thus we watch the military weakness of Russia acting as an incentive to the Germans to close down their operations on the Western Front, and, by means of their magnificent railway system, to reopen operations in Poland. In order to follow suit, the Allies, though knowing full well that the German forces in the West were inferior to their own, followed up this move with an attempt to capture Constantinople, so that, by gaining command of the Black Sea, the Russian armies might be supplied. In truth Russian strength did not lie in supplies, but, as in 1813, in retirement. Thus we see that though these supplies may have added to the moral of the Russian troops, by persuading them not to retire except through force of arms, they prolonged the war. What, I am of opinion, the Russians should have done was what the Germans did on part of the Western Front in February, 1917, that is retire to a Hindenburg line (not necessarily trenches), not a line twenty miles in rear, but two hundred, three hundred, or possibly four hundred.

In the Gallipoli campaign, the abuse of matériel was the main cause of its failure. " In 1906 the possibilities of such an attack had been examined by the British General Staff, and the opinion arrived at was that an unaided action by the fleet was to be deprecated; and if combined operations were to be undertaken, no landing could be effected on the Gallipoli Peninsula unless the co-operating naval squadron could guarantee with its guns that the landing force should reach the shore unmolested and find after disembarkation a sufficiently extended area, free from hostile fire, to enable it to form up for battle on suitable ground. In summing up, the General Staff stated that they did not consider that the co-operating fleet would be able to give this guarantee, and they recommended such an operation should not be attempted."[*]

[*] " Soldiers of the Prophet," Lieut.-Colonel C. C. R Murphy, p. 121

The Reformation of War

Though there was only one possible hope of such an attack succeeding, namely, that its initiation should come as a complete surprise, as early as November 3, 1914, the British Navy, by shelling the forts at the entrance of the Dardanelles, first drew the attention of the Turkish General Staff to a theatre of operations which offered decisive results. On March 5, 1915, a further bombardment took place, and on April 25, the first landing was attempted.

In these operations the mistake made by the navy was identical with the mistake which governed the operations of the army during this period in the evolution of the war. Surprise—the moral attack, was replaced by bombardment—the matériel attack ; cunning was ousted by steel, and the attack once again failed.

When considering the phases into which I have divided the war, it must not be supposed that any hard or fast dividing line can be drawn between them. To me they are comparable to a geological chart. The periods—tertiary, quaternary, etc., are shown by well defined bands of colour containing within each drawings of the types of animals, plants and minerals more especially belonging to each epoch. In fact there are no dividing lines, no fixed beginnings or endings, only a slow steady progression. Similarly with the phases of the Great War, which I am now examining : one period emerges from another, takes form, and then falls under the spell of some virile idea which the tests and trials of the war have proved sound. We see this clearly in the increasing employment of the most powerful of the older weapons—quick-firing guns and machine guns ; then of the newer weapons—aeroplanes and submarines, and lastly of altogether new weapons—gas and tanks

As traditional warfare merges into the war of matériel, every possible effort is made to enhance gun-power by air-power, in the form of fire-control and direction from the air, and yet, as I will show later on, this was not the main duty of the aeroplane. So also with the submarine ; at first she was considered as a minor adjunct of a fleet ; nevertheless, as the war proved, her main

The Last Lap of the Physical Epoch

power lay in her ability to dispense with fleet protection and to become the sniper of the seas.

As traditional warfare could find no solution to the problem of re-establishing mobility once battle fronts had become entrenched, and as soldiers, for the most part, could only think of war in traditional terms, the solution to this problem had, in the main, to be sought outside normal military thought, and the only place to seek it was among the civil sciences. Being a great chemical country, Germany turned to gas, and being a great engineering country, we, in Great Britain, turned to the petrol engine and produced the tank. The actual date when these two new means of war were first thought of does not much matter, for the ideas underlying them are very old, but a study of modern warfare in general and of modern industry in particular would have given the General Staffs of Europe a clearer idea of the probable nature of the next war than the one held by them in 1914. Unshackled by the traditional aspect of warfare, it was for this reason that Mr. Bloch, a pacifist, was able to visualize the nature of the next war more clearly than the most eminent of General Staff Officers. If it had only been appreciated that, failing an overwhelming initial success, such as a second Sadowa or Sedan, the next war would be a war of trenches, then it would have logically followed that not only would enormous quantities of ammunition be required, but to maintain mobility under the tornado resulting, armour would have to be reintroduced.

The last of the great siege wars was the war in the Crimea, and though this war had been studied by soldiers it had been little understood. Had it been carefully examined, it would have been realized that the conditions of 1915 were very similar to those of 1854, and that the difficulties of 1915 could be overcome by the solutions suggested to meet those which confronted the British Army in 1854.

In 1854, we find Mr. James Cowen, a philanthropist, suggesting to the British Government the adoption of a " locomotive land battery fitted with scythes to mow down infantry " : in other words the tank. The same year, Lord Dundonald, a noted admiral, suggested that gas could be usefully employed in order to asphyxiate the garrison of Sebastopol. Neither of these suggestions was adopted, because they did not harmonize with the traditional methods of waging war. They were considered too terrible to be contemplated. Curious to relate, however, the government which showed such qualms as regards killing the enemy showed none as regards inflicting a miserable death on thousands of our own men through their gross neglect of administrative arrangements and hospital necessities. The reason for this was that death by typhus, dysentery and neglected wounds did not violate tradition, while death by gassing or mowing down would have. In the Crimean war, tradition won through, and at what suffering and cost !

In the Great War, tradition once again formed phalanx against all innovation and improvement ; luckily for us, it went down before the hammer-blows of science, but unfortunately, though expectedly, immediately the Armistice had been signed, tradition rose like a phœnix from its ashes.

For a generation to come, tradition will fight against the new doctrines of warfare These will ultimately win through, as they must, and, in the internecine struggle between 1914 and 1918 organizations, will once again the next war be forgotten. Our only chance to escape this calamity is to change our outlook on history ; in place of solidifying reason, history should liquefy the imagination. History never actually repeats itself, for it constitutes one continuous transformation. Its tendencies may be ascertained by study, but foresight into these demands more than study · it demands meditation and a continuous use of the word " why ? "

I will now examine the next great period, that of the economic attack.

The enormous demands made for all types of munitions of war and warlike supplies during the phase of the matériel attack, brought into a clear light those economic foundations of the war which, in peace time, had lain too deep to be noticed much by

The Last Lap of the Physical Epoch

soldiers. First, these munitions had to be supplied; secondly, their supply curtailed the manufacture of luxuries as well as many everyday necessities. So visible did these economic foundations become, that it was not long before the General Staffs of the contending nations realized that, if the food supply of the enemy could be cut off, the will of the hostile civil population would be undermined, and with this loss of will to endure, their military forces would be rendered useless.

The first military problem of the Allies now became that of the circumvallation of the Central Powers; their second problem, their surrender by starvation. Consequently, during the third phase of the war, the problem of re-establishing tactical mobility was to a certain extent replaced by a direct attack on the enemy's stomach. The nature of this type of war is simple, yet, throughout history, it has been persistently misunderstood.

Starvation is a means towards an end and not the end itself, and I will repeat it again: the end, objective or goal in warfare is the imposition of the policy of one hostile government on another, the foundations of these respective policies being the wills of the contending nations. These wills must, however, be attacked in such a manner that their possessors are not permanently injured; for to weaken the enemy, either permanently or for a long period after the cessation of hostilities, is, as I have already pointed out, tantamount to wounding one's own body by a self-inflicted blow. Such a blow is immoral, not because it compels an enemy to accept a policy which is distasteful to him, but because, by reducing the physique of the enemy and especially of the enemy's children, it ultimately not only reduces his prosperity but the prosperity of the world—it is in fact a blow directed against civilization.

The encirclement of the Central Powers by the Allies resulted in the most gigantic siege in history, the lines of circumvallation running from Calais to Kermanshah, and thence through Russia to the Baltic. The establishment of this immense circle of bayonets took time, but what took longer still was the time taken by the British Government to realize that, once this siege had

The Reformation of War

been determined on, the lines of circumvallation were useless as long as supplies could be shipped in vast quantities to neutral countries and thence transported to Germany. The problem of starvation was virtually a politico-naval one, and the politician was afraid of enforcing it, not because it was immoral, but because it might prove detrimental to the pockets of neutrals who, like vampires, were feasting on the blood of the battlefields. Such neutrality as this is beneath contempt, and during the war its immorality was only exceeded by the vice of political fear.

The bottling up of the German fleet immediately after the declaration of war drew the attention of the German Government to the necessity of economy in resources, especially of all food stocks. In December, 1914, Professor Eltzbacher produced a book on this subject entitled : " Die deutsche Volksernahrung und der englische Aushungerungsplan,"[*] which dealt with this question in minute detail down to the tonnage of dog's flesh. Outside scientific circles, however, little attention was paid to this question in England, as may be gathered from Professor Poulton's " Romanes Lecture " for 1915. In this lecture he says :

> " Lord Robert Robert Cecil is reported in *The Times* of December 3rd (1915) to have said, ' Our policy was to secure our rights and to starve Germany first of all. Starving Germany was, of course, only a metaphorical expression—it was impossible ; he would rather say deprive her of essential articles.' What right had Lord Robert to say that the starving of Germany was impossible ? He is not an expert on food supply, and he quoted no authority. Has he studied the Eltzbacher memoirs and Dr. Waller's and Professor Ashley's criticisms ? Has he asked for a report from the Royal Society's Committee on the food supply of Germany ? What we really need to end this war is *knowledge* and firm action based on it. As it is, with the slipshod ways of conducting war and neglect of scientific authority, our own Government has done very much to help Germany out of the difficulty. It has ignored, as Dr. Waller says in the introduction to the English translation, ' the obvious fact that the food of a besieged nation, as of a besieged fortress, in

---

[*] English edition 1915, " Germany's Food and England's Plan to starve Her out."

The Last Lap of the Physical Epoch

tons of bread, meat and potatoes is as truly its ammunition as are its shells.' "*

From the above we see that while the War Office and the Admiralty were exerting all their strength to encircle and so besiege the Central Powers, the Board of Trade was forcibly feeding these Powers through the Dutch spout. Neutral countries may possess certain rights during war time, but to allow them to supply the enemy with food when he is being besieged is to turn even traditional warfare upside-down.

When, however, the blockade began to tighten, Germany had no intention of committing *felo-de-se* in order to maintain a naval custom or a humanitarian tradition. She was now fighting for her life, and not being able to hit above the belt she hit below it in order to make good by cunning her physical naval deficit. She was, consequently, outlawed. Though the infringement of international rules and customs is always dangerous, as it enables an adversary to call the kettle black, Germany, in my opinion, in the circumstances in which the blockade placed her, was justified in her turn in attempting to establish a blockade of her enemies' coast-lines by the unrestricted use of the submarine. If this action was an infringement of international law and the (fictitious) rights of neutrals, then those neutral countries which were affected should have supported their rights by declaring war on the lawbreaker. In place, most of these weedlings howled with injured innocence and continued to make money out of the battlefields they were too prudent or too cowardly to approach. There can be no doubt that, by instituting unrestricted submarine warfare, the Germans violated certain laws of war made long before the advent of this weapon ; but also can there be no doubt that, if the slow starvation of German men, women and children by means of investment did not contravene the spirit of international

* " Science and the Great War," E B Poulton, D.Sc., M A , pp 31-32. In December, 1913, Holland imported 1⅜ million tons of cocoa , in December, 1914, imports in cocoa rose to 7¼ million tons On account of the abnormal tonnage of oranges sent to Germany " on the Empress's birthday every German soldier was presented with a pot of marmalade ! "

98   The Reformation of War

law, then neither did unrestricted submarine warfare contravene it, though it may have infringed the letter of the tradition which this law had created. If starvation is right in one case it is right in both. The drowning of non-combatants is but an incident in the operation of killing by starvation, it does not affect the principle underlying this act. Further, it should be realized that, as long as international law is so worded as to permit of neutrals trading like ghouls on the blood of the belligerents, international law is immoral and, consequently, it is a virtuous act to destroy it. To foster it is not only to place a premium on greed and cowardice but also on moral prostitution.

During the period of the economic attack, the whole question of the security of property on the high seas was thrown into the limelight. This question is an old one, and a very brief summary of its history is instructive.

Up to the middle of the fourteenth century, capture at sea was practically unrestricted. Then we find several of the leading European nations binding themselves by an agreement known as the " Consolat-del-Mar," in which it was laid down that only enemy property, either ships or cargo, was liable to capture and that neutral ships and cargo were not. During the Crimean War, both Great Britain and France agreed not to capture enemy's goods in neutral ships or neutral goods in enemy ships. In 1856, Great Britain became party to the Declaration of Paris, and hung a millstone round her neck by agreeing to exempt from capture enemy's goods in neutral ships and neutral goods in enemy ships, subject to the exception of contrabands. In 1871 Lord Salisbury said: " Since the Declaration of Paris the fleet, valuable as it is for preventing an invasion of these shores, is almost valueless for any other purpose," and shortly before the outbreak of war, in 1914, Major J. A. Longridge wrote:

> " The Declaration of Paris curtails the offensive power of the only weapon with which, in the absence of an army of continental proportions, she (i.e. Great Britain) can make good her word when she speaks with her enemies in the gate."*

* " The Liability of Forfeiture of National Oversea Commerce," Major J. A. Longridge. " The Army Review," Vol. VI., April, 1914

The Last Lap of the Physical Epoch

If sufficient harm had not already been accomplished by depriving the fleet of an economic objective, shortly before the war, the British Government contemplated a further restriction of her naval powers by considering very favourably the terms of the Declaration of London ; fortunately for the Empire this Declaration was still unratified when hostilities began.

From the opening of the war onwards, few opportunities of a surreptitious nature were missed by Great Britain to file through the shackles of the Declaration of Paris, and when we view these attempts from an impartial point of view, there can be little doubt that, technically at least, Germany was right in stating that we had violated the terms of this Declaration, and that, consequently, she in her turn was free to torpedo ships at sight. Here, again, can we learn another lesson concerning the dangers of rules based on pseudo-humanitarian vapourings. The Declaration of Paris was a pacifical measure adopted to restrict the horrors of war ; it was not based on common-sense or human nature, and what happened was pre-ordained Having agreed to it in peace time, Great Britain tried to wriggle out of it in war time, with the inevitable result that Germany made these wriggles an excuse to institute a form of warfare which was, from the standpoint of the signatories of the Declaration, more barbarous than any type of warfare yet contemplated.

In the German economic campaign, one cardinal military error was made—it was declared too early. Had the Germans delayed their declaration until the end of 1917, and then launched an unrestricted submarine war backed by two hundred to three hundred of these vessels, they would have forced their will on Great Britain before the middle of the following year, and America would have been left completely out of the picture. In fact, like ourselves in the Gallipoli campaign, if they had not prematurely shown their naval claws, they might, in spite of the stalemate on land, have ended the war victoriously by the use of sea power. To-day, if we close our eyes to this fact and attempt to banish the submarine by incantations on the lines of the Declarations of Paris or London, we may, at some day in the future, suddenly open them to find starvation staring us in the face.

If we examine the basic ideas underlying this whole period of fighting, we shall find, as was the case in all former wars, that killing was the supreme object. Soldiers have killed soldiers since times immemorial; consequently, killing, which is but a means of enforcing the will of one nation on another, has monopolized the whole horizon of warfare. The submarine taught the civilized nations of the world that there were other means of compelling a nation to accept the will of its adversary, and, though its use resulted in men and even women and children being killed, the numbers destroyed were insignificant when compared to the numbers killed by traditional methods. Thus, we come to the conclusion that it was not the killing of non-combatants which was the real crime, for in modern warfare it is pure sophistry to attempt to draw a line between those who fight and those who assist the fighters, since entire nations go to war. Instead, that it was the novelty of the means, in spite of their low killing power, which horrified those who were attacked; for, not having grown accustomed to these means, they were not prepared to defend themselves against them.

Nearly all new methods of waging war have, in the past, humanized the art. Thus, the most brutal form of warfare is axe warfare, the hand-to-hand struggle which ends in the extermination of one side. Musket warfare humanized axe warfare, and, in the last great war, the submarine, aeroplane, gas and tank humanized that condition of warfare which, by 1914, had grown into a traditional art.

A novel weapon or means of warfare, like an unknown plague, fills the imagination of man with horror and intangible fear. Yet, no remedy to this is to be obtained by locking up terror in a mental dungeon; in place, the unknown must be examined in broad daylight, its nature diagnosed and its antidote discovered.

The underlying factor throughout the whole of this period of the economic attack was that, as the fighting forces are maintained by the country to which they belong, they can, under

The Last Lap of the Physical Epoch

modern conditions, be attacked indirectly by the delivery of direct attack on the nation itself. Siege warfare nearly always demands a costly process of attrition, and never more so than when an entire nation has to be besieged and starved into submission. In the next Chapter I will show that, towards the end of the Great War, a more economical method of attack was taking form, a method which in the future may compel an entire nation to throw up its hands and crave peace within a few days, possibly hours, of a war being declared.

V

THE FIRST LAP OF THE MORAL EPOCH

IN the last Chapter I examined the traditional aspect of the Great War and the main phases which out-cropped from it. I pointed out, as far as space would allow, that the theory underlying the war was that of enforcing policy by destruction of life and of property. The question may now be asked, if this theory is fundamentally unsound, how comes it that it has prevailed since times immemorable? The answer is not difficult to arrive at, when it is realized that national wars, in their modern aspect, are but correlatives of modern civilization, which, since the introduction of steam-power, especially in the form of the steamship and locomotive, has been completely revolutionized. With the adoption of steam as a motive force, we see simultaneously introduced a physical world contraction and an intellectual world expansion. While, in 1750, it took three weeks to travel from Caithness to London, to-day Bombay, Cape Town, San Francisco and Vladivostock can be reached in a similar time. Intellectually, what did this mean? It meant that, as space shrank, intelligence expanded through travel and rapidity of communication. In 1759, the news of the capture of Quebec took several weeks before it was received in London; yet, in 1921, the result of the Carpentier-Dempsey fight was announced to the whole of Paris within three minutes of the knock-out blow being delivered!

This intellectual and moral revolution, which was brought about through a growth in the physical sciences, was not grasped by the military mind. It was not realized that, while only a hundred years ago, it took days and weeks and months before a moral blow could be delivered, to-day it only takes minutes and hours. It was not realized that, while in the year 1800, the nervous system of a civilized nation was of a low and ganglionic order, by 1900 it had become highly sensitive and centralized. It was not realized that, as the whole aspect of civilization had changed, so also must the whole aspect of warfare be changed, and, as science had accomplished the civil changes, so also must science accomplish the military ones.

In 1914, what happened was this : unless the war could be won within a few weeks of its outbreak, armies, as then organized, could not, under probable circumstances, maintain or enforce the peace policies of their respective governments, because these armies, in constitution, belonged to a social epoch which was dead and gone. For over a hundred years civilization had been built upon science and steam-power, yet, in 1914, armies were still organized on muscle-power, the power upon which nations had been constituted prior to the advent of the steam-engine, the dynamo and the petrol-engine, the telegraph and the telephone. As the main target in war—the will of the nation—grew in size through intellectual expansion and sensitiveness, so do we see, in order to protect these targets, armies becoming, not more intelligent and more scientific, but more brutal, ton upon ton of human flesh being added, until war strengths are reckoned in millions in place of thousands of men.

This idea of human tonnage was a veritable hallucination, which became apparent when, in August, 1914, the first machine gun sent its bullets zip-zipping over the battlefield. This hallucination, thereupon, began to volatilize, for the soldier, however well he may have been trained, always remains a creature controlled by his instinct of self-preservation. What did this instinct do ? For the next four years, at first unconsciously, then more and more consciously, it urged the soldier to make good his hundred years of scientific neglect. Invention was thereupon piled upon invention, but the killing theory still held the field, until towards the close of the war it became apparent to some

104   The Reformation of War

that science was so powerful that it could even dispense with the age-old custom of killing and could do something far more effective—it could petrify the human mind with fear. It could, in fact, directly dictate the will of one nation to another, and with vastly reduced bloodshed. It could, in fact, enforce policy with far less detriment to the eventual peace than had ever been possible before. The idea of the moral shock, in place of the physical assault, was just beginning to flutter over the blood-soaked battlefields when the Armistice of November 11, 1918, brought hostilities to a close. Since that date this idea has been reduced from a dynamic force to a mere kinetic energy, by solemn international ignorance of the meaning and object of war. In 1921, at Washington, the aim of the Disarmament Conference was to restrict the outbreak of war and to render warfare less brutal, yet the action taken there, as I shall prove, was to render wars more likely and to maintain armies on a footing which, when the next great war engulfs society, will once again demand its million tons of flesh. I will now return to the war of 1914–1918.

If we examine the history of siege warfare, we shall soon discover that the causes of surrender, in order of importance, have been : treachery, starvation and assault. Here we obtain three different means of accomplishing a siege—the attack on the moral of the defenders, the attack on the resources of the defenders and the attack on the defences of the defenders   I have already dealt with the second and third of these means, I will now examine the first.

I will first inquire into the meaning of treachery as applied to war, for it is an ugly word* and its unenviable reputation may, in the minds of some, obliterate its tremendous power. Treachery is a violation of allegiance, the highest form of which is the co-operation of the individuals composing a nation in the maintenance of the nation's free existence. For an individual, who shares in common with others the prosperity of the nation to which

---

* An American writer defines strategy as follows : " When practised by Indians it is called treachery "—which is very true.

The First Lap of the Moral Epoch

he belongs, to refuse, for some selfish reason, to secure the nation against the aggression of an enemy, is an act of treachery. All acts of war ultimately aim at creating a state of treachery in an enemy; in other words, their object is to reduce the enemy's moral to so low a point that he is willing to set aside his national existence or policy, and accept the will of his adversary. Treachery, in its military meaning, is demoralization, and, if we once get the nasty taste of the word out of our mouths, we shall realize that, if by inducing a state of faithlessness or demoralization in an enemy we can more speedily win a war than by force of arms or starvation, we have every right to use treachery as a weapon. By this I do not mean that we should behave like barbarians, or that we should fire at an enemy under a flag of truce, or promise him terms of surrender we have no intention of carrying out; but that to attack the will of the enemy's army and his civil population by a rapid means is quite as honourable an act of war as to attack it by a slow means, such as shooting down his soldiers, sinking his ships and starving his women and children.

I will now examine this question from a very simple standpoint. In a besieged town or fortress, what human elements within it have, in the past, proved the most receptive to treachery? Undoubtedly the civil elements. The reason for this is self-apparent; soldiers are controlled by discipline, civilians by fear. Consequently, the main targets of the moral attack are the civil inhabitants of the country attacked, for if their will can be corrupted, however well disciplined may their soldiers and sailors be, their organization will become affected by the general rot which has undermined the stability of their government. A nation septic with revolution can no more wage an organized war than can a man, contorted with colic, shoot snipe. This was the lesson which Russia taught Europe in 1917, and yet, at that time, the Allied press was unanimous in pronouncing the revolution to be a glorious war-winning event!

On the declaration of war, in August, 1914, the moral attack

106　The Reformation of War

opened like a labour conference; the contending newspapers collected dirt from the gutters of their respective Fleet Streets and threw it into each other's faces. Later on in the war, the journalists were drilled into some form of order, and well-organized paper attacks were launched, treachery finding its extreme limit in the fictitious and comic discovery of the German Corpse Factories. Curious to relate that, though the power of the press, as a means of demoralization, was fully realized by the British Government, its enormous power to moralize the British Nation was never made use of. Being completely cut off from the realities of war by a short-sighted censorship, the press was never able to bring the people into touch with these realities and, consequently, into contact with their true responsibilities. The people being thus rendered inarticulate, the government was unable to ascertain the popular sentiment on any great question, and when a crisis had to be faced, not knowing how the nation might take it, decision was obscured by ambiguous action, which always permitted of numerous lines of retirement should eventually the people object. What the politicians never realized was that, during war time, the supreme duty of government is to take the nation into their full confidence; for, when national existence is at stake, popular opinion (intuition) is nearly always healthy and virile. The medium between the government and the people, and between the people and the nation's army, fleet, and air force, is the daily press; during the war, this medium, in place of being rendered fluid, was solidified by the chill blast of political fear.

Besides the newspaper-attack, the propitiation of neutrals was extensively made use of as a means of undermining the moral of the enemy's government. Looking back on the results, it is very doubtful whether this diplomatic attack did more damage to the enemy or to ourselves. The reason was that the government relied more on cajolery than on outspokenness. British diplomatic action in Turkey, Bulgaria and Greece, during 1914, was a grotesque failure, and there can be little doubt that, during the period which preceded America's entry into the war, the government was quite as concerned with pleasing the United States as with beating Germany In place of winning over the Americans—a virile nation—by frankness, this action, though it may have flattered President Wilson, withheld from the people of that great country the seriousness of the Allies' position in Europe. This want of straight talking undoubtedly lengthened the war. What no government appeared to realize, and Germany least of all, was that the poles of the magnet which attract all neutrals worth attracting are straight-fighting and straight-speaking, and why ? Because the winners of the war will, in the peace which must one day follow it, exert more control over neutrals than the losers; consequently, it was to the future advantage of the world that the "cleanest" nations should win.

Besides the purely civil means of attacking the moral of a nation I will now turn to the military means. In traditional warfare, it was the rule that armies attacked armies and not non-combatants. If this tradition were strictly adhered to, then the demoralization of the enemy could only be effected by the destruction of the enemy's army and fleet. This process proved a most bloody one, and, during the war, adherence to it resulted in appalling slaughter. It should here be once again remembered that the more bloodless a war is, the more prosperous and contented will the peace, which follows the war, be for all concerned. For example, if, during the recent war, Germany could have been forced to disband her army and scrap her navy by a sudden and enormous loss of national moral, which entailed little bloodshed and small damage to her industries, would not the world to-day be a more prosperous and contented habitation for man than it actually is ? There can be no two answers to this question. And, supposing even if this sudden blow had cost the lives of a few thousand German women and children, would this loss have rendered this novel type of warfare immoral ? Certainly, if the killing of men is to be considered moral while the killing of women and children, under all

108   The Reformation of War

circumstances, is an immoral act. The colossal fallacy of this argument is to be sought in the fact that traditional warfare will persistently and blindly think of killing or not-killing as objectives in war. When, however, it is realized that to enforce a policy, and not to kill, is the objective, and that the policy of a nation, though maintained and enforced by her sailors and soldiers, is not fashioned by them, but by the civil population, surely, then, if a few civilians get killed in the struggle they have nothing to complain of—" *dulce et decorum est pro patria mori* " And, if they will not accept these words as their motto, then, in my opinion, their governments should altogether abstain from war, however much they may be spat upon.

Morality is not a fixed quantity, it is not a law of Nature, but a dynamic and invigorating social force. It, again, is not an end in itself, but a means towards an end—peaceful national survival. Slaughter is the negation of survival; consequently, as the incidence of slaughter is reduced, the more moral, in the natural meaning of the word, does warfare become.

I will now examine certain means of warfare which were used during the Great War, the future developments of which, I believe, will, while minimizing bloodshed and ruin, prove adequate in order to enforce policy.

Nearly all new inventions in war, and not a few in industry, have been attributed to his Satanic Majesty, who must, indeed, be the greatest of all inventors, but, curious to relate, eventually all these inventions have made warfare more and more humane and less and less frequent. If this progress continue, it is quite conceivable that from the week-end wars of the Middle Ages, we may, in the future, expect wars once a century, once every two centuries, until warfare, as we know it to-day, is looked upon as a kind of international cannibalism and nations lose their taste for blood.

When warfare was very simple in nature, the soldier shot arrows at his antagonist; later on he fired cannon balls, and as these played terrible havoc when they bounded through close masses of troops, consequently the infantry opened their ranks

The First Lap of the Moral Epoch

in order to avoid destruction. This rather disconcerted the gunner, so he invented the shell and the shrapnel howitzer, and, when the opposing infantry found out, as they did very early in the Great War, that it was useless to open the ranks any further, they dug trenches and went to earth. Once again was the gunner disconcerted, and, while he was attempting to dig the infantry out of their trenches by means of shells, a very expensive operation, a cunning German, following on the lines proposed by Lord Dundonald in 1854, replaced steel particles by gas particles, so that a whole area and all the targets included in it, either above ground or beneath, might be hit.

On April 22, 1915, the Germans put this idea into practice east of Ypres, and inaugurated a mode of warfare which I believe is destined to revolutionize the whole art. They made, however, two cardinal mistakes: first, they used lethal gas—chlorine, which was totally unnecessary, especially so as the Hague Convention did not forbid the use of gases of a non-toxic nature; secondly, they did not use sufficient of it for the winning of a decisive battle. Had they really understood the meaning of gas they could have won the war.

The effects, though restricted, were immediate and appalling, the French and British troops fell back gasping for breath. They could do nothing else, for all their peace training and equipment were useless against this new death. Consequently, tradition was shocked to the marrow, and, without thought, the whole civilized world shuddered with horror, and gas, like gunpowder, chloroform and the locomotive, was pronounced to be the invention of the Devil.

The horrors of gas warfare have been so well advertised that the very enthusiasm shown by its execrators should make us pause and think. What are the facts? The main fact, as regards the brutality of this type of warfare, is to be discovered in the casualty lists. As regards their own losses, the American General Staff have carefully categorized them; they are as follows:

The total number of casualties resulting from all causes

110   The Reformation of War

was 274,217. Of these 74,779, or 27.3 per cent., were due to gas. Of the gas casualties only 1,400, or 1.87 per cent., resulted in death. Of the remaining 199,438 casualties, resulting from bullets, shell fire, etc., 46,659, or 23.4 per cent., proved fatal. Here, then, are the facts regarding these alleged horrors. Well may the compilers of this report conclude it by saying :

> "In other words, gas is twelve times as humane as bullets and high explosives. That is to say, if a man gets gassed on the battlefield he has twelve times as many chances to get well as if he is struck by bullets and high explosives."

Further than this, the permanent injuries resulting from gas-wounding are far less numerous than those inflicted by the use of traditional weapons. At the Meeting of the British Association of 1919, Brigadier-General H. Hartley, an expert chemist, said :

> "The death-rate among gas casualties was much lower than that among casualties of other causes, and not only was the death-rate lower, but a much smaller proportion of the injured suffered any permanent disability There is no comparison between the permanent damage caused by gas, and the suffering caused to those who were maimed and blinded by shell and rifle-fire * It is now generally admitted that in the later stages of the war many military objects could be attained with less suffering by using gas than by any other means."

I have already stated, more than once, that killing is not the objective in war. If this statement be accepted, then, as

---

* Pacifists and adherents of the traditional war school have deliberately attempted to discredit chemical warfare by stating that gas has blinded thousands of men and affected tens of thousands with tuberculosis. The facts of the case are as follows :

(i.) Blinding   During the war the Americans had eighty-six men totally blinded, forty-four partially blinded and six hundred and forty-four blinded in one eye   Of the gassed patients four were blinded in both eyes and twenty-five in one eye.

(ii) In the year 1918 there were one and a half times as many cases of tuberculosis per thousand among all American troops in France as there were amongst those gassed   In 1919 there were more than one and three-quarter times as many tuberculosis cases per thousand among all troops as there were among the gassed.

The Report of the Surgeon-General U.S.A. Army, 1920

The First Lap of the Moral Epoch

bloodshed is uneconomical, surely an attempt should be made to devise a means of forcing an enemy to change his policy by bloodlessly defeating his army. Gas warfare enables us to do this, for there is no reason why gases as weapons should be of a lethal nature. In the last war they were frequently so, because soldiers and the civil suppliers of soldiers had become so accustomed to think in terms of killing, that, when gas was proposed as a weapon, they at once looked upon gas in the form of a microscopic bullet.

On July 12, 1917, at the third battle of Ypres, the Germans gave up this idea, and, by making use of a chemical commonly known as mustard gas, disclosed to the whole world the future possibilities of gas warfare. Respirators to a great extent were now useless, for the persistent and vesicant nature of this chemical rendered whole areas, for days on end, uninhabitable and dangerous to cross. Men carried the oily liquid on their clothes, on the mud of their boots, and infected dug-outs, billets and rest camps far back on the lines of communication. Few died, but many were incapacitated for months on end. Here, curious to relate, is the true power of gas as a weapon—*it can incapacitate without killing*. A dead man says nothing, and, when once buried, is no encumbrance to the survivors. A wounded man will spread the wildest of rumours, will exaggerate dangers, foster panic, and requires the attention of others to heal him—until he dies or is cured, he is a military encumbrance and a demoralizing agent. Gas, as I will show later on, is, *par excellence*, the weapon of demoralization, and, as it can terrorize without necessarily killing, it, more than any other known weapon, can enforce economically the policy of one nation on another. I will now turn to air warfare.

For military purposes the aeroplane had been made use of before the advent of the Great War, both in Mexico and Tripoli, but it was only during the Great War that, in spite of traditional jealousy, its immense powers became manifest. At first a mere adjunct to the older services on land and sea, within three years it won its independence, for not only could it hop

112   The Reformation of War

over armies and fleets and attack the brains of these forces, but it could attack the moral of the government defended by these forces, and, above all, the will of the nation upon which the power of government is founded.

The Germans were, I believe, the first of the belligerents to bombard an open town from the air, and such action, being a novelty, met with universal execration. Nevertheless, it was not long before the Allies retaliated in what was known as baby-killing, but which in truth was the direct attack on the source of all military power—the nerves and will of the civil population.

As it cannot be more immoral to bomb a town than to bombard it, does the immorality of an aeroplane attack lie in the fact that, while in a bombardment the slaughter of women and children is but an unfortunate incident, in an aerial attack on a town the terrorization of its *civil* inhabitants becomes the main object ? I believe that this is the popular conception, simply because civilians have not yet grasped the fact that : when *nations go to war the entire population of each country concerned is ranged against the other*, and that the solidarity of their fighting forces is founded on the civil will. The justifiableness of such attacks was clearly pointed out by Mr. Lanchester as long ago as 1915, when he wrote :

"It is futile to attempt to disguise the self-evident fact that a serious attack on the capital city of an enemy, containing in its heart the administrative centre both of his Army and Navy, in addition to the headquarters of his Government, cannot be regarded other than as a legitimate act of war. No international agreement or contention can make it otherwise. . . . There is really no escape from this. Unquestionably the destruction of a capital city, such as London, with the administrative centres aforesaid, would be a military achievement of the first order of magnitude ; it would be, from an enemy standpoint, an achievement of far greater potential value than any ordinary success or victory on the field of battle."*

Apparent as this fact is, it was only towards the end of the Great War that the various belligerents began to realize what an attack on the social nerve-centres really meant. Simultaneously,

* "Aircraft and Warfare," F. W. Lanchester, p. 192.

The First Lap of the Moral Epoch

they also learnt that the body of an army attacked by low flying aeroplanes was all but helpless. In Palestine and Syria the routed Turks suffered seriously from this form of attack, so also did the retiring Austrians in Italy. Of the last-mentioned operations, Major-General the Hon. S. F. Gathorne-Hardy gives a graphic description in Vol. III., No. 1, of the " Army Quarterly." He says:

> " On these two days (October 29th, 30th, 1918), the Conegliano-Pordonone road was black with columns of all arms hurrying eastwards. On these the few British squadrons poured 30,000 rounds of S A A. and three and a half tons of bombs from low altitude. Subsequent examination of the road almost forced the observer to the conclusion that this form of warfare should be forbidden in the future."

Such advice as this is worse than useless, for difficulties are not banished by words, and, if such action were possible, either mankind would become a race of gods or all progress would cease. Curious to relate, a very similar suggestion was made by Baron de Jomini, who wrote his " Art of War " about one hundred years ago. He says:

> " The means of destruction are approaching perfection with frightful rapidity The Congreve rockets, the effect and direction of which it is said the Austrians can now regulate The shrapnel howitzers, which throw a stream of canister as far as the range of a bullet—the Perkins steam guns, which vomit forth as many balls as a battalion—will multiply the chances of destruction, as though the hecatombs of Eylau, Borodino, Leipsic and Waterloo were not sufficient to decimate the European races.
>
> " If governments do not combine in a congress to proscribe these inventions of destruction, there will be no course left but to make the half of any army consist of cavalry with cuirasses, in order to capture with great rapidity these machines; and the infantry, even, will be obliged to resume its armour of the Middle Ages, without which a battalion will be destroyed before engaging the enemy.
>
> " We may then see again the famous men-at-arms all covered with armour, and horses will require the same protection."

His prevision was right, comity of nations could do nothing; common-sense could do much, and his armoured man materialized in 1916 in the form of the tank, yet another invention which I will now examine.

114 The Reformation of War

For many years before the outbreak of the Great War the line along which tactical power was sought was fire, more fire and yet more fire. Protection, except by fire and by extensions, that is by reduction in the size of the target, had been neglected, and increased means of mobility, except for the railway, had scarcely been considered at all. In 1914 (and for all that still to-day), the marching-power of the soldier was about the same as it was in the days of Cheops and Sennacherib.

As the type of fire aimed at was rifle-fire, and as it was well known that a rifle bullet could be rendered perfectly harmless by about 8 mm. of armour, it is truly astonishing, when to-day we look back on the problem, that, before the outbreak of the war, no single soldier of note thought of using the petrol engine and chain track for the purpose of carrying armour in order to protect infantry. The problem is in nature so simple and so self-apparent, that the only answer to the question why then was it not thought of, must be that a tradition, when it becomes fixed in the mind of man, exercises a hypnotic influence over even the most intelligent, and over the less intelligent it is mentally a soporific drug and the most dangerous " dope " of all. So we find that, since 1870, the entire General Staffs in the world had been walking in their sleep. Then suddenly, in August, 1914, they woke up to discover that they were standing outside on the window-sill of a house forty-four stories high—the house of traditional warfare. Fire-supremacy, the very instrument of victory which, for forty-four years, they had been creating, drove friend and foe like rats to earth. Then a common-sense man—Colonel E. D. Swinton—came forward and suggested the tank, and the British War Office refused it !

Thanks to Mr. Winston Churchill, who, in 1914, was First Lord of the Admiralty, the first tanks were produced and, on September 15, 1916, they experienced their baptism of fire on the battlefield of the Somme. At once the British General Staff gave orders for the cancellation of all further production of tanks, but thanks to Sir Albert Stern this order was rescinded. From this date on to the battle of Hamel, on July 4, 1918, tanks had to fight for their existence, not against the enemy's opposition but against tradi-

The First Lap of the Moral Epoch 115

tion, and so well did they fight that, in 1921, General Von Zwehl was able to write : " It was not the genius of Marshal Foch that defeated us, but ' General Tank.' "*

I do not intend here to prove this assertion, for it has already been proved in many books ; in place I will simply take the tank as it existed during the Great War and show that in proportion as it was a life-saving invention so also was it a demoralizing agent, and, further, how it was on the point of revolutionizing tactics when the Armistice put an end to the war.

On the battlefield of the Somme, in 1916, it accomplished little of a startling nature and yet sufficient to have persuaded all but the traditionally blind that it was a weapon wherewith the war on land could be won at comparatively small cost. On September 25, one tank, followed closely by infantry, moved along about a mile of trench line and forced 362 Germans to surrender and at a cost to the infantry of five men killed and wounded. The point to note in this small operation is that the tank was in front of the infantry, a very common-sense position, for just as a man equipped with a shield carries it in front of him and not behind him, so when armoured machines accompany infantry their proper place is *in front !*

Common-sense has, however, nothing whatever to do with tradition ; for, as the tank operations which followed proved, common-sense is generally the antithesis of custom Because the manuals laid it down that infantry were the decisive arm, and because officers had been fed on the manuals, in spite of the armoured tank, the infantry continued from September, 1916, to November, 1917, to lead the assault. Then, on November 20, at the battle of Cambrai, tradition received such a blow between the eyes that even the most pessimistic asserted that the tank had at length come into its own. At this battle, an advance of 10,000 yards was made in twelve hours at a cost of 6,000 casualties, and 8,000 Germans and 100 guns were captured. At the third battle of Ypres a similar penetration took three months and cost over

* " Die Schlachten im Sommer, 1918, an der West Front," von H Von Zwehl, General der Infanterie a D.

8*

116   The Reformation of War

350,000 casualties. The traditional school was, however, only tank-shocked. In April, 1918, the Tank Corps was reduced from 18 to 12 Battalions because infantry reinforcements were falling short ! On July 4, 1918, at the battle of Hamel, tanks started once again *in rear* of the infantry ! The infantry attack was on the point of petering out when the 60 tanks co-operating caught up the leading wave of Australians and led them through to their final objective. The tank crews suffered no fatal casualties, the Australians lost 672 in killed and wounded and 1,500 Germans were captured. Then followed the battles of Soissons, July 18, and of Amiens, August 8, and the tank became the terror of Germany. On July 1, 1916, the first day of the battle of the Somme, the British Army suffered 40,000 casualties ; on the first day of the battle of Amiens the casualties were slightly under 1,000 !

During July, August, September, October and November, 1916, the British Army lost approximately 475,000 men, it captured 30,000 prisoners and occupied some 90 square miles of country. During the same months, in 1917, the losses were 370,000, the prisoners captured were 25,000, and the ground occupied was about 45 square miles. In July, August, September, October and November, 1918, the losses were 345,000, the prisoners captured 176,000, and the ground occupied was 4,000 square miles. If now we divide these losses by the number of square miles captured, we shall obtain a rough estimate of casualties per square mile gained. These figures are approximately as follows

(a) July to November, 1916 :
   475,000 ÷ 90 sq. miles = 5,277 casualties per sq. mile.
(b) July to November, 1917 :
   370,000 ÷ 45 sq miles = 8,222 casualties per sq. mile.
(c) July to November, 1918 ·
   345,000 ÷ 4,000 sq miles = 86 casualties per sq. mile.

In the third period alone were tanks used efficiently.

During the early days of the third battle of Ypres, in 1917, it became apparent to the General Staff of the British Tank Corps

The First Lap of the Moral Epoch

that, though it was always possible, granted the ground was passable, to break an enemy's front by means of tanks, by traditional methods of warfare it was most difficult to prevent this broken front falling back on its reserves or to prevent the reserves reinforcing the shattered fragments A project was, consequently, devised to overcome this difficulty. It consisted in the use of two types of tanks, one type, 26 feet long, to assault the enemy's front, and another type, 30 feet long, to move right through this front and deposit in rear of it a chain of machine-gun posts· Each long tank, besides its crew, was to carry forward within it 20 machine gunners with 4 machine guns. The point of interest in this novel form of attack was that its target was the *morally weakest point* in the enemy's battle body, namely, his rear

On May 24, 1918, the General Staff of the Tank Corps made out another project, which carried the attack on the enemy's moral a step further.

From 1914 onwards, traditional warfare had sought to overcome the enemy's resistance by defeating his fighting troops. Such a defeat would result in the demoralization of his command and his administrative services. The demoralization of his command would react on the will of the enemy's people, who might be reduced to so nervous a condition that they would either overthrow their government or force it to sue for peace. As the means of this method of warfare were superiority of weapon-power and man-power, that is brute force, and as, in the spring of 1918, the Germans were numerically superior to the Allies, there appeared no immediate chance of winning the war by traditional methods Consequently, it was considered that some other solution should be attempted. The proposals made were as follows :

The strength of the enemy's fighting forces depended on the solidarity of their organization, which, in its turn, rested on the integrity of the enemy's command and system of supply. If these two props could be knocked away, then the whole of the battle front supported by them would collapse. In order to effect this *moral débâcle* of the enemy's body, the Tank Corps

118   The Reformation of War

General Staff suggested that, for the 1919 campaign, two separate forces of tanks should be employed :

(i.) A force of fast moving machines which, under cover of darkness or smoke, would, at top speed, rush through the enemy's fighting body and, making for all Divisional, Corps and Army Headquarters, paralyse these brain and nerve centres by direct attack; simultaneously, other fast machines were to attack all railheads, supply and signal centres, and reduce the personnel at these points to a state of panic.

(ii.) A force of slower and more heavily armoured machines were to precede the attacking infantry and assault the enemy's front at the moment the faster machines were demoralizing and destroying the brains and stomach.

It was considered that if an attack of this nature could be delivered on a frontage of from 80 to 160 kilometres, such a demoralizing blow would be delivered that the greater part of the German front in France would crumble and produce such a condition of despair within Germany that the Germans would accept defeat.

The operation was a novel one, and it redounds to the credit of the Imperial General Staff in London that they accepted it in detail, and on July 20, 1918, communicated it to Marshal Foch, then Generalissimo of the Allied Armies, who agreed " in every way with the main principles of the study." Consequently this plan of operations was accepted as the basic tactical idea for the 1919 campaign.

Though Fate was to decide that this attack was not to take place, since hostilities terminated in November, 1918, it is nevertheless interesting to note the following evolution: that the war opened with traditional warfare ; that the underlying idea of all traditional operations is killing ; that by degrees this idea gave way to that of demoralizing, until, finally, a method of attack was devised which all but ignored brute force and which for slaughter substituted nervous shock, aiming a moral blow at the brain in place of a physical blow at the body of the enemy's army.

VI

THE WEAPON OF THE FUTURE

IN the last Chapter I showed that the tactical tendency in modern warfare was to strike at the moral rather than at the muscle of an enemy ; I also stated that, in my opinion, gas would prove itself to be the weapon which, of all weapons, could accomplish this blow the most economically. The tank and aeroplane, be it well remembered, are not weapons, but only vehicles—means of carrying weapons.

In this present Chapter I intend examining gas as a weapon. First of all it should be realized that the utility of gas in war is not a new idea. In modern times, this idea was thought of in 1812 and again during the Crimean war by Lord Dundonald. In 1864, Mr. B. W. Richardson, considering gas warfare, went so far as to write :

" The question is, shall these things be ? I do not see that humanity should revolt, for would it not be better to destroy a host in Regent's Park by making the men fall as in a mystical sleep, than to let down on them another host to break their bones, tear their limbs asunder and gouge out their entrails with three-cornered pikes ; leaving a vast majority undead and writhing for hours in torments of the damned ? "*

In 1899, the employment of lethal gas as a weapon was discussed at the Hague, and its use was forbidden, this prohibition only serving to give Germany, in 1915, a superior weapon to those wielded by her enemies. Possessing no protection against it, the British and French troops suffered accordingly, and anathematized the new weapon, not only because it was new,

* *Popular Science Review*, 3.176. (1864).

but because it was extremely powerful and Germany held the whip hand as regards its production. The evil name then given to gas has, in the popular imagination, clung to it ever since, for the people do not reason, because what their eyes have read their lips repeat. With the populace I have no quarrel, for they are docile, thoughtless creatures depending on others for their ideas; but with people like Sir Edward Thorpe, President of the British Association in 1921, it is otherwise, for they at least are presumed to be intelligent. Following in the footsteps of the worthy Baron de Jomini, some of whose ideas I have already quoted, Sir Edward has pronounced the use of lethal gas to be " one of the most bestial episodes in the history of the Great War. . . . Surely," he exclaims, " comity among nations should be adequate to arrest it " and then, deviating from the path of Jomini, the only means he suggests is to leave the solution of this problem to the unfortunate League of Nations, and to urge all scientists to set their face " against the continued degradation of science in . . . augmenting the horrors of war ! " Gas warfare is not, as Sir Edward Thorpe asserts, " the very negation of civilization," for it is, in fact, a product of civilization and an outcrop of science which will endure ; because, as Captain Auld says :

> " Chemical Warfare has come to stay. It is inconceivable that the light barriers of mutual consent or of edict can effectively close the road I speak of Military history and human nature are against it at every turn. No case is known of a successful new weapon or a tactical advantage having been discarded once its value was apparent. No agreement or treaty has proved strong enough to bind an unscrupulous enemy seeking an advantage, or for that matter one with its existence at stake. To avoid the new road is to risk being passed in the race of preparation and being outflanked and overwhelmed in the event of hostilities.
>
> " Whatever we do in the matter we can bind no one but ourselves. Until war ceases we must be prepared. Apathy is suicidal. Prejudice is a crime."[*]

There can be no doubt, outside Bedlam, of the wisdom

---

[*] " Chemical Warfare," by Capt. S. J. M. Auld, O B E., M.C., *Royal Engineers Journal*, Feb., 1922

of these words, just as there can be no doubt that the decision of the Hague Convention presented Germany, a country unscrupulous and fighting for her life, with a means wherewith, had she been wise, she might well have won the war Yet, at the Washington Disarmament Conference of 1921, at which were assembled intelligent human beings, what do we find was decided ? As follows:

> "The use in war of asphyxiating, poisonous or other gases, and all analogous liquids, materials or devices, having been justly condemned by the general opinion of the civilized world and a prohibition of such use having been declared in Treaties to which a majority of the civilized Powers are parties,
>
> "The Signatory Powers, to the end that this prohibition shall be universally accepted as a part of international law binding alike the conscience and practice of nations, declare their assent to such prohibition, agree to be bound thereby as between themselves and invite all other civilized nations to adhere thereto."

Then, in place of defining what is meant by " all analogous liquids, materials or devices," a veritable witches' cauldron of mysteries, this Conference, in the footsteps of Sir Edward Thorpe and others, indulges in abuse. The Report continues:

> "It undertakes further to denounce the use of poisonous gases and chemicals in war, as they were used to the horror of all civilization in the war of 1914-1918.
>
> "Cynics have said that in the stress of war these rules will be violated Cynics are always near-sighted, and oft and usual the decisive facts lie beyond the range of their vision."

Before I examine the first part of this astonishing agreement, I will examine the question of the cynics:

Giordano Bruno died at the stake because he was a cynic. Galileo perished in prison and Copernicus just died in time to escape persecution because they were cynics. Roger Bacon, a terrible cynic, hid the secret of gunpowder in a cryptograph. Solomon de Caus was locked up in a madhouse for proclaiming that ships and vehicles could be moved by steam. Simpson, who first made use of chloroform in obstetrics, was considered an agent of the devil, and so was Jenner, the introducer of vaccination against smallpox. George Stephenson, probably the greatest

The Weapon of the Future

of all cynics, was virtually outlawed. His invention, the locomotive, was declared to be " contrary to the law of God," because " it would prevent cows grazing, hens laying, and would cause ladies to give premature birth to children at the sight of these things going forward at the rate of four and a half miles an hour ! "

With reference to the locomotive, I cannot forbear quoting from the *Quarterly Review* of 1825, for the quotation is in character so traditional.

> " What can be more palpably absurd and ridiculous than the prospect held out of locomotives travelling TWICE AS FAST as stage coaches ! We should as soon expect the people of Woolwich to suffer themselves to be fired off upon one of Congreve's ricochet rockets as trust themselves to the mercy of such a machine going at such a rate. We will back old Father Thames against the Woolwich Railway for any sum. We trust that Parliament will, in all railways it may sanction, limit the speed to EIGHT or NINE MILES AN HOUR, which, we entirely agree with Mr. Sylvester, is as great as can be ventured on with safety."

Gunpowder, the most revolutionary military discovery prior to that of gas, was anathematized beyond belief. In the Middle Ages wars were very frequent, because weapons were very simple and unscientific. Knights boasted of their courts and codes of chivalry, but, when battles took place, there was usually, as one chronicler puts it, " a horrid slaughter among the common folk." The reason for this was that the common folk were not worth taking prisoners—they had little in their pockets. Then came Roger Bacon's gunpowder, and, as Carlyle says : " this logic even the Hyperborean understands," for, " it makes all men alike tall. . . . Hereby, at last, is the Goliath powerless and the David resistless ; savage animalism is nothing, inventive spiritualism is all." Mind has in fact triumphed over body, and upon gunpowder is modern democracy founded.

Needless to say, the knight, who, dressed in steel plate, was immune from democratic sticks and stones, strongly objected to be shot by a poltroon, that is, a peasant armed with an

124   The Reformation of War

arquebus. To give such a knave power over the knight was an insult which could not be tolerated; it was utterly barbarous, and as late as 1626 we find a certain Mr. Monro writing:

> "It is thought that the invention of cannons was found first at Nuremberg for the ruin of man . . how soone the trumpet did sounde, the enemy was thundered on, first with those as with showers of hailstones, so that the enemies were cruelly affrighted with them, men of valour being suddenly taken away, who before were wont to fight valiantly and long with the sword and lance, more for the honour of victory; than for any desire of shedding of blood; but now, men are marterysed and cut downe, at more than half a mile of distance, by these furious and thundering engines of great cannon, that sometimes shoote fiery bullets able to burn whole cities, castles, houses or bridges, where they chance to light, and if they happen to light within walls, or amongst a briggad of foote or horse, as they did at Leipsigh, in the grave fon Torne his briggad, spoiled a number at once, as doubtless the devilish invention did within Walestine, his leaguer at this time."

Mr. Monro was wrong, because gunpowder humanized sword and lance warfare. The cynic of 1626 was right, and so, in 1922, will the cynic once again prove himself right, because gas will humanize the type of warfare Monro objected to, but which the members of the Washington Conference wish to maintain. Just as William Napier objected to the introduction into the British Army of the Minié rifle, a weapon with a range of one thousand yards, because, as he said with some heat, " it would turn infantry into long-range assassins," so, to-day, do we find many eminent people objecting to gas warfare, because, being a novelty, its meaning is only sufficiently understood by them to realize that it may disturb their preconceived ideas, which, through long acquaintance, have become cherished personal belongings.

I will now turn back to the compact and examine the peculiarly ambiguous wording—" other gases and all analogous liquids, materials or devices." What do these words mean? They vaguely and all embracingly can mean nothing outside everything. In fact they mean that no chemical whatever may be used in war. This is absurd, because no nation can accept a decision which excludes all harmless lachrymators and smokes

The Weapon of the Future

which may save life, as well as high explosives which give off carbon monoxide. If this compact be carried to its ultimate conclusion, then the use of petrol gas in military motor cars, and of coal gas in officers' billets, are also forbidden ! The above words exclude and debar so much that they really include nothing, for all that an enemy has got to do, in peace time, is to prepare vast quantities of various gases, for he knows for a certainty, from the wording of this compact, that innumerable excuses will always be found on the battlefield, such as the use by his adversary of T.N.T. or picric acid, which will provide him with an excuse to retaliate with the real " stuff." " To us," to quote from an American scientific journal, " the endeavour to abolish chemical warfare throughout the world by the resolutions of the present Conference reminds us of the experience of King Canute in commanding the tides not to rise." Personally, it reminds me of that " cunning " bird the ostrich.

I will now inquire into the military reasons why I believe that gas will prove itself to be the weapon of the future.

First of all what is a weapon ? A weapon is a means of imposing by force a policy upon an adversary. The policy of a nation, as I have explained, should be enforced with the least loss possible to either side and to the world at large. The less this loss the better will the policy enforced flourish. The security of peaceful prosperity is the object of war, not slaughter. A weapon should, therefore, possess the following characteristics :

(i.) Its production should not detrimentally affect prosperity.
(ii.) It should be simple to manufacture in peace or war.
(iii.) Its nature should be unknown to the enemy.
(iv.) It should economize time on the battlefield.
(v.) It should incapacitate without killing.
(vi.) It should permit of an antidote being known to the side using it.
(vii.) It should effect no permanent damage to property.

The weapons of traditional warfare do not permit of these characteristics being developed, as they are all based on the idea

126   The Reformation of War

of physical and material destruction. Gunpowder revolutionized the means of war but not its underlying idea, and it only gave rise to the use of more powerful weapons of the killing type ; and so all the more frightening and, consequently, less destructive. I will now show that gas as a weapon will not only effect an equally great revolution of means, but also a revolution in idea.

(1.) *Economy in Production.* Armies and navies are of necessity expensive organizations, because they detract in place of adding to peaceful prosperity. During the last hundred years they have become more and more costly in proportion as the means used by them have diverged from the civil means. At the beginning of the last century a good fowling-piece differed little from the musket of the day, and a merchantman could rapidly be converted into a ship of war. To-day the rifle and machine gun have no civil uses outside Ireland, and a super-Dreadnought not only possesses no commercial value, but detracts from commercial prosperity by costing about £8,000,000, or considerably more than the whole British Navy did in 1823.

Gas is an article of commerce, and most of the gases employed during the Great War were manufactured not only by the normal commercial processes but from chemicals in everyday use. Modern civilization could scarcely exist if such chemicals as chlorine, phosgene and hydrocyanic acid were removed. Thousands of tons of all these substances are yearly made use of for bleaching, disinfecting, dyeing and killing rodent and insect pests. Consequently, we see that, in gases and war chemicals, we possess not only a means of securing national prosperity, but also a means of fostering it. This in itself constitutes a stupendous economic revolution. To-day, Germany possesses seventy per cent. of the organic chemical output of the entire world. In the next war she can use, if she so will, the whole of her chemical plant for the production of warlike chemicals Great Britain possesses but eleven per cent. of the world's output. What does this mean ? It means that, in spite of the treaty of Versailles, which limited the size of Germany's army, navy, and air force, Germany still possesses gas supremacy, and, of this supremacy in 1915, Mr. Balfour, at the Washington Conference, said that, " the result had been very near to a complete disaster for the allied armies." Should not we, therefore, do our utmost to foster organic chemistry at home ; yet how can we create the necessary supply unless we create a demand for it. If gas becomes our predominant weapon, then a demand for it will be created, and in seeking for new war gases we shall undoubtedly discover chemicals of great commercial utility. " The Chemical Warfare Service," says Mr. R. S. McBride, " furnishing as it does an important link in the chain of chemical industries, contributes to peace-time welfare of the community." This alone sufficiently justifies its cost, " even though its military value as a measure of defence were entirely ignored."*

Compared to the cost of the means employed in traditional warfare, the cost of war chemicals is insignificant. On January 16, 1922, in a speech before the Compressed Gas Manufacturers' Association, New York City, Brigadier-General Amos A. Fries, chief of the U.S.A. Chemical Warfare Service, said :

"Chemical Warfare cost the United States in the World War just about $150,000,000. The total cost of that war to the United States is estimated at $30,000,000,000, or two hundred times the cost of Chemical Warfare, and yet Chemical Warfare had a profound influence in causing the Germans to surrender. Briefly, Chemical Warfare was as cheap as it was effective and humane. If the United States wants economy in peace while at the same time being prepared for any emergency, gas is the weapon above all others."

(ii.) *Simplicity of Manufacture.* Simplicity of manufacture of weapons during war time is frequently a synonym of victory. Men are generally forthcoming, but unless weapons can rapidly be produced in bulk these men are useless, and, unless the nature of the weapons made is simple, bulk production will not be rapid. During the recent war, the training of the British New Armies was seriously delayed on account of shortage of weapons, and it was not until the beginning of 1918, or after more than

* "Chemical Warfare and the Arms Treaty," R. S. McBride, *Chemical and Metallurgical Engineering*, February 22, 1922.

three years' strenuous effort, that sufficient shells were produced to satisfy the demands made. If, before the war, we had devoted our attention to war gases, it is quite conceivable that we might have discovered a gas against which the Germans would have possessed no immediate protection, and that, by firing a few thousand projectiles loaded with this gas from the existing field guns, we should have attained greater results than we did by multiplying high explosive shells by the million; which, in their turn, demanded thousands of extra guns and gunners to fire them. During the war, we multiplied the nature of our guns and so complicated training What gas enables us to do is to use the same gun and only change the nature of the chemical inside the shell, which scarcely, if at all, affects the training of the gunners. Further still, gas is, what may be called, a universal weapon; that is to say, "in the mechanics of firing chemical ammunition there is no difference whatever from the mechanics of firing high explosives or shrapnel."

For any weapon to be manufactured rapidly, it is necessary to have its components at hand. If a country cannot produce these, then at any crisis it may suffer from a weapon-famine. What is the main source of chemical warfare? Coal—coal-tar and oil, from which also most of the medicines and dyes of the world are produced In Great Britain we possess vast resources of coal; consequently, for chemical warfare supplies we are not dependent on foreign products. Not only is it unnecessary for us to obtain from abroad our raw material for weapons, but, in place of spending our money on foreign nitrates, we can spend it on home-mined coal. Germany is also a great coal producing country; if in another war, as in the last, she loses her command of the sea, is it humanly likely that she will placidly accept defeat because of a shortage of traditional weapons when gigantic resources for the production of chemical weapons are actually but a few yards under her feet?

(iii) *Secrecy of Nature.* Secrecy in the nature of weapons is the foundation of tactical surprise, and surprise, as I have shown, is the most economical principle whereon to build grand

The Weapon of the Future

tactics. In war, surprise is the pivot of victory. In the past, the brute-force theory of warfare has to a great extent been foisted on to the armies and navies of civilized nations on account of their inability to keep their weapons secret. And, when they have attempted to do so, as in the case of the French mitrailleuse in 1870, training has suffered so severely that on the battlefield the weapons have proved useless. The difficulty has been, and still is, that once a weapon is in the hand of the soldier its characteristics soon become known to other nations, the most noted exception to this being the recoil system of the French 75 mm. field gun. In this case, however, it was unnecessary for the soldier to examine it, yet once in the hands of the soldier this contrivance might easily have been sold to a foreign country.

It is not practically possible to keep a bullet or a shell secret. It is, however, possible to keep the contents of a shell secret. A new explosive may be discovered and may be kept secret, but in effect it will only be a modification of existing means of destruction. A new gas may, however, be kept an absolute secret, and, what is equally important, its antidote may be kept secret as well. During peace time, let us suppose that a gunner is trained to fire shells filled with chlorine gas and that the container of his respirator possesses the necessary antidotes to chlorine. On mobilization he is given shell X and he changes his training respirator for one possessing substance Y, which is an antidote to X. X and Y are absolute secrets, he has not the faintest idea what they are, and yet they may enable him to defeat his adversary within a few minutes of the first attack being launched I will corroborate this self-evident advantage possessed by chemical weapons by again quoting from Mr. McBride.

> "Gas as a military agency can be developed by research and its manufacture continued in secret indefinitely, if any nation wishes, despite any number of international agreements to the contrary. In this respect it differs fundamentally from battleships and fortifications, which cannot be so secretly constructed and preserved"

(iv.) *Economy of Time.* The activities of war, even more so than those of peace, are controlled by time, for in war speed

130   The Reformation of War

and improvisation are predominant conditions. As regards weapons, time, in its military sense, is a correlative of effect. Thus, the speed of fire, such as is possessed by the machine gun, would be useless if the bullets were ineffective, and ineffective they frequently are when fired against an earthwork, or a tank, or into the blue. With gas the actual rate of fire may be much slower than that of traditional projectiles, though as it is normally carried within these projectiles, it is the same. But, if volume of fire be considered, it will at once become apparent that no traditional weapon possesses this quality to the extent of gas. From a rifle ten aimed shots can be fired in a minute, from a machine gun six hundred, from a field gun twenty shells, and, if shrapnel, each will contain 365 bullets, so that in a minute 7,300 bullets will be fired. Gas is, however, composed of chemical molecules each of which can disable; consequently, the projectiles of a gas bombardment cannot be reckoned by thousands per minute but by thousands of trillions. In fact, so immense a number, that it is not even necessary to know the position of the target; all that is necessary is to know in what area it is, and then to inundate this area. Unlike a bullet, the effect of gas does not cease once the force generated to propel it is spent, for, while the bullet is " dead " the gas molecule is " alive," and may remain alive for days after gas has been projected. If the reader can imagine a machine gun which can fire millions of bullets a second, each bullet drifting on after the force of the original discharge has been spent, creeping through trees and houses, wandering over walls and into shelters and dug-outs, then he will have some idea how gas can be used to economize military time.

(v.) *Economy of Life.* I have already repeatedly accentuated the fact that, in modern warfare, the object is to enforce a policy and not to kill and destroy. I realize that, in all probability, for many years to come killing will be an unavoidable attribute of battle, but it stands to reason that, if killing can be reduced, warfare will become more economical and the object of war will be the better attained. I have already examined the alleged horrors of gas warfare and have shown definitely that, during the recent

The Weapon of the Future

war, it was twelve times as humane as traditional warfare. In my opinion it can be made more humane still directly the idea of killing is replaced by that of incapacitating. A bullet is essentially a lethal weapon, for it is impossible to design a non-lethal bullet which would be of any practical use in war. It is, however, quite as feasible to employ non-lethal gases as lethal ones, and their power to incapacitate is enormous. During the third battle of Ypres, General Fries states, " that the British had over 160,000 gas casualties, but only 4,000 deaths—2½ per cent." Whether these figures are correct I am unable to say, but, as a partaker in this battle, I can vouch that after mud, mustard gas was the severest resistant encountered.

On the three days preceding the attack, on March 21, 1918, it is estimated that the Germans fired 250,000 mustard-gas shells against the British Third Army, which suffered a loss of 500 officer casualties

> " In spite of the fact that the Germans had no reserve gas for many days after the beginning of the Argonne fighting—the greatest battle in American history—the gas casualties among the Americans, according to the best information, amounted to 27.2 per cent. of all American battle casualties This is all the more remarkable when we consider that about one half of all American battle casualties occurred in the battle of the Argonne, where the Germans had practically no gas They had used up all reserves of that material against the British and the French earlier in the season, and hence had only daily production to draw upon "*

These are a few examples of the direct effect of gas as an incapacitating weapon ; I will now examine its indirect effect If soldiers, in order to protect themselves against bullets, had to don armour, even if this armour could be made proof, the bullet would not lose its whole value, for, by forcing the soldier to wear armour, it would soon reduce him to a state of physical exhaustion In place of attacking his body it would attack his mobility. Gas, by compelling a soldier to wear a respirator, can accomplish this important military result " Physical vigour," writes General Sibert (Director Chemical Warfare Service, U.S A , in 1919), " is

* Extract from United States War Department Annual Report, 1919.

one of the greatest assets in any army. Gas, used properly and in quantities that will be easily obtainable in future wars, will make the wearing of the mask a continuous affair for all troops within two to five miles of the front line, and in certain places for many miles beyond. If it never killed a man, the reduction in physical vigour and, therefore, efficiency of an army forced at all times to wear masks would amount to at least 25 per cent."

If the statistics of the total casualties of the Great War, so far as they are ascertainable, are examined, it will be found that by far the greatest number of casualties were suffered by the infantry, and that these casualties were inflicted by infantry weapons—bullets fired by rifles and machine guns. It follows, consequently, that, if infantry could be abolished, warfare would be made much more humane and economical than it is to-day, and, as one writer puts it, " without infantry, the ravages of war would be reduced something like eighty per cent.," and then adds, " When the frock coats get about the long table and begin to talk about limiting war's barbarity, they want to realize that they won't do much good by omitting a little of the millinery of war. What the world wants them to do is to keep the infantry at home."*

Gas will accomplish this very effectively, as I will now show.

An infantry soldier cannot go into action in a diver's suit with a mile or two of piping played out from a spool on his back, yet so powerful are certain modern gases, such as Lewisite, that they will penetrate without difficulty all ordinary clothing and burn the skin beneath it. To put a man into an air-tight suit is impracticable, as in battle he will die of heat apoplexy. Infantry, as infantry, can play but a small part in gas warfare, and with their disappearance can war be humanized, as I will show later on.

There are two further reasons why gas warfare will economize life by reducing casualties. The first is that, as I have explained, gas is a universal weapon, it can be used by all arms ; consequently, the result will be what I will call a universal type of casualty. The nature of all wounds will be very similar, because the means of inflicting them will be similar ; consequently, medical

* Racine, Wisconsin, Call, January 7, 1922.

The Weapon of the Future

arrangements on the battlefield can be simplified. The second is that, since new war gases can be kept secret, surprise in war will become more frequent and, consequently, the winning of victories will be speeded up. The shorter the war the less, normally, is the loss resulting.

(vi.) *Assurance of an Antidote.* In traditional warfare the only universal antidote to being killed is to kill, hence its barbarous and blood-thirsty nature. From time to time means have been sought to reduce casualties—such as body armour, helmets, shields and entrenchments. Gas is, however, unlike all traditional weapons in that, if a new gas is discovered, immediately an antidote can be provided for it. Consequently, it is now possible to send men into battle equipped with weapons against which the enemy may possess no protection, while our own men are completely protected. This in itself constitutes such a colossal tactical revolution that it is difficult at present to see where it will lead. In my own opinion it will sound the death-knell of infantry as we know them to-day, and how this will be accomplished I will explain in a future Chapter. One fact requires, however, to be accentuated, namely, no nation can hope to protect their fighting forces effectively against gas unless offensive gas warfare is studied during peace time and the troops themselves trained to understand what this form of warfare entails.

(vii.) *Economy of Property.* As the objective in war is to guarantee and safeguard prosperity, destruction, even of the enemy's property, should be avoided. In modern warfare the means of destruction have become so great that no nation considers its frontiers safe unless it possesses an army sufficiently powerful to destroy the enemy before the enemy can destroy it. The horror of the results of invasion was one of the causes not only of the Great War but of the armed peace which preceded its outbreak.

The war of 1914-1918 was a war of high explosives, and traditional methods of destruction were carried to such a pitch that entire towns were demolished, villages completely vanished, not a stone remaining, and the surface of hundreds of square miles of fields, vineyards and orchards was literally blown away. It is incredible that anyone, who has the welfare of humanity at heart, can wish to repeat this devastation. Yet it cannot be avoided as long as traditional warfare is maintained. Substitute gas warfare for high explosive warfare and a remedy presents itself; this is what the short-sighted cynic wants, but the professional humanitarian will have none of it. Why? Because he is blinded by tradition, and should he happen to be a politician, he is unable to forget his votes—truth must be obscured so that he may continue to rule the blotting-paper brained multitudes.

After reading through what I have already written, I cannot conceive how any rational person can have the face to maintain that traditional warfare is more economical and humane than chemical warfare. I can understand anyone wishing to abolish war, for the world is full of those who have no stomach for a fight; but I cannot understand how it is possible for people judged sane, people who have lived through the last war, even if at a safe distance, wishing to repeat its destruction This they are doing as long as they prevent armies and fleets developing on scientific lines For the prosperity of the world, scientific military research is essential. "Scientists are making," says General Hartley, " very rapid advances, and many of these will have a direct bearing on the next war. It is absolutely essential to make adequate provision to continue research on gas warfare problems, as otherwise all preparations for defence may prove valueless. . . . Such research can only be made effective by the closest sympathy and co-operation between soldiers and scientists, and unless their co-operation is much closer than it was before the late war, there will be little chance of success. It is for the scientists to explore the possibilities and to develop such as are thought likely to be of value, and for the soldiers to apply the results to their investigation of war problems."[*]

At least a military generation will have to pass by before a stock of soldiers is bred which can fulfil their part in this contract,

[*] " British and German Gas Warfare," Brig.-General H. Hartley, C.B.E., M.C , *The Journal of the Royal Artillery*, February, 1920

The Weapon of the Future

and then it will take another generation of soldiers to work out scientifically the changes which traditional tactics must undergo. Those of us who believe in the inevitability of war are nevertheless apt to think, as great wars only occur at about fifty year intervals, that, whatever changes science may demand, we have ample time to rest before seriously setting to work to discover what the next great war will require No assumption could be more fallacious, for, before a new military idea is accepted, a whole school of obsolete ideas, religious in their intolerance, has to be converted to the new idea, and not until it is converted will efficient training take place, and training is an all essential of victory. If the truth must be known, should the next great war explode in 1972, then, if we work hard, we may just be able to convert the traditional school in time and replace it by a school of military scientists. Not brawny halberdiers skilled at the game of push of pikes or push of bullets or push of shells, bullets and shells which strike down fool and sage alike ; but intelligent thinkers who will push their ideas to the detriment of the enemy's beef, who will pit brain against muscle, and, if opposed by muscle alone, will win a war quite possibly in a night without a day, as in the next Chapter I will explain.

VII

THE FUTURE OF AIR WARFARE

IN the last Chapter I stated that gas was a universal weapon because it could be employed by all types of arms. In this Chapter and the two following, I will substantiate this statement by showing that to-day we are approaching the adoption of a universal means of military movement which will more completely than ever before enable the universal weapon to be employed.

In the past, the motive force of all military movement on land has been muscular power, and, tactically, this was the main motive energy used throughout the Great War, which, in my opinion, will definitely close a military epoch stretching from the cave man to the present day. This muscular power was of two degrees—human and animal. Tactically, the soldier is simply a weapon mounting of about one-eighth h.p. energy, which limits, to a considerable extent, the nature and power of the weapons he carries. In the past, in order to increase the speed of the soldier the only means available was to mount him on an animal of greater muscular energy than himself, and if, when so mounted, he was unable to carry a certain weapon, this weapon was either carried on an animal or hauled by one or more animals. In the South African War we see as many as thirty-two oxen harnessed to a five-inch gun, and each animal requiring fodder added enormously to the complexity of war.

As the limitations of muscular energy in their turn limited the nature and power of weapons, consequently we see, especially in modern times, the introduction of a great variety of weapons, each attempting to make good certain deficiencies in the others

The Future of Air Warfare

due to the deficiencies in their mountings Thus, for example · if it were possible for an infantryman to carry a machine gun and several thousand rounds of ammunition, the rifle would long ago have been scrapped. And, again, if it were possible for six horses to haul at high speed a six-inch gun and one hundred shells, eighteen-pounder field guns would no longer be required. But such changes have not been possible because muscle power possesses definite limits.

To-day, we possess an all but universal means of movement —the petrol engine, which will influence land weapons as it is to-day influencing air weapons, and as steam has and is influencing naval weapons At sea, in capital ships, we see a tendency towards a universal weapon—the big shell; and in auxiliary craft a tendency towards a universal weapon— the torpedo. These weapons are very similar in nature, though the first is used for out-fighting and the second for in-fighting, for both are but metal containers filled with high explosives.

In the air there is a greater difference, two entirely different weapons being used. The big aeroplane carries the bomb and the small the machine gun. In the future, I believe that these two weapons will more closely coincide; this I will discuss presently, meanwhile, I will examine the most universal means of movement yet devised, namely, the aeroplane, with its power of movement in three dimensions.

Though the power of three dimensional movement by aircraft is generally recognized, the influence of this power on the future of warfare is in continual dispute, because, so I believe, we have not yet learnt to think of war from its third dimensional aspect.

Hitherto strategy, or the art of moving fighting units—armies or fleets—has been either one or two dimensional in nature. On land, the major strategical movements are normally one dimensional, because armies, and particularly modern armies, cannot move or supply themselves rapidly unless movement is directed along roads, railways, canals, or rivers. These constitute *lines* of advance, each line possessing two directions, that is facility to move forwards or backwards. Where these

138   The Reformation of War

lines do not exist, the nature of war tends towards that of partisan operations; in other words, wars in countries devoid of communications are tactically small wars, however large the forces employed may be At sea, naval movements are in nature two dimensional, because the vehicle of movement is an *area* and not a line; the exception to this rule is the power of movement of the submarine, which I will discuss in Chapter IX.

Bearing in mind these three dimensions of movement, it will at once be recognized that the future strategical problems of war are closely connected with the protection of land roads, sea roads, and air roads, in order that trade may prosper, and, in the event of it being threatened, may be secured by military force.

As the powers of aircraft include the dimensions of movement made use of by armies and fleets, it stands to reason that, of the three great defence forces of civilized nations, the air force is the only one which can closely and continually co-operate with the other two On account of this ability to co-operate, that is to move with armies or navies and yet independently of them, we are faced by the following portentous strategical problem · may not this power of aerial co-operation become so perfect that, in place of aircraft co-operating with navies and armies, these forces will instead co-operate with aircraft, and that possibly, at some date in the future, the utility of armies and navies will be reduced to zero, aircraft entirely replacing them? I will shortly examine this problem, which embraces the following three sub-problems :

(i.) The influence of aircraft on land warfare.
(ii.) The influence of aircraft on sea warfare.
(iii.) The independent action of aircraft in air warfare.

Before examining these sub-problems, it is necessary to make certain of the tactical limitations of aircraft, for this will enable us to consider these problems logically.

Aircraft are of two types—the lighter and the heavier than air machines. I am of opinion that the main purpose of the airship

The Future of Air Warfare

in future warfare will be the carriage of supplies rather than offensive action, though these vessels may assist this action by long-range reconnaissance. The airship is virtually the tramp steamer of the air, and there is no reason why vessels should not be built which could circumnavigate the globe, or carry a hundred tons and upwards for distances ranging over thousands of miles. Compared to an aeroplane, the airship is a slow moving craft with a lower ceiling on account of the danger of rising above the hail line, it is conspicuous even at high altitudes, readily picked up by searchlights and easily held within their rays. It is easily attackable and cannot well be armoured, it requires a numerous personnel to maintain it, an expensive housing and mooring system, and it is a gluttonous consumer of gas. Its one predominant characteristic is that it can remain motionless in the air without the expenditure of energy.

The chief characteristic of the aeroplane is speed of locomotion in three dimensions. This speed to-day is well over 150 miles an hour, and, when diving, 300 miles an hour; further still, many aeroplanes can climb at 1,000 feet the minute. When in movement, an aeroplane can proceed straight from point to point, motion in the air encountering no physical obstruction as on land and sea. Its predominant limitation is that it cannot remain motionless in the air, to which may be added that the ceiling of a useful war machine is unlikely to exceed 30,000 feet.

From the above we may deduce the elements of its tactical nature—a high offensive power and limited means of direct protection, that is protection by armour. The greater its radius of action the less offensive it becomes on account of petrol replacing armament, and the more it is protected by armour the less will be its range of action on account of steel replacing petrol. From these deductions, I will extract three tactical requirements which later on I shall refer to, namely·

(1.) Aircraft protection is to be sought for in the height they can operate from the ground.

(ii.) Aircraft offensive power, if the above protection is to be maintained, depends on the size of the target.

(iii.) Aircraft radius of action depends not only on the amount of petrol, etc., carried, but on refilling while in the air.

Bearing in mind the aeroplane's three dimensional power of movement and that the air presents to it no physical obstacle, the size of an air force is, in theory, unlimited. In practice, however, this is not true, for as aeroplanes cannot remain motionless in the air, the factor which limits the numbers which can usefully be employed is landing ground, which is more and more difficult to find as aeroplanes increase in size.

Besides this limitation, the following are of secondary importance: it becomes readily "bogged" in a ground mist, sense of direction is frequently lost in cloud and fog, landing at night and in foggy weather on unprepared landing grounds is dangerous, and further, though an aeroplane is not tied down to definite tracts of country, as wheeled vehicles are, or to definite expanses of water, as ships are, it is to a very considerable extent tied down to its landing grounds. In the Great War, on account of its static nature, no great difficulty was experienced in providing these; nevertheless, in France during the last eighteen months of the war, the average wastage in aeroplanes was between fifty and eighty per cent. per month. Of these casualties but one quarter were due to hostile action, the greater number resulting from crashes on landing. Will crashes in future be less frequent? This is doubtful in spite of improvements to be expected. Consequently, as belligerents may have to replace their entire equipment of machines once every two months, either an immense number of reserve machines will have to be maintained during peace time, or co-operation with the slow moving land forces abandoned, or a plan of attack evolved which will decide the war within a few weeks or days or hours of its outbreak.

I will now turn to the three problems of this Chapter:

The Influence of Aircraft on Land Warfare — At present we

The Future of Air Warfare

do not posses a tactical theory of aerial warfare. Our outlook during the recent war, and to a very great extent to-day, was and is a Homeric one. Hero met hero in hand-to-hand fight, and victories were based on individual contests. From this primitive type of warfare we must expect in the future to see evolve an elaborate tactics, for in the next great war capture of the air will become of supreme importance, because of all tactical "positions" the air is the one which commands all others. Once this supreme point of vantage is gained, the next tactical operation will be to deliver an aerial attack on the land forces, not only on their bodies—their men, horses and guns, but on their brains—their command headquarters; on their nerves—their system of communications; on their internal organs—their bases, supply depots, chemical and engineering works and workshops.

The ultra-traditional school does not hold these views; its adherents possess little if any imagination, and what was good enough for the army and navy in 1914 is good enough for these forces to-day. Such is the opinion which they hold, in spite of the fact that armies and navies as organized and equipped in 1914 *did not* win the war. But to these bats blinded by light this is the fault of the war and not of the 1914 organization. Their ignorance is colossal and is only excelled by their lack of vision. On Armistice Day, 1918, a typical adherent, without a smile on his face, said to me : " Thank God ! we can now get back to real soldiering." Aircraft are quite useful in order to assist the other arms, to range their guns and to fly about with cameras and bombs ; they can co-operate, of course ; but act independently—never ! As to replacing infantry or Dreadnoughts—absurd ! Such are the views held by the older and fruitier traditional vintage.

The new and raw wine, still not quite fermented, thinks otherwise. It realizes that the aeroplane is a new means of waging war, and it applies it to the old end—killing and destruction. Consequently, in place of humanizing war and so rendering it less costly and wasteful, these thinkers are frequently terrified

142 The Reformation of War

by their own thoughts. What do they see? They see columns of foot and horse wending their way towards their battle area, whole divisions twelve miles long toiling along dusty roads Then they see in the distance tiny specks on the horizon, they grow bigger, there is a droning of engines—twenty low flying armoured battle planes top the rise in front, and, before the wretched infantry have time to unstrap their limbered vehicles and mount their machine guns, there is a rattle of musketry from twenty times twenty machine guns. In ten minutes the whole column is traversed from van to rear, 250,000 bullets have been pumped into it—not 30,000, as on the Conegliano-Pordonone road—and the very dust of the highway is churned into a porridge of blood.

Such warfare as this is truly horrible, because it is so one-sided. To shoot down infantry in this manner is mere massacre. But such slaughter must continue so long as infantry exist and so long as tactics are controlled by the traditional school. Further, this school believes in material destruction. In the aeroplane they behold a means of accentuating destruction to such an extent that killing in bulk will become unnecessary. Here at least we see a glimmer of light, economic destruction replacing the killing of human beings. Of this type of attack Mr. Lanchester writes:

> "Depots of every kind in the rear of the enemy's lines would cease to exist, rolling stock and mechanical transport would be destroyed, no bridge would be allowed to stand for 24 hours; railway junctions would be subject to continuous bombardment. . . In this manner a virtually impassable zone would be created in the rear of the enemy's defences, a zone varying, perhaps, from 100 to 200 miles in width . . not only will the defence be slowly strangled from the uncertainty and lack of supplies of all kinds, but ultimately retreat will become impossible The defending force will find itself literally in a state of siege under the worst possible conditions. . . . Thus, in the extended employment of aircraft, we have the means at hand of compelling a bloodless victory."[*]

I do not intend to waste my ink in proving that the old vintage is wrong. To all beings, possessed of any intelligence,

[*] "Aircraft in Warfare," Lanchester, pp 187, 188

The Future of Air Warfare

this must be apparent. Instead, I intend showing that though the new wine of war is perfectly right in asserting that aeroplanes can destroy infantry like vermin, and devastate whole districts, it is extremely foolish to use such means of imposing the will of one nation on another, when non-lethal gases will enable this same end to be attained with incomparably greater economy of life and property.

Let us picture to ourselves again the infantry toiling along the road. The aeroplanes approach ; they do not skim a hundred feet above the road, but fly at an altitude well outside effective bullet range. They open their chemical tanks and a fine spray and fog envelopes the astonished column of men. Suppose that this gas is a deadly poison, all these men will shortly die ; such an end is anyhow better than being shot to pieces. Suppose this gas is a vesicant chemical, like mustard gas, all these men will be wounded and only one per cent. *may* die. Cruel though such an attack is, it is incomparably better than being shot to pieces, and, if not killed, probably maimed for life. Suppose that this gas is but an anæsthetic, then the whole column will fall, as Richardson poetically wrote in 1864, " into a mystic sleep," and when its twenty thousand men awake, if they do not find themselves prisoners, they will have anyhow lost several good marching hours. What general on earth is going to win decisive battles, battles which need the most careful assembly and speedy concentration of troops, if whole divisions and army corps are going to be put to bed for several hours at a time, two or three times a day ? Consequently, traditional infantry, the greatest slaughterers of all, have no place on the future battlefield, not because they are harmless but because they are absurd ! And with them must depart cavalry and all horse-drawn guns and vehicles ; in fact, the whole of the traditional army of 1914 will have become a phantom.

I will now turn to Mr. Lanchester's picture. Why drive the car of Juggernaut over entire areas ? Why destroy depots, bridges, railways and workshops in order to strangle, bloodlessly though it may be, the enemy's troops which are in advance of

144 The Reformation of War

them ? Even to-day a depot drenched with a sneezing mixture would cease to fulfil its duties, and a mile of roadway or railway drenched with a strong lachrymator would become impassable for days on end. More impassable than if the road were smothered in barbed wire or the rails removed from the permanent way Why destroy, when no one really wants to destroy ? When I ask Mr. Jones to sign an agreement, I do not knife him if he refuses, for if I do so he may die, and then his signature, my objective, will be unobtainable. To destroy a nation is to destroy the very objective of peace ; consequently, the less the destruction the more complete to the winner is the victory

Some time back, I made mention of three tactical requirements, the first of which was that aircraft protection is to be sought for in the height the machines can operate from the ground ; and the second, that the offensive power of aeroplanes depends to a great extent on the size of the target. I will now examine the relative value of machine guns, bombs and gas as aircraft weapons. For a machine gun to be effective the aeroplane must fly low, which means that it must forgo its natural means of protection or hamper its mobility and restrict its offensive power by carrying armour. For a bomb to be effective the target must be sufficiently large to be hit easily ; the higher the aeroplane flies the smaller does the target appear to be. Here we are faced by two difficulties which would seem to be irreconcilable. This is, however, not so, for liquid gas sprayed from a machine or dropped in bombs, which burst in the air like shrapnel, will form a gas cloud which, within certain limits of height, increases in size in direct ratio to the height of the machines from which it is dropped on account of the liquid atomizing as it falls through the air. A bullet or bomb maintains its form until it strikes the target or the ground ; gas acts otherwise, its form increasing in size as it nears the ground ; consequently, a gas attack delivered from a height against a small target is likely to prove a much more effective attack than one made with bullets and bombs Again, if a high wind is blowing, it is not necessary to aim at the target, but in place to manœuvre for wind, which an aeroplane

The Future of Air Warfare

can always do, and then drop the gas at a distance from the target and let it drift over it. Yet again, suppose that the traditional arms—infantry, cavalry, and field guns—are strongly protected by anti-aircraft artillery and machine guns and the attacking aeroplanes are afraid to approach them, all that these machines need do is to fly ahead of the hostile column and drench sections of the road it is marching along, preferably defiles and road-junctions, with persistent lethal or non-lethal gasses, which will compel the traditional arms to wear their respirators continuously. What will their rate of march then be, seeing that the infantry carry fifty to sixty pounds of arms and equipment?

The answer is : at best two or three miles a day, for marching in respirators, especially in hot weather, is not a practical military operation. In my opinion, the fact of the case is that THE TRADITIONAL SOLDIER IS DOOMED

The Influence of Aircraft on Sea Warfare. I will now turn to the second problem—the influence of aircraft on sea warfare.

I have already accentuated the fact that the main theory of all past naval warfare was that fighting at sea is a two dimensional operation. However, during the recent war, two weapons possessing three dimensional powers came into use—the submarine and the aeroplane (or seaplane). The first caused consternation, and the second proved a useful adjunct for purposes of reconnaissance and observation, but the combined use of these two weapons was not understood. Combined, their offensive power may well prove enormous.

What does the traditional naval attack entail—slaughter in an accentuated form. On land, military units are seldom exterminated, at sea the extermination by drowning of entire ship's crews is the rule and not the exception. Off Coronel, the *Monmouth* and the *Good Hope* went down with the loss of all hands, and, of Admiral von Spee's squadron, very few were saved from the icy waters of the South Atlantic. Of all forms of warfare, sea fighting is the most prodigal , in ten minutes a ship, costing £8,000,000, manned by 1,250 sailors, may be sent to the bottom. Destruction by maximums is what the naval mind aims at.

Besides a new vintage of soldiers, there is growing up amongst us to-day a new school of sailors; men who, though they are considering the new means of naval warfare, are still obsessed by the old idea—destruction. They picture a fleet of Super-Dreadnoughts pursued by aeroplanes like bears pursued by bees. High above they swoop and whirl. Thousands of small smoke bombs are loosed into the air, they whistle downwards, strike decks and sea, and a minute later all is lost in an immense cloud of rising smoke. A veritable volcanic eruption has been projected from heaven Under cover of this cloud and the loss of fighting efficiency caused by every sailor having to wear a respirator, dive down torpedo aircraft, while submarines race over the surface of the water towards their prey. Immense explosions throw into the air great columns of water, and vortices of smoke vibrate upwards Little by little the smoke clears. Where is that proud fleet? It is gone: £100,000,000 worth of steel is swirling downwards through the depths below, and the surface of the sea is dotted with thousands of human forms as if they had been shaken out of some giant caster. There are oaths and groans and shrieks; then, with horrible gurglings, one by one they vanish to join their ships: there is silence and the victory is won!

What a senseless waste of good steel and better human life. What an inane and barbaric attempt to gain more prosperous peace terms than those which existed before the outbreak of hostilities. Why destroy, why not capture? Here then is another picture.

The fleet of Dreadnoughts is steaming in line ahead, preceded by a cruiser screen Then again do the aeroplanes approach and the smoke bombs are showered down. They are toxic, and the crews are killed and disabled, but the ships are saved. They are vesicant, and the decks are splashed with mustard gas; the ships are saved and the crews are mostly disabled. They are filled with a colic-producing chemical, and, as the submarines once again approach, they emit immense clouds of the same irritant. Respirators are adjusted, but the chemical penetrates them as cloud after cloud sweeps over the great vessels. Men groan, they are doubled up, the crews are demented, gun stations are abandoned, discipline is cast to the winds, there is panic and pandemonium, and not a shell or a torpedo is fired. A motorboat puts out from a submarine and skims over the water towards the enemy's flag ship. A rope ladder is fired into the air, it whirls upwards and its grapnels become engaged with the bridge. A man in a mask swarms up it, to the bridge he goes; the commander-in-chief is squatting in a corner groaning and holding the pit of his stomach The man in the mask says: " Hoist the white flag, or the whole of your fleet will be sunk in five minutes ! " Up goes the signal of surrender, and a few days later £100,000,000 worth of steel rides at anchor in a hostile harbour, and thousands of foreign sailors are eating biscuits and bully behind the wire of the prisoners' cages. Not a ship has been lost or damaged, and the casualties have been under five per cent., and most of these were caused by fright and panic.

The question may now well be asked, how can such an operation be carried out in the middle of the Pacific ? The answer is not a difficult one, if the third tactical requirement I laid down is remembered, namely, that the radius of action of aircraft depends on refilling with petrol while in the air, and in this case, also, while on the water

Aircraft carriers can proceed anywhere a battleship can steam They will form the sea bases of the air attack, but they possess this disadvantage, that to refill, and especially during battle, aeroplanes will be forced to leave their protective element—the heights of the air, and descend to dangerous altitudes, and eventually to the still more dangerous surface of the sea. Consequently, I believe that airships will be used as air bases, on the envelopes of which aeroplanes can alight to refill and refit at ease. In the future, such moving bases should be able to carry a hundred tons or more of supplies and could, in their turn, replenish their stock from large supply submarines which, possessing power to

148   The Reformation of War

submerge, would be able, without great danger, to proceed unescorted to various rendezvous in the oceans and seas in the neighbourhood of the theatre of war.

The Independent Action of Aircraft. Whether I have solved the two preceding problems I must leave it to the reader to judge. I have purposely avoided detail, and have merely elaborated an idea which I believe to be possible; yet, nevertheless, I believe both the above problems and the solutions I have outlined to be subordinate to the third problem, which I will now examine.

I have, earlier in this present Chapter, hinted at the possibility that, in the future, air forces may replace armies and navies. Actual replacement is, in my opinion, a misconception of the objective in war. Armies and navies are lethal instruments of security, but the true object, as I have frequently stated, is not to kill soldiers or sink ships, but to change a policy which these soldiers and ships are protecting. If, in the event of war, an air force can change this policy with less physical destruction than in the past it has been possible to attain by means of armies and navies, and this may be the case, then the air force will not absorb the military purpose of navies and armies, which in nature is tactical, but will instead establish a new conception of war, a conception in which naval and military forces will have either no place at all or one which is subordinate to their present purpose, and by subordinate I mean the occupation of land and sea *after a moral victory has been won on land* by aircraft

This problem is the most vital military problem of to-day, for, if my supposition be correct, not only will our present-day armies and navies be valueless *in war*, but the immense sums of money spent on them during peace-time will be squandered

I have already pointed out that the policy of a nation is founded on the will of its civil inhabitants, and that the supreme military power of aircraft is their ability " to hop " over armies and fleets and attack what is in rear of them. Here then is this vital problem in brief : can a hostile nation be forced to change its will by means of an independent aerial attack ?

The Future of Air Warfare

That such an attack is possible was visibly demonstrated to all who inhabited Paris and London during the Great War. At first, being in nature a novelty, it was dubbed immoral. Is this assertion, however, true ? Only so far as all warfare may be classed as immoral, in which case the less the ethical and economic damage done during a war the more moral will the waging of it become. This leads us to the following question : will aerial warfare in the future, should it supersede land warfare, do more damage than the damage resulting from land warfare as to-day conceived and accepted ? I believe that it may, if the object is to obliterate towns and cities by means of high explosive bombs. I believe that it will not, if the nerves of the people are attacked by an offensive directed against their bodies by means of non-lethal gases. I have shown that the statistics of the gas casualties suffered by the American Army during the Great War prove that gas warfare, including the use of deadly gases such as chlorine and phosgene, is twelve times as humane as bullet and shell warfare. Further, I have pointed out that the general assertion that gas warfare is immoral is founded on the fact that nations have not yet realized that great wars are national wars in which the attack on the will of the so-called non-combatants is the objective. Further, I believe that the civilian will fight this idea to the death, because it is far more comfortable to raise forces of men called soldiers and let them slaughter each other, not always to the disadvantage of the civilian, in place of the civilian being attacked directly. In the past such attacks have been difficult to deliver because warfare was two dimensional in nature, and where armies moved (on a plane surface, the crust of the earth) other armies met them and blocked their way. This condition still holds good for armies and navies but not for air forces, and as the object of war is to attack the will of the enemy's people, and as aircraft possess the ability to avoid armies and navies, is an air force going to be so foolish as to attack these forces in place of attacking this will ? Whatever the civilian may desire or squeak for, to put it vulgarly, in the next great war he is going to be " in the soup," and what kind of soup will it be ? A pretty hot one !

150   The Reformation of War

I have pointed out in a former Chapter that destruction can be avoided by the use of non-lethal gases, and that the "political" danger of such chemicals is that they can incapacitate and terrorize without killing. I believe that, in future warfare, great cities, such as London, will be attacked from the air, and that a fleet of 500 aeroplanes each carrying 500 ten-pound bombs of, let us suppose, mustard gas, might cause 200,000 minor casualties and throw the whole city into panic within half an hour of their arrival. Picture, if you can, what the result will be. London for several days will be one vast raving Bedlam, the hospitals will be stormed, traffic will cease, the homeless will shriek for help, the city will be in pandemonium. What of the government at Westminster? It will be swept away by an avalanche of terror. Then will the enemy dictate his terms, which will be grasped at like a straw by a drowning man. Thus may a war be won in forty-eight hours and the losses of the winning side may be actually nil !

If a future war can be won at the cost of two or three thousand of the enemy's men, women and children killed, in place of over 1,000,000 men and incidentally several thousands of women and children, as was the case in France during the recent war,* surely an aerial attack is a more humane method than the existing traditional type. Further, the material damage done will be insignificant when compared to the damage effected during the recent war, the cost of which can only approximately be reckoned in thousands of millions sterling.

Here then is the moral of this Chapter :

In the future, when once the storm clouds of war burst, a nation dare not depend on gaining time wherein to make good its deficiencies in preparation. In place it must be ready to act, and act at once. The only arm which can so act, which can mobilize and fight within twenty-four hours of an outrage taking place, is an air force. This liberty of immediate action is, in fact, its

* The total soldiers, sailors and airmen killed during the Great War has been estimated at between nine and ten millions. The loss among the civil populations, excluding Russia since the close of 1918, due to killed, diseases directly attributable to the war, and fall in birth-rate, has been estimated at twenty millions.

supreme duty, and, however important co-operation with the navy and army may be, first and foremost must an air force be prepared to act alone. The morality of such action is beyond question, for self-preservation is a human right To commit *felo-de-se* by denying to an air force power of retaliating against the will of the enemy, is the act of a nation which has become insane.

VIII

THE FUTURE OF LAND WARFARE

THE recoil of a fire arm is in proportion to the force of the explosion of its charge, and, before buffer springs were fitted to cannon, this recoil was detrimental to a high rate of fire. Human ingenuity overcame this difficulty, not by restricting the recoil, by bolting the gun down to a fixed mounting, but by utilizing the force of the recoil to reload the piece. The result of this wonderful economy of energy was to increase the rate of fire of a field gun from about five rounds to 30 a minute and to enable a machine gun to deliver sixty times the aimed fire of a breech-loading rifle.

Like a weapon, every human activity possesses its recoil, which, as it grows, by degrees transmutes the original force into something new. This novelty, in its turn, possesses its recoil, so the process continues, progress moving along its predestined path impelled forward by the force engendered through the friction and integration of opposites.

In the last Chapter I peeped beneath the veil of future war in the air, and, as I fathomed its mysteries, I beheld that traditional armies and fleets were of things doomed, for I saw that their sand was running out and that soon they must take their place in the Valhalla of war. Will they be followed by other soldiers and other ships? I think so; for, potent though the aeroplane is, it can never become perfect, for perfection does not exist on earth. In its day it will be eaten up by its own recoil and its powers digested into something new.

My ignorance, I hope, is not so invincible that I dare to guess at what the nature of this novelty will be. All I intend to do is

The Future of Land Warfare 153

to examine the recoil of aircraft and then attempt to point out its direction

What is its nature ? This question demands another : how can we frustrate the powers of the aeroplane ? We can secure ourselves from them by going to earth like foxes, but this will not master them. We can build up a superior air force and destroy our enemy's air fleet ; this is a common-sense action, but it is one based on brute force and is, consequently, uneconomical. We may discover its weaknesses—its lack of power, and by using our brains, our human cunning, accentuate these weaknesses until they grow into defects so large that they out-balance its powers.

To understand these defects, even if only to see them, we must impartially dissect and analyse the powers of its prey—the traditional arms, for it is their defects which accentuate the power of aircraft. This I have done sufficiently in the last Chapter in order to render it unnecessary to consider this subject in much detail.

In the last Chapter, I pointed out that the three great tactical requirements of aircraft were (i.) for protection—height of flight ; (ii.) for offensive power—size of target, and (iii.) for mobility— rapidity of supply. I explained how the use of gas as a weapon enabled the aeroplane to equate the first two and how airships might be used as mobile aerodromes. I also pointed out that the paramount limitation of the aeroplane was that it could not remain in the air without the expenditure of energy. This limitation is the Achilles' heel of air warfare. Gravity is, in fact, the tactical recoil of the machine.

For the aeroplane, what are the main joints in the harness of present-day armies ? They are the enormous targets they offer ; the vulnerability of men and horses to bullets and gas ; the slowness of their movement and the dependence of their supplies on roads, rivers, railways and canals—fixed communications which from the air can be followed at ease.

What have we got to do ? We must reduce the target, that is, make it so small that the aeroplane is forced to fly at low altitudes in order to discover it. But, say you, it need not do so, because gas is an area and not a target hitter. Well then, we must completely protect our land forces against this weapon and compel the aeroplane to risk flying at low altitudes, which will demand the replacement of gas by bullets. Consequently, we must protect our troops from bullets as well. Further, we must enormously increase the speed of our troops. For example, let us picture to ourselves the power of the British Army had it been able, in August 1914, to march in one night from Boulogne to the forest of Crecy, a distance of 50 miles; lay hidden there; marched on the next night to the forest of Mormal, 100 miles away; lay hidden there; marched the following night to the woods in the vicinity of Waterloo, 75 miles, and then, like a tiger, have sprung on von Kluck and von Bulow as they advanced westwards from Liége. But, granted that by some magic power this army had been supplied with seven-league boots, the roads and railways would never have permitted of even 100,000 men and their impedimenta moving at this rate. Very well then, in place of crying " Kamerad ! " we must scrap roads and railways, the traditional means of movement, and move over areas, that is straight across country like ships over the sea.

Studious reader, are these problems impossible? Far from it, for the tank, and especially the tank of the future, solves them all !

(i.) It reduces the target, for it does away with great march columns and immense battle formations.
(ii.) It can be made gas-tight, so completely that even unknown gases will lose their dread.
(iii.) It can be made bullet-proof, even against bullets of enormously enhanced powers to existing ones.
(iv.) It can be made to move at 20 miles and more the hour or 200 miles the day for several days without refilling.
(v.) It can move across country, and, consequently, free itself from the dominion of roads and railways.

It, in my opinion, is the product of the recoil, for it can, by being made gas-tight, force the aeroplane to fly low and to use

The Future of Land Warfare 155

bullets. Then the tank will reply with bullets and the aeroplane will armour itself against them. Then the bullets will grow bigger and the aeroplane armour thicker, and as the tank on the ground is less affected by gravity than the aeroplane in the air, the tank will attack, not so much its powers, but its preponderating limitation—its weakness, and in spite of Professor Einstein, the tank WILL WIN !

It may be argued here that, should the aeroplane be unable to incapacitate the tank crew by means of gas, it will make use of a gas which will prevent the tank engine from firing, but just as its crew can live on oxygen or compressed air, when their machine is rendered gas-tight, so may the energy required to move it be stored in accumulators which temporarily will do away with the necessity of combustion. Again, may it be asserted, if the aeroplane be forced, on account of the thickness of the tank's armour, to replace machine guns by cannon, that is volume fire by fire which requires precision, why should not the high explosive bomb be used, for it would not require a very large one to destroy a machine protected by armour of even two inches in thickness. In other words, why should not a tank be attacked in the same manner as I have shown a battleship may be attacked ? This is not impossible, but the difficulties are considerable. First of all, I agree that though 20 torpedo carrying aeroplanes may be able, under cover of smoke, to sink a Dreadnought, it should nevertheless be remembered that a battleship offers vastly greater hitting area than a tank. Again, it must not be overlooked that the offensive value of a weapon is correlated to its cost. Thus, a Super-Dreadnought costs £8,000,000, and a torpedo carrying aeroplane about £3,000 ; consequently, the cost of one Super-Dreadnought equals the cost of 2,700 torpedo carrying aeroplanes. To risk, therefore, 20 or even 200 of these machines in the destruction of one Super-Dreadnought is an economical operation. Not only is a tank a much smaller target to hit than a Super-Dreadnought, but its cost should not exceed £6,000, or the cost of two torpedo carrying aeroplanes. Would two be sufficient for its destruction, seeing that a tank can so completely cover itself with smoke that the two aeroplanes would have to descend within a few feet of the ground in order to aim their bombs, and, while diving into the smoke to nose for their prey, would be met by an upwards spray of large calibre bullets or possibly small calibre gas shells, which would penetrate an inch of armour at 500 to 1,000 feet range ? If two aeroplanes be insufficient, the addition of others at once renders the attack uneconomical ; that is to say : if it costs more to destroy a tank by aeroplanes than the tank is worth, for equal sums of money more tanks than aeroplanes can be built ; consequently, with the increase in the production of tanks is decreased the net value of aeroplanes as a means of destroying them. Finally it may be asserted that one aeroplane dropping a shower of medium-sized bombs will be sufficient to destroy the tank. This assertion has, however, no foundation in past experience. In the recent war no single tank was ever hit by an aeroplane bomb. But, say you, aeroplane bombing was still in its infancy. I agree, but must add that so was the tank. As a matter of fact, in 1918, the aeroplane was 15 years old and the tank only two. For one aeroplane, carrying, let us suppose, 20 anti-tank bombs, to hit a tank moving at 20 if not 30 miles the hour under a pall of smoke, would appear to me to be almost as difficult as to attempt, in a London fog, to hit a snipe with buckshot.

Having now dealt, at some length, with the influence of the tank on the aeroplane through the power it possesses to hit at that Achilles' heel of the air—gravity, I will turn from the aeroplane to the traditional arms of to-day and examine the influence the tank will exert on their transformation.

From what has gone before, it may seem unnecessary to do this, for, if it be accepted, as it certainly is not by the traditional school, that in the future aeroplanes are likely with impunity to destroy infantry, cavalry and gunners, and, in all probability, will only be able to destroy tanks with great difficulty, it would appear to be a common-sense action to replace the traditional arms by tanks. Of course it would be a common-sense action, but, of all reasons, this is the last one which will persuade the traditional school to accept it, since their theory of war is not founded on

The Future of Land Warfare 157

common-sense but on custom, or the imitation of actions, the utility of which is long dead and buried and gone to dust. I will, therefore, in order to supply the reader with the ammunition of argument, consider the power of tanks against the traditional arms, and the restriction of their power when attached to them. I will now show that the tank of the near future is likely to be as superior to the traditional arms as a modern destroyer is to a British coracle, and that to link the traditional arms to tanks will be as uneconomical as linking sailing frigates to a squadron of battle cruisers.

In Chapter V., I briefly outlined the general influence of tanks on the tactics of the Great War, that is on traditional fighting, and, in spite of the fact that soldiers are still found who believe that the tank was merely a war freak,* I will assume that the reader is a sane civilian who will not fall into a frenzy if I assume that tanks will play an important part in future wars. I will lay down, therefore, the following assumption : at some future date two armies meet in battle, each possesses infantry, cavalry and artillery as equipped to-day and two types of tanks—a light cavalry tank possessing a speed of 25 miles the hour, and a heavily-armoured infantry tank with a speed of 15 miles the hour. What will happen ?

I will assume forthwith, if the lessons of the recent war are of any value, and if human nature remain what it is, that, by the time the two armies are within striking distance, the infantry will be in rear of the tanks and the artillery in rear of the infantry. Tank will, consequently, engage tank, and a battle for tank supremacy will result. As cavalry cannot take part in this battle, unless it be employed in galloping towards the hostile machines and scattering land mines in their path, an operation which might more efficiently be carried out by a mine-laying tank or by an aeroplane, the cavalry tanks will be detached from the arm they

* " Possibilities of the Next War," Major-General Sir Louis C. Jackson, K.B E., C B , C.M G. (R.U S I Journal, vol lxv , February, 1920) "The tank proper was a freak. The circumstances which called it into existence were exceptional and are not likely to recur If they do they can be dealt with by other means " (p. 74). These other means are not mentioned ! What are they ?

are protecting and will manœuvre behind the infantry tanks ready to move forward should the enemy's tank front be pierced, or preparatory to attacking this front in flank.

The question now arises, what can the infantry do? These troops can do nothing outside playing the part of interested spectators. What can the gunners do? They can do next to nothing, for, being distant from the field of action, upon which in a minute a tank may have changed its position by a quarter of a mile, they dare not promiscuously bombard any area; besides, in order to fire at all, they will generally have to employ direct laying, which, in most cases, will require them to be either with, or in advance of, the infantry. In such positions, as the gunners, in order to protect themselves, cannot lie flat like infantry, their pieces will soon be silenced by hostile machine gun fire.

I will now carry the battle to its next stage. One side will gain tank supremacy and the shattered remnants of the other side will retire. As the pursuit will be rapid—at from ten to twenty miles the hour—the defeated tanks can either retire with their infantry, which delaying them will jeopardize their retreat, or else abandon their infantry and let them be destroyed. Falling back on their artillery, what can the gunners do? They cannot move their guns without their horses, which are very vulnerable to fire, and they cannot fire them while in movement. They must therefore, remain stationary and, if the ground in front of the guns be an obstacle to tank movement, they may possibly hold up the enemy's infantry machines, which, nevertheless, if they advance behind a smoke cloud, will be very difficult targets to hit. Meanwhile, the enemy's cavalry tanks will be racing round the artillery flanks in order to attack in rear the guns, wagon parks, teams and command headquarters. We see, therefore, that, even if the artillery can halt the hostile infantry machines, in nine cases out of ten the guns are likely to be destroyed in a few hours. The only arm which will be able to save itself from destruction is the cavalry, not by charging the enemy, but by galloping off the field.

In the main this picture is not overdrawn, because to-day

The Future of Land Warfare

tanks exist which can move at twenty-five miles an hour. True, they are not reliable—neither was the motor-car in 1901, nor the aeroplane in 1909—yet the tank to-day is as old as these two means of movement were twenty-two and fourteen years ago ; consequently, there is no reason why reliability should not be accomplished within a few years of to-day. Are existing cavalry, artillery and infantry then doomed to extinction? Yes, and certainly as regards the former two, their death will be followed by their resurrection. I will examine this assertion.

No operation in war can have been more terrible and awe-inspiring than that of a massed cavalry charge—a blare of trumpets, the thunder of hoofs, and the flash of steel. When such operations were possible, only the steadiest infantry could withstand the assault, and even the best troops, once they had been pounded by shot and shell, frequently succumbed to the cavalry charge. Of all operations in war it was the most rapid and the most effective, for though its killing power was seldom as great as that of infantry, its disorganizing and demoralizing power was terrific.

During the recent war, any side which could have made use of its cavalry, as Alexander or Frederick the Great did, would have shortened the war by years, and this, I believe, the future will prove, for so essential to land war is the cavalry charge that it must be reinstated ; besides, the problem is so simple. Picture a brigade of tanks moving at thirty miles an hour charging through an infantry division. What can the infantry do ? What can the gunners do ? A few tanks will be destroyed, but this is all. As long as cavalry depend on the horse, the charge is dead ; only can it be revived by replacing the horse by the tank ; then, against an unarmoured enemy, the result is certain.

But has not present-day cavalry still a part to play in the initial and final stages of battle—reconnaissance and the pursuit ? None, if economy of time is of any value in war. A light scout tank, with a maximum speed of thirty miles an hour and a mean speed of fifteen miles, can easily travel one hundred and fifty miles in a day, with a few exceptions, such as narrow mountain tracks

160   The Reformation of War

and very thick woods, a machine of this nature can pass over all ground negotiable by a horse and can traverse many obstacles which a horse cannot look at. It can lie up hidden for days if needs be without consuming petrol ; it can carry its own supplies for a long period, and its crew have little to fear from hostile cavalry or *francs-tireurs*. It possesses so many advantages over the horse, and so few disadvantages, that its adoption for purposes of reconnaissance is as near a certainty as can be predicted

There are two types of pursuit ; the first against a retiring enemy, the second against a routed foe. Against the first cavalry can do no more than annoy ; against the second their use is great, because they can move at three or four times the pace of infantry in flight   Tanks will move, however, at twice the pace of cavalry and will carry their own protection ; further, at night-time, under the rays of their searchlights, they will be able to carry on the chase. Onwards they will go, rousing hostile bivouacs by the shrieks of their sirens, flashing their searchlights along hedgerows, over fields and through villages ; they will reduce the enemy to a demented mob. Thus will they destroy his moral, and his soldiers will cease to be fighting men. Cavalry can do all this and more, if they will exchange flesh for steel. The idea is the same, the means of movement is alone different.

I will now turn to artillery   A fortress is merely an artillery emplacement. If, in the past, it had been possible to move fortresses in open warfare, this would have been done   In fact, in the days of Alexander and Cæsar it was done, for fortresses were made of wood, and could be moved slowly over the ground by means of rollers. To-day this is no longer practical since reinforced concrete has replaced wood. Yet, in its very nature, the tank is a mobile strong point, a moving bullet-proof box in which is mounted a gun.

A field gun, in the open, can be attacked by bullet, shell, gas, or bomb, and during such attacks it can seldom move. Because of the vulnerability of artillery to bullets, the normal position of the guns is in rear of the infantry, and if not so protected, then must an escort be provided ; that is to say, infantry

The Future of Land Warfare

and cavalry must be immobilized in order to secure the gun against infantry and cavalry attack. If the guns are attacked by tanks, this escort is useless; if attacked from the air the gunners and their teams will probably suffer heavy casualties; further, no certain protection can be provided against gas All these difficulties can be more than overcome by mounting the field gun in a tank.

Let us picture to ourselves the following weapon. A tank which can move at least fifteen miles an hour, and which, when necessary, can be rendered gas-proof. In it is mounted a field gun, an anti-aircraft machine gun, and two ordinary machine guns. What can such a weapon do ? It can move at twice the speed of a horse-drawn gun, it can operate behind infantry, with infantry, in front of infantry, or on the flanks of infantry. It can render itself gas-tight, can defy all aeroplane bullets, can attack aeroplanes, and can hide itself from them by means of smoke. It can change its position when attacked, can fire while in movement, and does not require an escort. It has nothing to fear from infantry, nothing from cavalry, little from a horse-drawn field gun, and, if attacked by fast moving tanks, it has at least a chance of escape. It is in fact a movable fortress, which, if rendered floatable, may virtually become a small man-of-war. If, in the next war, the gunner wishes to pull his weight, then he also must get into a tank.

I will now turn to the last of the arms of traditional armies namely, the infantry. First of all, it should be realized that, even though infantry may still be " the queen of battles," for eight hundred years during the Christian era foot troops were mere pawns in the game. When the armoured knight ruled the battlefield, infantry was employed merely to garrison castles, or to hold tactical points such as swamps, forests and hill-tops, that is, in localities in which the knights could not move. I believe that the armoured tank is going to create a tactical condition similar to that created in the past by these armoured horsemen, and that, in the near future, infantry, if they exist, will only continue to do so as police and the defenders of positions

―rail-heads, bridge-heads, workshops and supply magazines. As this is a point which is likely to be hotly debated, I will trace the evolution of this assumption.

To provide infantry with an escort of tanks detached from the main force of these machines is no guarantee that, in battle, should the tank *versus* tank engagement be likely to fail, any but a totally incapable commander will not at once withdraw all these protective machines in order to support his tanks, for on their success will depend victory or defeat. Assuming that there will be a capable commander, his initiative can, of course, be restricted by supplying him with protective tanks the speed of which does not exceed the pace of infantry. Such a restriction is, however, absurd ; it not only violates the principle of the offensive, but these slow machines will be no match against the faster hostile ones.

Another solution must be tried. The infantry may be equipped with a heavy machine gun, which will weigh seven times the weight of a rifle, and, therefore, an infantryman will not be able to carry it. It will have to be mounted on a transporter, and, as off this machine it will be immobile and on it unprotected, the first thing its crew will ask for is protection by armour. We are once again back to the tank, and an indifferent one at that, for the effective range of the tank gun against a lightly armoured tank is far greater than that of a heavy machine gun against a heavily armoured machine. In addition to this objection, there is nothing to prevent the heavier tank being equipped with a heavy machine gun as its in-fighting weapon.

As it would appear that the heavy machine gun will not fulfil the purpose for which it is intended, it would seem preferable to give infantry a high velocity gun such as the tank six-pounder If this be done, the evolution will be the same as in the case of the heavy machine gun. Starting on its wheels, it will end in a small six-pounder tank, and, if it be found to be an efficient tank destroyer, then the proper place for it is in the tank battle and not behind it.

I consider that the main deduction to be made from the

The Future of Land Warfare

above is that, whatever offensive weapon is given to the infantry, it will have first to be motorized; secondly, armoured; and thirdly, will be taken away from these troops at all critical periods —periods when it is most required by them. If this be a correct judgment, then we must seek for a solution of this problem in a purely defensive weapon, that is to say a weapon which cannot be used when in movement. Such a weapon is the land-mine, which, to hark back to mediæval warfare, will take the place of the old-fashioned moat. It may, therefore, be predicted that tank mine-layers will accompany future infantry, siege artillery and the administrative services. In order to keep in the vicinity of the battle, though always at a safe distance from the actual front, the infantry and administrative troops will be carried forward in cross-country transporters, the descendants of the present motor-bus. These transporters will be lightly armoured and constructed so that they may be made gas-proof, and endowed with a sufficient speed to enable them to escape from their strongholds should the tank mine-sweepers, which tank mine-layers will render necessary, succeed in clearing a way through the minefields. Lastly, as warfare is likely to become more and more mobile in nature, the slow digging hand spade will be replaced by the fast digging cross-country trench digger, so that, when halted, the infantry and their transporters will be able to seek cover by ground in order to protect themselves from aircraft attack.

From the above we may predict that the tank will rapidly revolutionize *existing* modes of warfare. Cavalry is likely to disappear, except perhaps as mounted police; infantry may become the " queen of fortresses," but on the battlefield the rule of this monarch is rapidly drawing to an end, for without offensive power this queen is bereft of her crown. Artillery will become doubly important, and, as speed is added to this arm, the old naval struggle between gun and armour will find its counterpart on land. Then will the infantry tank, as we know it to-day, disappear and be replaced by the heavy gunned and strongly armoured land battleship—the artillery of the future.

164   The Reformation of War

then will the cavalry tank, relying on less armour and greater speed, become the battle cruiser. Numerous auxiliary machines may be built, but, as long as armies are obsessed by the idea of killing, I believe that, on these two types, the land battles of the future will be founded, battles which will be fought after the fashion of Alexander—the *hoplites* disorganizing and the *cataphracti* annihilating the enemy.

Before depicting a battle between these armoured packets of men, I will examine how they can be supplied before, during and after battle, for, in the future, as in the past, so long as humanity wars, so long will armies continue to march on their stomachs.

In war, the chief concern of the soldier is not to kill, but to live. He fixes his eyes on the communications of the army to which he belongs, and is terrified if they are threatened by the enemy. Why is this? Because on their integrity depends the supply of his bread, beer and beef. It is mainly for this reason that communications play so important a part in land warfare. In naval warfare they are also important, but in a smaller degree, for, while the average road is only thirty to forty feet wide, the sea offers a vast area which can be traversed in four directions in place of two. If it were possible to move armies as we move ships, we should entirely revolutionize the art of war. Curious to relate we can do this, for, I have shown that, not only must infantry get into tanks, but gunners and troopers must do the same, and, if all these arms do get into tanks, it would be truly a comic organization should, for means of movement, their administrative services continue to depend on the horse. Naturally they will not do so, but will equip them selves with cross-country tractors and transporters. Wheels will disappear from lorries, cookers, and limbered vehicles, and tracks will replace them.

What shall we then see? Armies liberated from roads; armies ceasing to move like gigantic human serpents; armies which can move deployed if their commanders so wish it, with all their necessary supply vehicles immediately in rear of them,

The Future of Land Warfare

and not at the tails of columns a day's march in length The administrative personnel and garrison troops can be carried in cross-country omnibuses ; the fighting troops can be supplied not only with the munitions of war, but with tents, hot meals, cool drinks, bedding and blankets.

Roads, though they have proved a strategical blessing, have frequently proved a tactical curse. In the past, in roadless countries, the soldier has often fared but little better than a neolithic savage, and in well-roaded ones, such as Flanders, scarcely as well as the inhabitants of a slum, and all because wheeled vehicles demand roads, and where roads do not exist pack animals or coolies alone can be used ; and, where they do, they seldom permit of more than two streams of vehicles passing along them simultaneously, and then only if they are clear of troops. The tank carries its own roadway in its tracks ; it does not, therefore, need a road ; it can, therefore, look upon a road or roadless country with unconcern, and in this indifference, without probing very deep, we may discover an entirely new epoch in the art of war—the epoch of roadless tactics.

When we contemplate the wars of the future, the recent war with its trenches and its canteens will appear a very leisurely affair. There will be no ten days' mobilization, and less getting in and out of trains, for war in the air will force pace upon the earth. There will be no time to select and prepare landing-places, or to take over some friendly harbour ; besides the obvious landing points will have been marked down by the enemy, and will be drenched with persistent gases long before we reach them. Further than this, we do not want the enemy to know where we are going, for, as surprise is always the most powerful of weapons, we wish to take him unawares, suddenly springing at his throat. Therefore, when the crash comes, we may expect to see our tank army of the future mobilize in a few hours and make for the coast, either to take to the water or to crawl on to tank carrying ships, which, under cover of darkness, will speed across the sea or possibly under it. These ships will make for some prearranged point, perhaps a desolate stretch of sand dunes, where the tanks will either crawl ashore or take to the water from the ships and swim towards the land.

As machines of great size will be difficult to hide, smoke clouds will be formed to cover them; meanwhile numerous other smoke clouds will be created so that the enemy's aeroplanes may be misled. Of a hundred such clouds, perhaps only two or three will cover tank forces, and then, at a given hour, all the clouds will move towards the frontiers, for they will be emitted by cross-country machines, which will leave a spoor behind them still further to bewilder the enemy's airmen. Presently the clouds will coalesce into one vast expanse of smoke, which, like a gigantic storm cloud, will roll over the enemy's land. Only when it bursts, when the thunder of the guns is heard, and the flame-projecting tanks advance on their prey, spouting forth sheets of fire, like tongues of lightning, will the enemy discover which parts of the typhoon are alive. It may then be too late for him to manœuvre his own tank army to meet the invader, or, if he has gauged their position correctly, then will a battle of mechanical monsters take place, each monster controlled by a tiny brain—its crew, upon the pluck and determination of which, even more so than in the past, will victory depend, for the machine is, after all, but the weapon of man; once a sword, to-day a rifle, and to-morrow a tank.

Rolling forward on its tracks, the war of the future will resemble a conflict of mobile fortresses, followed by moving supply dumps. The skeleton of the battle will be as heretofore; there will be the search, the grip, the clinch and the overthrow, but on this skeleton will be built up muscles of steel. Man will remain the same, a cunning human creature; his means of movement, his weapons and his methods of protection will alone have changed. If mechanically both sides are equal, then, on the valour, obedience and self-sacrifice of the soldier will victory depend. But if one side relies on these virtues alone, and neglects to safeguard them by the most powerful weapons obtainable, then will they be of little value, as little as all the valour of the Soudanese was at Omdurman. Moral

The Future of Land Warfare

is the most precious virtue which a soldier can possess, and as we value it so must we protect it.

In the van of the battle of the future may we watch the scout tanks, the light cavalry of the army, retiring before the side which has gained the initiative, falling back on their heavier machines, or away from them to a flank to draw the enemy into a false position. Wireless reports will be sent back from the air fleet and telephoned on from the flag tank to the squadron leaders, which will manœuvre for ground, for position, for light and for wind. Great clouds of smoke will roll over the battlefield, under cover of which mine-laying tanks will move forward to deny to the enemy's machines certain tactical positions, or in the hope that, by a calculated retirement, they may be induced to attempt to advance across them. Destroyer tanks will dart forward to attack the huge artillery machines, the capital ships of the battlefield, and succeed or be driven back by their like. Then, at length, will the two sides clinch, and, amidst the whirl of smoke and gas, the thunder of the guns and the crash of steel, will one human being impose the will of his army on that of his antagonist. Lastly, the pursuit, the roaring of engines and the race to destroy.

The battles of the future may be something like this, or even something still more different from the conflicts of the recent war. Different they will be; so different, when it is realized that we are now entering a new epoch in warfare, that no man can, with any semblance of certainty, say that the above picture is impossible. In it infantry, cavalry and artillery, as they are armed, mounted, or moved to-day, have no place—NONE! It is impossible even to imagine them partaking in such a struggle; as well pit a fleet of coracles, triremes and galleys against destroyers, submarines and Dreadnoughts, as to pit the frail arms of to-day against their more powerful descendants. All things material change, but one thing immaterial will remain constant—the will to win, the soul within the machine.

How different may the battle be; let us for a moment think,

and then offer one more speculation. The battle of machines, is this the ultimate goal in warfare ? I do not think so, for a machine is but a means of waging war, a tool whereby men seek to impose their will upon each other. Once the machine was a bow and arrow ; to-day it is a rifle or a machine gun carried on a mounting called man ; to-morrow it may be an aeroplane or a tank. Yet, whatever it be, it is the will and understanding of man which the machine forces man to accept Just as in a telephone the vibrations of the voice are transmitted by an inaudible current of electricity, so also in war is the silent will of one nation transmitted to its antagonist by means of roaring tools. Tools change, and though in the past the soldier has generally been no designer, in the future he must become one if he is to continue to impose his will on his enemy.

What does this mean ? It means that invention is an important branch of strategy. It means that we must never be content with what we have ; without halt we must everlastingly seek for something better. If a tool can be found, or designed, against which the enemy possesses no immediate protection, then this tool alone may constitute ninety-nine per cent. of victory, even if every general in the enemy's army is as cunning as Napoleon, and every private soldier as brave as Marshal Ney.

For a moment, I will turn back to the battle of machines. The two great mechanical forces surge forward over the land, while high above in the air another terrific conflict is being waged. Suddenly the whole of the machines of one side stand stock still, and the whole of the aeroplanes of this same side swoop down to earth and crash upon the ground. Would not this mean ninety-nine per cent. of victory to the side which could continue to move and fly ? It would mean more, it would be victory itself. But how could such a catastrophe take place ? The answer is simple. The victorious side, all unknown to the enemy, has discovered how to derange, by means of etheric waves, the mechanism of the hostile tanks and aeroplanes. Perhaps the antidote is but a leaden box or a glass container

The Future of Land Warfare

costing a few shillings, which could be turned out by the tens of thousands in a few days. What does this matter, so long as the enemy does not possess it, for in twenty seconds his entire army will be immobilized by perhaps *one man* !

Does this mean that tanks and aeroplanes are useless, and should, consequently, be scrapped ? Certainly, if the means of safeguarding them are of as little value as a woollen jacket against a bullet ; otherwise, no ! It means this . that nothing devised by human brains is perfect, there is ever a recoil, there is always room for improvement, and that side which gains supremacy in invention and design is the side which is going to win the next war In the past, wars have frequently been decided by man-power ; in the future they will almost certainly be decided by machine-power, begotten of brain-power—possibly in a single test-tube may be discovered the secret of the conquest of the world !

IX

THE FUTURE OF SEA WARFARE

IN this Chapter I will first recapitulate what has gone before, so that the reader, before considering the future of sea warfare, may be certain of his starting-point. In Chapters IV. and V., I examined the nature of the Great War and its tendencies, and I showed, how out of the cavern of brute-force timorously crept forth, like a wee mouse, the idea of the moral attack Then in Chapters VI. and VII., I examined the instruments of this attack—gas, which would humanize the bullet, and aircraft, which would transport gas and, by directing it against the will of a nation, reduce the horrors of bloodshed and destruction. Thus were opened before us the portals of a warlike Eden; yet, like Eden of old, within dwelt the serpent closely twined around the ancient trunk of the tree of life, whose sap is drawn from the blood of warriors and whose ever falling leaves are battles lost. In Chapter VIII., the snake moved its coils, unwound itself, and offering to us the gas-proof tank, seduced us from the narrow path which leads to the true objective of war Like Adam, we eat of the fruit of death and are fallen; yet without this fall there can be no redemption, and, as good is the recoil of evil, so shall we discover that, out of the horrific struggle of monstrous machines, nations may advance yet one march further towards the bloodless battlefields of the future.

Studious reader, remember ever that we can only progress from evil to good, and that, as the good in humanity grows old, in its perfection is begotten its corruption, within which is conceived its redemption. I have shown how, by gas and air,

The Future of Sea Warfare

warfare may be humanized, and how, by petrol and steel, it may become re-brutalized. But, pause before you deliver judgment, for the battle of petrol-driven steel, appalling as it may seem, is not so brutal as the battle of blood-driven muscle. Why is this ? I will explain.

Time is the controlling factor in war, it is the urge of armies. The more rapid the assembly, the quicker the battle ; the quicker the battle, the more speedy the victory, and victory is the postern of peace. Petrol economizes time in war, caterpillar tracks or aircraft propellers economize space. Economy in time and space are the sire and dam of surprise, and surprise is the true sword of victory.

Power to move in all directions introduces into strategy and tactics a new meaning, which will demand a higher type of mind than has ever been required in past wars. The more cunning this mind becomes, the more deadly will be the result of its overthrow. Heretofore, war minds were small and war bodies were big ; armies were like certain reptiles—their brain could, on occasion, be actually removed without influencing the wrigglings of their bodies. War is fast outgrowing the reptilian stage, and, when mind expands, man will realize what the objective of war demands. Then will the desire of the soldier be to avoid rather than meet the army of his adversary, so that in place he may be free to attack the will and nerves of the hostile nation. Frequently, he will not be able to do so, nevertheless, he must never lose sight of his main objective, for, as in war, moral is to the physical as three to one, so is a successful moral attack not only three but thirty, possibly three hundred, times as effective as a physical onslaught.

While battles are raging in the air, battles which may be won in hours or days in place of months or years, on land must an army not only seek out the enemy, but must race towards his vitals—his aerodromes, dockyards, chemical factories, workshops and seats of government. Undoubtedly will the enemy attempt to protect these by means of his military forces, and undoubtedly will his adversary attempt to hack his

172 The Reformation of War

shield to pieces, and, if it be shattered, what then? A withdrawal followed by reconstruction? No; for, within a few years, it will be possible for a mechanical army to sweep from the Seine to the Vistula in seven days.

If the shield is, however, not hacked to pieces, what shall we see? While the axe is being wielded against it, aircraft, like arrows, will speed over it; and fast moving tank forces, like javelins, will shiver past its flanks, and these will transfix the civil brains of the enemy with terror. Which side will outlast the other, this has always been a vital question in war? In the recent war, over four years were required wherein to undermine the German moral; in the days of Napoleon it took twenty-two years to undermine that of the French In the recent war, had the Germans won the battle of the Marne, the war might have been won in six weeks, and, be it well remembered, the German muscle-moving armies took four weeks to cover the 150 miles which separates Liége from the outskirts of Paris. To-day, the aeroplane can cover this distance in one hour, and, in a few years to come, a tank will be able to accomplish this journey in one day. Bearing in mind such rapidity of movement, it becomes almost a certainty that, in the next great war, the endurance of civil moral will be in direct proportion to the speed of the war machines used; consequently, the duration of wars will be short, and, as I will now show, the power which can command the seas is the power which will hold the winning card.

Sea warfare, like land or air warfare, is but a means towards an end, and as man is a terrestrial animal and not an aquatic or aerial beast, he lives and breeds on the land, and over ninety per cent. of his activities are connected with the land; consequently, of all the military means employed by a nation to impose its will on another, sea warfare is the least direct.

The military objective is attained through two great activities : liberty of movement and liberty of action. The first I will call the strategical objective and the second the tactical. The aim of the first is to place an armed force in such a position that it

The Future of Sea Warfare

may attain the second—namely, victory, at the lowest cost in men, money, material and honour. Normally, victory is to be sought on land, because man primarily belongs to the earth. In primitive times this condition was absolute, but, as civilization advanced, nations became more and more dependent on each other's efforts for supply of food, clothing and other commodities, with the result that sea roads were added to land roads and highly organized fleets to armies. The first, to-day, constitute the great strategical forces, especially in maritime powers, and the second the great tactical forces.

As the military policy of a virile nation is to impose its will on its antagonist, the sooner it can do so the less commercial capital will it expend, and the less disorganization of existing markets, whether in its own hands or in those of its enemies and allies or neutrals, will result.

In wars originating through trade competition, the object is visibly not to kill, wound, or plunder the enemy, but simply to persuade him, by both moral and physical force, that acceptance of this policy will prove more profitable than its refusal ; for to kill, wound and plunder is to destroy or debilitate a future buyer —it is, in fact, a direct attack on the competitive impulse which is the foundation of prosperity

I have already shown that the most rapid method of enforcing a policy is not to destroy but to capture, morally and physically, an enemy's government and so compel it to agree—a man pinned down with a pistol pointed at his head does not argue. Enemy governments, being land organizations, must be captured on land. In order to prevent so dire a fate they protect themselves by armies, and, if the countries they govern possess sea coasts, they raise navies in order to protect their communications with other countries and so prevent the invasion of their territories, or to assist in their invading those of their enemies. If we carry this analysis a little further we shall find that fleets exist for four primary purposes in war :

(i.) To protect the transportation of armies, as took place

174   The Reformation of War

in the Crimean War, the Russo-Japanese War and the Great War of 1914-1918.

(ii.) To compel an enemy to disperse his main army by landing or by threatening to land troops, such as the landings in Portugal and Spain during the Peninsular War, and the Gallipoli, Salonika and Archangel landings during the Great War.

(iii.) To protect the transportation of supplies, as took place in the Dutch Wars of the seventeenth century, the Napoleonic Wars and the Great War.

(iv.) To impede or completely prevent supplies of all natures being shipped to the enemy's country, as was attempted during the Dutch Wars, the American Civil War and the Great War.

The four primary purposes of a fleet may be condensed into two—namely, the military purpose of a fleet and the economic purpose, which together may be expressed in one term : " Command of the Sea," or the power of controlling movement over the water in order to maintain and secure national policy, which in its highest form, is survival with prosperity, honour and contentment.

As the ultimate aim of a fleet is to gain or maintain command of the sea—that is, liberty of movement and action on the water—consequently, its object is to clear the sea of all hostile ships, either by sinking or blockading them, and until this objective has been gained, the purposes of a fleet cannot, without grave risk, be accomplished.

For any nation to possess complete freedom of the sea, it is necessary for its fleet to be in a position to guarantee its military and economic purposes. Before the invention of the submarine this was difficult enough, even when surface superiority was most marked, as was the case with the British Fleet from 1806 to 1815, during which period, nevertheless, hundreds of merchantmen were yearly sunk or captured by the enemy. Since the introduction of the submarine, a complete guarantee or anything approaching secure command is no longer possible; consequently, the question which should now be perplexing naval brains is not that of battleships *versus* submarines, or *vice versa*, but rather, what constitutes the intrinsic values of these two types of vessels in the maintenance of command of the sea against all prospective enemies?

It must first of all be realized that the submersible vessel has introduced a third dimensional movement into the art of naval warfare, which differs fundamentally from third dimensional means of movement in the air, in that, while the air offers no direct protection to aircraft, water offers a more complete protection to the submarine than does a trench to a soldier A submarine, in fact, possesses the power to enter her "dugout," at most points on the surface of the sea, at will, and thus protect herself from hostile attack, but while submerged she possesses no more offensive power than does the soldier in his underground shelter. The main characteristic of the submarine is, in fact, her power to evade a fight and not her power to seek combat on equal terms with surface craft.

This power of evasion introduces a new problem into naval warfare. On the surface, the submarine in fighting power is inferior to the surface warships, because, at present, she cannot give the same number of blows or withstand an equal hammering, but by diving she can normally avoid, even at close quarters, receiving any blows at all. Though this protective power possessed by the submarine has greatly influenced the economic purpose of a fleet, because on the surface the submarine is far more powerful offensively than an armed merchantman, up to the present this power has had little influence on the military purpose of a fleet, because this purpose is still accomplished on the surface, and on the surface her power of evasion is lost. If, however, this military purpose could be accomplished under the surface, surface craft would be all but impotent to prevent it. Such a possibility would reduce the actions of a fleet to that of commerce protection, surface craft becoming but mere escorts to merchant vessels.

Before examining this stupendous possibility, which, if feasible, will revolutionize the whole outlook of naval warfare, I intend returning to the question of surprise, which I have called—the true sword of victory.

In the past, sea power, when properly used, has enabled innumerable surprisals to be effected, such as the landing of Sir John Moore in Portugal in 1809 and the Japanese at Chemulpo in 1904. These surprisals have, however, normally demanded one condition—command of the surface of the seas, and, in order to gain this command, the enemy's fleet has either to be destroyed or blockaded. In the days of sailing ships temporary command frequently sufficed. In 1805, Napoleon hoped to gain such a condition, by enticing Nelson and his ships away from the English Channel to the West Indies. Since the introduction of steamships, this temporary ability to evade, and so attack the will of a hostile nation overseas, has become more and more difficult, until, to-day, however perfect the surface command may be, as long as the enemy possesses a few submarines, not necessarily supremacy in submarines, such operations become exceedingly hazardous.

I have already shown in Chapter VII. the extreme danger that large battleships will run if they are attacked simultaneously by submarines and aircraft. Day by day, evidence is accumulating to show that the age of the present naval Brontosaur is nearing its end For ten or fifteen years, these immense and costly ships, veritable Titans of brute-force, may continue, but their dotage is in view, because the objective in naval warfare is not to sink steel, but to impose a policy on the enemy. Supposing, however, that I am wrong and that a Super-Super-Dreadnought will be able to keep afloat in face of a dual three-dimensional attack, even then will not the submarine greatly restrict her activities?

" As an engine of destruction," writes Admiral Daveluy, " the submarine is admirable, because—a fact unique in history —she does not come under the law of numbers by reason of her invisibility : one unit of small tonnage can attack enemy's forces,

The Future of Sea Warfare

no matter how numerous or powerful."* A submarine in the Pacific Ocean, as Mr. Bywater points out, though she might not be able to sink an American battleship, she can normally injure her. To tow a Super-Dreadnought across several thousand miles of water " would be hopeless if enemy submarines were about."† Besides direct attack, submarines can indirectly attack a fleet by sowing mine-fields in the neighbourhood of naval ports, by forcing an enemy to cease offensive construction and concentrate on the building of protective anti-submarine craft. Again, with fleets based on oilless countries, the submarine can strike at the capital ship economically by sinking her oil tankers. As regards this very important use of the submarine to starve the engines of a fleet Mr. Bywater writes :

" . . . if experience in the world war counts for anything, the losses among these vessels would be enormous. During that conflict no less than 244 colliers and 44 oil tankers in the service of the British Admiralty were sunk, mainly by enemy action . Ships of this type are peculiarly vulnerable to submarine attack owing to their great length and low speed. So serious were the casualties suffered that the reserve of oil fuel for the British Fleet was gradually reduced to an eight weeks' supply . . . The bulk of these losses were suffered . . . a few hundred miles from the English coast in an area which was closely patrolled."‡

From the above it would appear that the unanimity of the British press, on the receipt of Mr. Balfour's declamation against the submarine, made during the Washington Disarmament Conference, was not due to her uselessness in naval warfare, but to the fact that her power is so great that the British surface supremacy of the seas is imperilled. If this be the true cause, then it would be wise to acknowledge it. To force the head of the British public under the sands of untruthfulness is scarcely an action which deserves applause

Now that I have examined the influence of the submarine on

* " Les Enseignements Maritimes de la Guerre Anti-Germanique," Contre-Amiral Daveluy, Part I , Chapter I.

† " Sea Power in the Pacific," H. C. Bywater, p. 290.

‡ Ibid , pp. 274, 275.

the military purpose of surface craft, I will show how this purpose can be accomplished by moving an invading force not on the surface of the water but under it.

The object of a fleet, as I have stated, is to maintain command of the sea in order to enable both traders and soldiers to move freely across the waters. This objective is gained by compelling an enemy to accept a policy which guarantees this free movement, and, if the enemy refused to accept this policy, in accordance with the old theory of naval warfare his fleet was either destroyed or blockaded, that is immobilized.

In itself, this destruction or restriction of the enemy's naval power was but a means of accomplishing one of two naval purposes. Once command had been secured, the hostile will could either be attacked, directly, by landing an army on the enemy's shores, or indirectly, by striking at his stomach by cutting off his food supply. If the enemy's country were self-supporting, then the second action was normally so prolonged that it was ruled out of account. As generally the enemy's fleet had to be destroyed or captured before complete command could be guaranteed, by degrees these means obscured the end, so that a tradition was created that the sole object of a fleet was to destroy another fleet.

As submarines can, however, move under the surface, the commanding surface fleet can be avoided. This means that the economic purpose can still be fulfilled. To carry out, however, the military purpose, as long as a traditional army is maintained, would demand such an enormous number of submarines that it becomes impracticable. Should, however, the nature of such an army be so changed that a powerful force could be moved by submarines under the water, it would then be possible to gain command of the sea, not by destroying the enemy's fleet or by blockading it, but by avoiding it and attacking the will of the hostile nation upon which the stability of the fleet is based. In fact, what is contemplated here is, in place of hopping over an army by using aeroplanes, to dive under a fleet by using submarines; in both cases the objective is the same, namely, the will of the hostile nation. If this can be accomplished, then the sub-

The Future of Sea Warfare

marine will become the most potent of naval weapons, surface craft simply being maintained to protect merchantmen from submarine attack. This will mean that the big capital ship will eventually go out of commission and be replaced by smaller and more mobile vessels

During the Great War, the British Navy obtained surface control so completely that it accomplished, within the limitations of the existing land forces, its military purpose to the full Though the command of the surface of the sea was guaranteed, surface craft were so powerless to maintain their economic purpose that Great Britain was almost brought to her knees by the German submarine attack, during which 8,500,000 tons of British shipping were sent to the bottom.

There are two ways of attacking a ship physically; the first, when she is at sea and the second when she is in harbour, and the submarine is no exception to this rule. Successful invasion and the seizing of the enemy's naval bases is, from the general military standpoint, a severer blow than the mere destruction of his fleet at sea. To strike at his ports is to strike at the focal points of his sea communications. A fleet alone can seldom do this, neither can the army of an inland power accomplish such an operation single-handed

The Russo-Japanese war of 1904-1905 illustrated clearly the paramount importance of military co-operation in naval enterprises of this nature, and accentuated the fact that " the destruction of the enemy's ships in harbour is as important as their destruction at sea."* Curious to relate, however, these object-lessons were entirely lost on British military and naval thought ; the " blue water " school killed the " coast attack," and the declaration of war in 1914 found the British Navy and army entirely unprepared to carry out such operations, which the war, throughout its course, constantly demanded.

Lord Jellicoe writes. " Against Ostend and Zeebrugge, no *permanent* result could be achieved by the Navy alone. . . ."

* "Combined Operations," Major-General Sir George Ashton, K.C.B , Journal of the R.U.S.I., February, 1920.

180   The Reformation of War

And again : " The feasible landing-places, so far as we were concerned, were unsuited to military strategy. . . ."* Why? Because either naval action would have to be heavily supported by costly land attacks, or else troops must be landed from innumerable lighters, barges and small craft. I will now show that, by means of submarines, it will be possible, in the near future, to land, on any ordinary beach, a formidable military force as a complete surprise

The first tank operation ever planned was for a landing on the Flanders coast. In 1917, this idea was revived and an account of it is given in Admiral Sir Reginald Bacon's book, " The Dover Patrol " Within ten years of the present date it is all but a certainty that a reliable self-propelled water-crossing tank will be invented, a machine of under twelve tons with a speed on land of over 20 miles an hour and an extensive radius of action. It is not impossible to suppose that a submarine could be built to carry six of these machines, and that a squadron of ten of these submarines, supported by a few submarine monitors and submarine gas-projecting vessels, might appear off the enemy's coast-line or a selected harbour, and, at the most unexpected of moments, and far distant from any land supporting forces, suddenly, under cover of gas and smoke clouds and fifteen-inch gun and howitzer shells, land sixty tanks in a quarter that number of minutes. Within an hour or two, the point selected might be destroyed and the tanks re-embarked, making their way home on the surface or below it. There is nothing impossible in such an attack, there is nothing impossible in such a landing; it is feasible, it is commonsense, and it is yet another answer to the submarine peril, for the navy which can effect such an operation first is the navy which is first going to destroy its enemy's submarine bases. Here, then, is a new reading to Sir Walter Raleigh's famous exclamation :

> " I say that an army to be transported over sea and to be landed again in an enemy's country, and the place left to the choice of the invader, cannot be resisted on the coast of England without a fleet

* " The Crisis of the Naval War "

The Future of Sea Warfare

to impeach it. . . . For there is no man so ignorant, that ships without putting themselves out of breath, will easily outrun the soldiers that coast them."*

But the difference is this : a fleet will not know how to impeach such a landing, neither will the soldier know where to run, for, in the words of Bacon : " Secrecy and celerity are the life of despatch in all military operations," and here this secrecy and celerity will be accentuated in their maximum degree, and may be assisted by a simultaneous attack from the air.

The above example of a physical attack delivered by tanks transported by submarines against a military or naval objective should only be regarded as a stepping-stone to a moral attack on the nerves and will of the hostile nation. Indeed, such an attack is less difficult, since military objectives can hit back, while the civil population, deficient of military protection, is at the mercy of an invader.

In the last Chapter, I showed that, on account of the tank being able to protect itself against the aeroplane, the brute force theory of war would find a new outlet in the tank versus tank battle. Further I showed that, though the enemy's tank army would demand a concentration of an equal or superior force of tanks against it in order to restrict its activities, every effort should be made by small detachments of machines to avoid the main hostile force, so that they may strike at the moral of the civil population behind this force. A moment's consideration will at once cause us to realize what a potent weapon the submarine-carried tank will be in the moral attack.

For a continental power to invade the British Isles by means of submarine-transported tanks would be a difficult operation, unless the blow were delivered as a complete surprise. But for an island power, such as Great Britain, to raid a continental power by this method is much more feasible ; it is, in fact, so possible that I will consider it in some detail

In the past the main difficulty in harmonizing a combined naval and military operation is closely connected with movement.

* "History of the World."

The Reformation of War

A fleet which possesses command of the sea can normally steam to any point on an enemy's coast-line and effect a surprise before the land forces can be assembled to meet it. To-day, this operation has become an exceedingly dangerous one, seeing that the aeroplane can watch the approach of the invading force which, *en route*, may be attacked by submarines.

On arriving at the point selected for disembarkation, the main difficulty begins. The ships cannot crawl on to the land, and the military forces to be landed cannot swim to the shore, and because of these limitations, the means adopted to transfer a muscularly organized army from mechanically propelled ships is little superior to those used by Julius Cæsar, and much more complex, for his triremes drew very little water. The result, in the past, has frequently been (and as long as traditional armies are maintained will remain so) that all surprise is lost and that, before the army landed can move forward, it will be confronted by an enemy in superior strength.

Now let us consider a floatable tank carried in a submarine. As the embarkation can take place at night, the initiation of the operation will be secret. As the machines will mainly be transported under the water their voyage will be secret. As their destination will alone be known to the invader their landing will be secret. From their floating mechanical base will be launched a floating army. This force will propel itself ashore, crawl up the beach, and in place of converting it into the condition of Epsom Downs on a Derby morning, will move straight inland at a speed varying from 10 to 20 miles the hour. Within 24 hours of landing it will be 200 miles within the enemy's country. Freed from railways, and let us suppose possessing one week's radius of action, it will be able to terrorize the enemy's people, and if threatened by superior force, it will generally be able to make for the coast, possibly several hundred miles away from its original point of landing, and swim out to the submarines and re-embark.

Let us now visualize three or four such forces operating at different points against an enemy, and some picture may be formed of the confusion resulting. Then, let us suppose that,

The Future of Sea Warfare

while these raiding forces are disorganizing the enemy's plans and command, and demoralizing the civil inhabitants, as the Vikings disorganized and demoralized half Europe a thousand years ago, a determined invasion is launched at some vital point; it will be a difficult operation for the enemy to collect his disintegrated forces to meet it, even if these forces are mechanical.

The whole of such an operation depends on sea-power, the only difference, when compared with the past, being, that while formerly an army, using muscle as its motive force, could seldom make good what the navy rendered possible, a mechanical army *can* make it good, it can take advantage of a naval surprise and accentuate this advantage by the speed with which it moves inland.

Think now what such possibilities mean to us islanders. No longer will our sailors belong to the Great Silent Fleet, but to a fleet which belches war on every strand, which vomits forth armies as never did the horse of Troy, and which will swallow them up again, if the land appears unpropitious, and carry them safely home beneath the ocean.

Think of the naval bases seized and the landing-places protected. Think of the paralysation of government and the terrorization of mind. Think of the channel which separates us from Europe. It has been called a " ditch "—it may become a veritable tube railway for hostile armies.

Munchausen! Munchausen! Perhaps; but do not let us disparage our inventive genius like a certain Italian alchemist did his own at the beginning of the sixteenth century. He promised to fly from the walls of Stirling Castle to France. He attempted to do so and, falling, broke a leg. He attributed his failure to the fact that he used for his wings feathers of fowls, which, he said, had an affinity for the dung-hill! It was not his feathers which possessed an affinity for this unpleasant heap, but his brains! He had been thinking backwards of Icarus; he should have been thinking forwards in terms of the Wright Brothers.

184   The Reformation of War

Here then is the moral: Do not let us now, in the year 1923, continue to think backwards to 1914; let us think forwards to 1930, 1940, 1950 and beyond, or we shall become pillars of salt in an arid and unproductive wilderness. Let us look ahead; the world is getting small, but science is vastly huge. Every rational thought is a true thought which may lead to realizable effect. There is nothing too wonderful for science, and the fighting services must grasp the wand of this magician and compel the future to obey their will.

If we meditate for a moment on the above possibilities, rendered practical by wedding tank to submarine, two facts will strike us forcibly; these are:

(i.) The secrecy and celerity of the operation.
(ii.) The vulnerability of the civil target.

If to these two weapons we add the aeroplane, this secrecy and this vulnerability becomes enormously enhanced. Consequently, we may well ask ourselves, as Fontenoy courtesies have become completely out of date, will not formal declarations of war follow suit. Bearing in mind that the main tactical problem in war is to hit without being hit, is it common-sense to expect a nation, reduced to fight for its life, a nation which possibly possesses scientific weapons of tremendous power, and the development of the power of which demands surprise in its positive form—an unexpected and terrific blow, moral or physical, according to the theory of warfare held—to place its adversary on guard by saying: " On August 4 I am going to hit you." What is far more probable is that the enemy will say nothing at all, or : " On August 4 I will agree to your terms," and then launch a surprise attack on the 3rd. Such action may be proclaimed as immoral; this, however makes it none the less likely, because war is not a boxing match; far from it—it is a life and death struggle. To say to a would-be murderer, " In five minutes I am going to shoot you," would be the act of a fool, and, in the struggle for national existence, aggressive nations are murderers and not prize-fighters. Surprise in its

The Future of Sea Warfare

positive form—an unexpected attack—possesses yet another virtue: it enables bloodshed to be reduced to a minimum; in fact it enables a policy to be enforced with a minimum of killing or destruction of property—*it is the true sword of victory.*

I predict that, when nations comprehend the purpose of war, wars will not be declared, and that, consequently, small mobile striking forces will be kept ready, like fire engines, to extinguish at the shortest possible notice any conflagration which may break out. In Chapter IV., I showed the brutal nature of warfare based on muscle. In Chapter VII., I showed how liquid gas dropped from an aeroplane would reduce slaughter. In Chapter VIII., I showed that the tank would introduce a reaction towards bloodshed, but that wars would, in duration, be short and that surprise would become, more than ever it has been in the past, the main instrument of victory. In this Chapter I will outline yet one more form of battle and yet one more war-road to peace.

It is a lovely day, not a cloud in the sky, as humanity wends its daily path to work, toil and leisure. Two nations have long been competitors for power which to-day is represented by trade, one is Great Britain the other the Unknown. The Unknown determines to strike. Its people know nothing of the impending blow, for they are all socialists and consequently are subjected to an iron discipline. Less still do the inhabitants of the isle " set in the silver sea " realize that the day is anything other than of the most perfect. Besides, being highly educated democrats, they are all busily reading the last " Girl Bride Divorce," which provides a vent for their hunting spirit.

The Unknown possesses submarines, tanks and aircraft. The numerical strength of which is immaterial, but what is material is that, relatively, these forces are superior in type to those in England. The submarines can carry six large tanks each, the aeroplanes can carry seven tons of liquid gas apiece, or a small tank of an equal weight. The Unknown general staff have studied war. Why kill, why destroy ? War is but a means to an end, the end is a more prosperous peace, and prosperity demands international co-operation, possibly the serfdom of one nation to another, but it cannot mean international destruction, for this is to turn prosperity upside-down.

The night of August 4 is purple and azure, and under the twinkling stars the Unknown fleets set out : some high in the air, some on the surface of the water ready to dive beneath it should necessity demand.

It is day; the advanced guard tanks have descended from the air and proceed at a steady pace down the Edgware Road or any other road which will take them to Westminster. They emit an odourless gas, which causes the crowd now gathering from all quarters to laugh irresistibly. Peals of laughter greet the tanks, roars of laughter, shrieks of laughter, groans of laughter, for to be unable to stop laughing at a tank is veritable agony. In Whitehall a sneezing mixture is emitted. A policeman on traffic control sneezes and involuntarily lowers his hand ; an elderly lady sneezes and gets knocked over by a motor-bus, the driver of which sneezes and sneezes again. The War Office and the Admiralty sneeze and cannot stop sneezing, sneezing becomes an excruciating torture. At the Cenotaph the Unknown Commander signals " Increase speed," and in a minute his machines occupy New and Old Palace Yards and the Victoria Tower Gardens. The nozzle of a hose-pipe is thrust through a window of the House of Commons and a tap is turned on. The gas emitted is a powerful melancholic mixed with hot air, and, as the members breathe it, they become suicidally despondent. Then the Unknown Commander, carefully protected by a gas-mask with a megaphone protruding from it, like a second Cromwell, strides into the House and says :

" In the air above you there are five hundred aeroplanes loaded with several thousand tons of a deadly gas. The garrisons of London are confined to their barracks by a stink barrage which they are unable to cross. In Hyde Park and elsewhere by three p.m. will be assembled five hundred formidable tanks.

What can you do ? You can sign this scrap of paper by which you will agree to :

- (i.) Subscribe £500,000,000 towards the cost of building the Tokio-San Francisco tube railway.
- (ii.) Remove all protective duties on the exports of the Unknown nation.
- (iii.) Sink your fleet and disband your army.
- (iv.) Pull down your slums and build decent houses for our socialist brothers in Great Britain.
- (v.) Create an earldom for the Editor of the *Daily Herald*, etc., etc."

What tomfoolery, how ridiculously absurd. Granted ; but what can the Prime Minister do, this is the vital question ? The five hundred machines overhead *do* carry lethal gas and the tanks in Hyde Park *are* equipped with thermite shell. If the Prime Minister hesitates, the Unknown Commander is quite man enough to burn down or gas up a district or two to show him that he is in dead earnest. Besides, the War Office and Admiralty are still sneezing and are helpless. The Prime Minister signs and then, with a sigh, turns to the masked commander and says : " What country do you represent ? " The Unknown bellows, " Eurasia," through his megaphone, and, just before the Prime Minister swoons away in the arms of the Secretary for War, the reporters allege that he murmured : " Et tu, Brute ! "

The above I acknowledge is an exaggeration ; but, through years of contact with my fellow men, I have learnt that it is by exaggeration that man's mind is aroused, for of the meticulously proportioned man takes little heed. Granted that it is a gross exaggeration, then an exaggeration of what ? Not of traditional methods of war, for these can no longer be exaggerated, having reached the very apex of exaggeration at Verdun, on the Somme and at Ypres. In place, an exaggeration of a new type of warfare, warfare based on surprise and on science, in one word, on brains ! A war which does not aim at killing and destroying, but merely at imposing the will of one nation on another as economically as brains can conceive On victor and vanquished alike, because, during peace-time, the welfare of both forms the supports of the bridge we call prosperity. Destroy one support and the other is rendered useless until the stones are replaced and the bridge is rebuilt. Not by victor or by vanquished single-handed, but by both unitedly. In the future, wars will be looked upon as a means of creating a better peace and not as a means of bruising a worn-out one. So I believe that a day will arrive when wars of righteousness will evolve from the present-day wars of commerce ; when nations which will not work or rule *for the benefit of the world* will nationally be stamped out of independence, so that the world may become a fairer and a cleaner place to live in than it has ever been before.

X

THE PROBLEM OF IMPERIAL DEFENCE

AS diplomacy is the art of maintaining policy by persuasion, so is strategy the art of maintaining policy by force, and, as policy depends on the ethical and economic conditions of the nations, it is, consequently, changeful in nature, and strategy, unless it can keep pace with these changes, must of necessity become unethical and uneconomic It is, therefore, my intention in this Chapter to examine this question, which not only confronts ourselves—a far flung empire—but every independent country in the world.

To-day, the Empire is loaded with an immense debt accumulated during the recent war and is suffering from acute nervous unrest, which, in itself, is not altogether an unhealthy condition, but which, at any moment, may become so, should it lead to a nervous breakdown ; in other words to revolution Outwardly, the relationship of the Empire to foreign powers is uncertain, for to-day no balance of power exists between the nations of the civilized world. From this state, if past history is to be relied upon, we can, however, with some certainty predict that until the balance of power is re-established, and until one or more demented nations again attempt to upset it by grasping at world dominion, as Philip II., Louis XIV , Napoleon I. and William II did, a great war, in any way comparable to the recent war, is unlikely. Our immediate strategical problem is, therefore, not a great war but a problem of small wars and internal security in militarily and politically backward lands Both these problems are primarily problems of movement and particularly of movement in roadless and railless countries.

In examining this problem, I think it will simplify our ideas if we look upon movement from its dimensional aspect, thus :

(i.) One dimensional movement, road, rail and river.
(ii.) Two dimensional movement, sea and cross-country.
(iii.) Three dimensional movement, air and under-water.

The first includes the traditional method of military movement, and the second of naval ; the third includes both these dimensions, but with this important difference, namely, that, on the actual surface of the land or sea the mobility of aircraft is not generally useful.

Bearing in mind these three dimensions of movement, our future strategical problems are closely connected with the protection of our land roads, sea roads and air ways, in order that trade may prosper and, in event of it being threatened, may be secured by force. If we can guarantee a high condition of prosperity, we shall simultaneously attain to a high state of contentedness, which will mean that our policy will possess a sound economic and ethical foundation. I mention this here as it must never be forgotten that policy is as dependent upon strategy as *vice versa*.

The problems of Imperial defence may be divided into three categories—great wars, small wars and domestic tranquillity, the objectives of which are the maintenance of policy internal and external. Each of these problems is different in nature. Thus, a great war is a contest between highly civilized and similarly equipped opponents, in which tactical values are of the greatest importance ; while a small war is normally the pursuit of an ill-equipped enemy by a well-equipped antagonist, in which rapidity of movement is the predominant factor and in which physical geography plays a leading part. In the maintenance of law and order the limiting factor is the law of the land, for while rioters and rebels are at liberty to break it, seeing that they have cast the law aside, the forces of the Crown are not similarly placed, for, as their object is to reinstate the law, their actions must be within the law until such time as the rebellion develops into a

The Problem of Imperial Defence

small war, when the maintenance of the law by persuasion is replaced by its enforcement. The mere proclaiming of martial law in a disturbed district in no way entitles the defence forces to cease regarding the insurgents as citizens, for a rebel, however hostile, is not an alien.

As I have already examined the possible future of great wars, in this Chapter I will restrict my inquiry and my suggestions to small wars and the maintenance of domestic peace. Are our present means adequate, are they economical, and, if not, can they be improved ? These are the main questions I will attempt to answer, first of all inquiring into the premises of these two questions and then examining how the three great means of defence—the army, air force and navy, can assist us in the solution of these problems.

(i.) *The Small War Problem.* While a great war is a struggle between organized forces raised by civilized nations possessing an intricate political system and an elaborate social organization which is easily deranged by nervous shock, a small war is generally waged against congeries of tribes or a loosely organized community united by ties of blood rather than by the political and social bonds of civilization. The organization of such a society, like the organism of the lower animals, is controlled by a series of nervous ganglia rather than by a centralized brain, consequently the moral targets are small and numerous in place of being large and few as in the case of a civilized power.* On these facts may be built the following theory, namely, that in small wars against uncivilized nations, the form of warfare to be adopted must tone with the shade of culture existing in the land, by which I mean that, against peoples possessing a low civilization, war must be more brutal in type (not necessarily in execution) than against a highly civilized nation ; consequently, physical

* Through not realizing this difference many curious mistakes have arisen in the past, e g : *The Graphic*, September 30, 1899 : " The Strategy of the Boer Campaign," by Charles Lowe : " Once Pretoria is in possession of our troops all resistance in the Transvaal must collapse, for the simple reason that all further supply of war material to the Boers must cease." Simple here is an equivalent of silly !

blows are normally more likely to prove effective than nervous shocks. If this theory be correct, then war on land will predominate over war in the air (moral warfare), as I shall explain later on.

As regards small wars generally, two main problems face us, the first is dependent on time and space, and the second on organization and administration. Translated into military terms these two problems are ·

(i.) How are we going to secure our Empire by means of our small army, small air force and depleted navy ?

(ii.) How are we going to establish a higher co-operation than at present exists between our army, navy and air force ?

The first of these problems I shall deal with in this Chapter, and the second in the following one.

The first problem is virtually one of fitting means to ends. Our army is smaller than it was in 1914, and yet costs twice as much ; our Empire is larger than it was in 1914, and is in a very unsettled and nervous condition. How, then, are we to protect it ?

Because we lack money, we cannot increase the size of the army to fit the Empire ; consequently, there is only one thing which we can do, namely, reduce the size of the Empire to fit our army, and there are two ways of doing this. The first is based on the factor of space and the second on that of time.

(*a*) We can abandon large tracts of the Empire and so cut down our liabilities until they balance our securities

(*b*) We can increase our present speed of military movement so that our securities, through enhanced mobility, may be brought to balance our liabilities.

If we believe in the value of the Empire, then there can be no shadow of doubt that duty demands that we should at least attempt the second solution before putting into force the first. I will explain this by means of a very simple example.

Aldershot is thirty miles from London An athlete will walk this distance in about ten hours and will be dog-tired at the end of it ; a soldier will take two days—say thirty-six hours ;

The Problem of Imperial Defence

he also will be dog-tired at the end of the second day. In place, I get into a Rolls-Royce car and travel to London in one hour, and am perfectly fresh when I arrive there. What have I done? In terms of time I have reduced space by nine-tenths when compared to the athlete and by thirty-five-thirty-sixths when compared to the soldier, and have to all intents and purposes expended no physical energy in the process. Fit this picture to the Empire, and suppose that, by means of a cross-country tractor, we only double the mobility of the army, well then, in terms of time, we shall have halved the size of the territories we are at present called upon to protect. I will now turn to land protection.

We, as the inheritors of a world-wide Empire, possess an all but unlimited knowledge of the nature of small wars; we have engaged in them for over two hundred years, and throughout this long period our difficulties in winning them have been very similar. Looking back on the small wars of the past, we find that in character they may be classified according to the topographical nature of the countries in which they most frequently occur, namely:

(i.) Mountainous land.
(ii.) Desert land.
(iii.) Bush land.
(iv.) River land.

Generalizing the main characteristics which are coincident with most small wars, they are found to be as follows:

(*a*) A lack of communications
(*b*) A badly equipped and ill-disciplined enemy.
(*c*) An unhealthy climate.
(*d*) A lack of local supplies and water.

To summarize still further, it may ultimately be said that small wars consist in overcoming physical geography in order to chastise unorganized and ill-armed savages or brigands. The enemy himself is frequently beneath contempt, but Nature in small wars has hitherto proved herself, as often as not, to be

194   The Reformation of War

omnipotent ; consequently, the solution of the problem is not to be sought in men or weapons but in movement. Any weapon with which our men may be armed will almost certainly be superior to the enemy's ; but unhindered as he is by the paraphernalia which a civilized force requires for its welfare and subsistence, his leg-power is frequently so superior to theirs as to render inoperative the use of whatever weapons they may carry.

Concerning this problem, one thing is certain, and this is that civilized leg-power cannot compete with uncivilized, and throughout the history of small wars, from the earliest ages to present times, the principle of " setting a thief to catch a thief " has frequently been adopted.* When this has not been possible, small wars have generally been won by seizing whatever communications may exist, by picketing these and so denying their use to the enemy. Small wars, even more so than great wars, are wars of communications. This being so, should we not cease to base them on leg-power and, instead, substitute machine-power as typified to-day by the tank, cross-country tractor and aeroplane ?

Accepting this suggestion as eventually feasible, if not immediately so, it is interesting to deduce the simplifications and economy which will be effected by the introduction of machinery in the four main small war theatres—mountain, desert, bush and river land.

In mountainous countries, the main characteristics of past operations have been as follows :

The dissatisfied area is entered by one or more of the natural

---

* E g , in 1725, four companies of Highlanders were raised " for the protection of the country against robbers." In 1739, this number was increased to eight companies and the whole constituted into the 42nd Royal Highlanders. In a book entitled, " A Short History of the Highland Regiments," published in 1743, we read : " The Highlander wears a sort of thin pump or brogue, so light that it does not in the least impede his activity in running, and from being constantly accustomed to these kind of shoes, they are able to advance or retreat with incredible swiftness, so that if they have the better of any engagement it is scarcely possible to escape from them, and, on the other hand, if they are overpowered, they soon recover their hills, where it is impossible to reach them " So with all other hill tribes

The Problem of Imperial Defence

avenues of approach, usually river beds along which an indifferent road has been constructed. The force operating consists of a small fighting advanced guard, a lengthy supply train and a considerable force of men to protect it. This protection is normally guaranteed by " crowning the heights," that is by picketing the summits of all positions of vantage within rifle shot of the column wending its way along the valley. This elastic square of infantry, which is drawn round the supply train, both by day and by night, at varying distances, is only necessary because the men and animals in the valley are pervious to bullets ; were they impervious it would be unnecessary. This imperviousness can at once be obtained by replacing infantry by tanks and pack mules by bullet-proof cross-country tractors.

I will picture a mechanical punitive expedition operating against Kabul. The distance from Peshawer to this town is about 150 miles. Moving at four miles an hour for eight hours a day, Kabul can be reached in five days. The Afghans crown the heights as the column approaches, but gain no further advantage than an unquenchable thirst which sooner or later will drive them once again back to the valleys. Road-clearing tanks equipped with " grabs " lead the advance in order to clear boulders and other obstacles from the road ; bridging tanks follow, then the fighting machines and the supply tractors. Having arrived at Kabul, the expedition is supplied by aeroplanes, which, with impunity, can ferry supplies through the air from the base and bring back the sick and wounded to the hospitals.* If police garrisons are required to occupy the city while the mechanical force moves on, these can be transported by airship to the " bridge-head " established by the tanks.

No communications need to be maintained ; the whole operation is really too simple to be considered as partaking of warfare. Is it feasible ? No, not as yet, but it can be made so within a few years. Is it worth instituting ? Yes, if lives, man-power, money and time are worth economizing.

In desert warfare, what is the problem ? Not the enemy, who

* All field hospitals will disappear from the front and be relegated to the base.

The Reformation of War

is armed with anything from a matchlock to a maxim, but water. Water regulates the operation, and, as frequently it will not drop from the clouds, why not make a certainty of it dropping by using aeroplanes ? In desert warfare, if the wells are 20 miles apart, marching becomes difficult ; if 40, an extensive train of camels has to be used. In 1885, Sir H. Stewart took 21 days to cross from Korti to Gubat,* a distance of 180 miles ; a fast moving tank would take 48 hours and an aeroplane only one and a half. In marching order, a man carries one and a half pints of water, a mule 16 gallons and a camel 32 gallons ; there is no difficulty in constructing a tank which will carry 1,220 or 2,240 gallons, or an aeroplane which will carry 224 to 336. The whole problem is so simplified by machinery that it again practically ceases to be a question of warfare at all. A few aeroplanes would have saved Gordon, and El-Teb, Maiwand, or Isandhlwana could each have been turned into decisive British victories by a single tank.

Bush warfare forms a rather more intricate problem, as the nature of the country may frequently, be difficult for roadless traction Ordinary bush and scrub land should prove no hindrance even to existing types of machines. Dense forest land, however, forms a real obstacle, especially if swamps also exist. As we are so seldom confronted by this type of warfare, it would, in my opinion, be uneconomical to attempt to construct giant floating machines which could crash through the trees and splash through the thick waters.

The problem in normal bush warfare is very similar to that already dealt with in mountain warfare, for it resolves itself into one of the protection of the administrative services. Supply trains have again to be protected by means of an elastic square of men moving forward through the jungle, sufficiently far from the carriers and pack animals to prevent these from being pelted with pot legs and chopped up telegraph wire. A small tank needs no such protection and but a slightly better road than carriers require, and its supply by aeroplane should generally be feasible, even if the country be covered with thick bush.

* The chief difficulties of this expedition were those connected with supply.

The Problem of Imperial Defence 197

In river warfare it is hardly necessary to accentuate the possibilities of an amphibious tank In the attempted relief of Kut during the Great War, the supreme difficulty was one of communications—the command of the Euphrates. If supply ships could have proceeded up the river, the garrison would not only have been relieved, but there is every probability that Bagdad would have been occupied months before it was, and quite possibly the war shortened. The movement of the ships was restricted by gun-fire from the river banks. If amphibious tanks could have been employed, these would have preceded the ships, landed at suitable points and turned the flanks of the Turkish gunners. As a matter of fact good land machines would probably have proved as useful.

In each of the four types of small wars examined above, one outstanding tactical deduction may be made if muscle-power is replaced by machine-power, and this is that : *small wars will cease directly an ill-armed antagonist is denied the support of natural obstacles*.

Whatever may be the demand for future great wars, for present and future small wars motorization is essential. Recently, a rising of the Senussi was quelled by three armoured cars. During the South African War, de Wet was never caught, but when at the beginning of the last war he again took to horse, he was run to ground by an armed motor-car in a few weeks If a wheeled vehicle can do this, a tracked vehicle can do several times as much ; it can, in fact, indirectly reduce the size of our Empire by endowing the soldier with increased power of movement—this is our immediate small-war problem.

The problem of the use of aircraft in small wars is very different from that in great wars. Moral attack is localized on account of the loose system of government which exists in most uncivilized lands and on account of these lands possessing a very rudimentary nervous system—lack of newspapers, telephones, telegraphs, railways, postal service, etc., all of which link individuals into one corporate nervous organization Physical attack is rendered difficult on account of natural obstacles—mountains, forests and deserts, and on account of paucity of fixed communications—roads and railways.

Bearing these two means of attack in mind, I will examine the following small war difficulties from the point of view of the use of aircraft.

- (i.) Reconnaissance, due to lack of maps and definite or fixed objectives.
- (ii.) Movement, due to lack of roads and innumerable physical obstacles.
- (iii.) Protection, especially of lines of supply.
- (iv.) Offensive Power, lack of, due to the mobility of the enemy.
- (v.) Supply, due to a lack of communications.

Reconnaissance. In mountainous regions and over vast expanses of desert land, tactical reconnaissance by aeroplane presents many difficulties. Known towns and villages may be visited, but villages among mountains are difficult to locate and in desert countries may be inhabited one day and abandoned the next. I consider it probable, therefore, that one of the main intelligence duties of aircraft will be that of photography, for the past has shown that no less that 100 square miles of country can be photographed by a flight of from four to six aeroplanes in one day. Such work as this must be of the utmost value to the troops engaged.

Movement. Aircraft being able to dispense with roads and fly over physical obstacles may, in certain cases, be able to transport small garrisons from point to point. But, until they can land on very restricted areas of ground, this will not generally be possible. Their main duty, in this respect, will be to transport staff officers from place to place, either for the purpose of controlling military operations or for that of parleying with the enemy or with neutral and friendly tribes.

Protection. For protective work, aircraft will undoubtedly be of the utmost use, for not only can they protect the troops on the ground by co-operating with them, ranging their guns and re-

The Problem of Imperial Defence

porting concentrations of the enemy, but they can protect our own communications and attack the enemy's as they did those of the Turkish Army during the final operations in Palestine, in 1918.

Offensive Power. Their offensive power, though local, is great. At Kabul, in May, 1920, the single attack of one machine caused extensive damages to the arsenal, which formed, however, a tactical objective not frequently met with in small wars. For attacks on villages and positions out of reach of the troops, they are the only means possible; further, they can frequently attack the economic resources of the enemy, his wells, coops and herds, and so, on occasion, force him to surrender.

Supply. I am of opinion, however, that the greatest of the many uses to which aircraft can be put in future small wars is that of supply work, which is, at present, the pivotal difficulty in these operations. At the siege of Kut and in the final advance on Aleppo supplies were sent by air. In the autumn of 1917, the German naval airship, L 59, loaded with supplies and so constructed that her frame and covering could be made use of by troops, sailed from Bulgaria to German East Africa and though, through an error, her journey was made in vain, she nevertheless covered a distance of 4,500 miles in 96 hours. Bearing in mind that an aeroplane carrying three tons can feed a battalion for one day and that an airship carrying 60 tons can feed a battalion for three weeks, the possibility of overcoming the age-long difficulty of supply in small wars becomes manifest, a difficulty which faces us to-day in a more acute form than it faced Alexander 2,300 years ago.

As in great wars, so in small wars, the chief hindrance to the full use of aircraft lies not in the difficulty flying machines experience in co-operating with the troops, but in the difficulty the troops experience in co-operating with aircraft. They can move swiftly and bomb fairly accurately, for rifle fire is, normally, the only anti-aircraft defence they have to meet. They can destroy wells and pipe-lines, and can cause local panics, but, as their crews can seldom occupy the positions attacked, their influence is transitory. Surely this is not the fault of the aeroplane but of the

200 The Reformation of War

soldier with his speed of two and a half miles an hour and fifteen miles a day. If he will abandon his legs and take to tracks he can move at an average speed of ten miles an hour and one hundred miles a day. In one day he will then accomplish what he can seldom now accomplish in ten days, and, by doing so, he will not only accentuate his own importance but he will enhance, out of all present recognition, the influence of aircraft on the problems of small wars.

Since piracy is, to all intents and purposes, a thing of the past, small wars are restricted to land operations except for guerilla warfare at sea, and possibly, in the future, in the air as well; nevertheless, opportunities in small wars will frequently arise in which the navy can assist the land and air forces. This will more particularly be the case when an amphibious tank has been produced, for then, as I have already shown in Chapter IX., ships will virtually be able to shoot armies onto the shore; consequently, tank-carrying vessels, which can steam at high speed, are likely to become recognized naval craft. As these tanks, when once on shore, will require aeroplane co-operation, both tactical and administrative, aeroplane-carrying vessels will also be needed. With these two types of ships and the war ships themselves, a fleet will become a completely self-contained fighting force capable of operating on and in the three elements of water, earth, or air. The possibilities of such a force, for the major police work of the Empire, need no accentuation, for they must be visible to all.

Still one more question confronts the navy, the type of vessel with which it intends to picket the seas and oceans. Hitherto, this all-important duty has been carried out by cruisers; but the naval operations of the Great War showed quite clearly that, though the few scattered German cruisers were able to do considerable damage to their enemy's shipping, their life was a short one, because the German High Sea Fleet could not support them. The war also showed, as I have already pointed out, that the only vessel which is able to dispense with fleet protection is the submarine; consequently, though cruisers may still be used for out-

The Problem of Imperial Defence

post duties, there can be little doubt that ocean-going submarines will, in many cases, be able to carry out this work more efficiently. I will now turn to the second main problem of this Chapter.

(ii.) *The Problem of Internal Security.* Peacemongers, who are ever crying loudly for universal and total disarmament, seldom if ever seem to realize that domestic peace is based on military force, and that the maintenance of domestic peace is a more important problem than that of foreign invasion. Disband the Home Army in England to-morrow, and either the police forces will have to be quintupled *and armed*, or, at any moment, a revolution may overthrow the government Revolutions have many causes, but the immediate cause of practically every revolution in the past has been weakness of military power to maintain law and order. It is for this reason that anarchists, communists and socialists are ever active in directing their energies towards disarmament or the socialization of military power, not because they hate war but because they loathe peace and know full well that if the watch-dog of the State is shot or poisoned, they will be free for a space to plunder, ravish and burn to their hearts' content. What they really desire is civil war, and if the reader does not believe me, then I can only suggest that he study the works of Weishaupt, Clootz, Babeuf, Fourier, Blanc, Proudhon, Marx, Bakunin and the present-day Bolshevists—a wilderness of howling blood-intoxicated gorillas.

The maintenance of law and order requires two forces, one mobile and one stable. The mobile force is represented by the police, who do not so much enforce the law as, through their uniforms, express it. They move everywhere, and, though little is said, they endow peace-lovers with a confidence in security and peace-haters with a fear of punishment. The stable force is the army, which, quite rightly, is little seen in public ; nevertheless, silently it stands behind the police ever ready to enforce the law when persuasion not to break it fails to impress the lawless.

The Reformation of War

The problem of internal security, as concerns the Empire, may be examined under two main headings.

(i.) The maintenance of law and order in civilized countries.
(ii.) The maintenance of law and order in undeveloped countries.

The maintenance of law and order is guaranteed by a state of peacefulness; consequently, when force has to be resorted to, *its object is to prevent violence, first, by the moral threat of its application*, and secondly, when this has proved useless, *by the least possible expenditure of violence compatible with the re-establishment of quietude*.

All social upheavals, such as riots, rebellions and revolutions, are at base psychological, they are like attacks of intermittent fever, they give little public notice of their advent and they prostrate a district rapidly and frequently are highly contagious. In all these disturbances, there are two main difficulties: first, their suppression normally demands bloodshed; and secondly, it is difficult to shed the blood of the rioters or rebels without shedding the blood of the innocent as well. Though in the past man has had no qualms as to killing alien enemies, he, in modern times, has shown the greatest concern, and quite rightly, in killing the most demented of brother citizens. So much so, that, through delaying the social cupping, society has on occasion succumbed through a rush of blood to the brain. The whole difficulty, it will be seen, is one of killing. First, is the dog mad, for otherwise I do not want to shoot him; secondly, if I fire, I shall probably hit the old lady on the other side of the street. But why kill, why shoot, why fire? Why not instead use common-sense? What then is the antidote?

The object of an antidote to revolution, according to the premises I have laid down, is the maintenance of law and order without bloodshed. To kill sick men is no cure, and it frequently exasperates the surviving relatives.

The Problem of Imperial Defence

The main requirements of the antidote lie in accomplishing the following acts without harm to the individuals concerned :

(i) The breaking up of crowds and revolutionary meetings.
(ii.) The stopping of riots and acts of violence.
(iii.) The protection of houses and public buildings.
(iv.) The isolation of areas infected by revolution.

The whole question of revolution must be looked upon as a social disease and not as an act of felony. Reason must, therefore, be exercised and not anger ; common-sense and not violence.

The means at our disposal must be sought for in the realms of chemical sciences and not in those of military law and musketry. Innocuous gases which anæsthetize crowds or temporarily blind them, cause them to sneeze violently, vomit, go to sleep, laugh irresistibly, or acutely irritate their abdominal regions, producing a violent though harmless distemper of the bowels, should be sought for by our chemists, who are far too prone to seek for lethal gases in place of those the effect of which is sedative, soporific, mirthful, or comic.

In thinking out a plan of action, the old methods of violence must be banished from our minds, for the employment of truncheons and rifles only leads to the loss of life among valuable though misguided citizens, and frequently among perfectly innocent people as well. Besides this, violence is apt to inflame a crowd and to glorify its disease in the eyes of affected and unaffected onlookers. Why, then, adopt so unintelligent a procedure when a little gas will produce, among the most truculent *sans-culottes*, so violent a distemper that they will not only be prevented from proceeding with their nefarious task, but that the onlookers, watching them at a safe distance, will be merrily amused by their contortions Ridicule is a potent weapon, and when coupled with acute colic, is apt to become irresistible. The *reductio ad absurdum* method, and not that of *lex talionis* is the more effective in dealing with revolutions as with many other dissatisfactions.

As to the methods which might be employed in order to carry out the above requirements, they are innumerable, and the following are merely examples of what might be done.

Crowds and seditious meetings, which are usually dispersed by some form of violence, might be broken up by a simple sneezing mixture. Men cannot talk and sneeze simultaneously, and unless they can talk a meeting loses its interest. Riots might be stopped by a colic gas or a local anæsthetic or some sedative mixture. Houses and public buildings could be protected by similar means, or by a laughing gas which would make a burglar the best of friends. Dissatisfied areas could be completely isolated by a strong lachrymatory solution sprinkled in the streets surrounding them by a tank, which would operate as a tear-producing water cart. Surely such a method as this is more economical and reasonable than a cordon of hundreds of police. Such, at least, are a few of the means which might be employed, and certainly they appear to me to be more common-sense than those which had to be resorted to in Sidney Street a few years ago, when a powerful force of police, a battalion of infantry and a battery of guns besieged a single house occupied by *three* desperadoes!

If the above suggestions are worthy of consideration, then steps should be taken to create an organization capable of putting them into execution immediately trouble arises. This is a very simple matter, once our chemists have agreed upon the means, for all that is necessary is to issue anti-riot appliances to every police and fire station, and to hold central reserves of these under military control in dissatisfied areas. The actual operators of colic gas, etc., should of course be provided with respirators, or otherwise they may be seriously affected before they have completed their patriotic task.

The first consideration which will strike the average Englishman, who is entirely wanting in imagination, is that his fellow countrymen will not tolerate gas because it is a Hunnish invention. Such a contention is not only untrue but absurd, for when social upheavals are viewed in the light of crowd

The Problem of Imperial Defence

diseases, surely it is no more Hunnish to draw, under the influence of gas, the fangs of a riot than it is to do so in the case of a patient sitting with ill-favoured teeth in the dental chair. Chloroform was discovered by an eminent Scotsman and not by a Hun. To shoot down a mob is like operating on a patient without an anæsthetic, and if the use of anæsthetics is considered humane in the case of individuals, it is only commonsense to apply them also to crowds temporarily affected with the fever of rebellion. Once this has been done, their leaders can be carefully extracted by a method guaranteed to be absolutely painless to the crowd itself, and the leaders are not only the teeth but the brains of every revolution.

Having now arrived at a system whereby the stability of domestic peace may be attained in the hubs of the Empire—the highly civilized centres and especially in England—I will move outwards towards its circumference. First, let the reader never forget that every British citizen, according to the ethics of British rule, has a right to live, even when temporarily demented, and consequently that law and order must be maintained and enforced by as bloodless a process as possible. To kill a man may destroy the ravages of disease, but it is no cure.

To-day the police-soldier is armed with weapons of war, and I consider that, so far as it is possible, he should be equipped with weapons which neither kill nor permanently injure—what he requires is a chemical "strait-jacket" he can clap on the offender. Is any Imperial benefit gained by shooting down several thousand Hindoos in Amritsar or Moplahs in Madras ? For the greater part of their lives these unfortunate victims were useful, law-abiding citizens ; for a few days or weeks they were demented maniacs. Dementia is not cured with the axe.

To-day the British police-army may be likened to a poor overworked country doctor who, possessing no carriage or car, is compelled to walk from patient to patient in order to tend them as best he can. On his feet he can manage to visit about twenty scattered patients in the course of a day, but in a motor-car he can visit forty, and, therefore, it would appear wise to provide him with one, for it will double his utility.

Our present problem of the maintenance of domestic tranquillity in undeveloped lands is identical with the problem of the above doctor. Law and order constitute the health of a people, unrest its disease. Those who judge and govern us are the specialists, and our soldiers are the general practitioners upon whose skill the social health ultimately depends. Sometimes the soldier is called upon to perform a surgical operation, sometimes to administer an anæsthetic, sometimes a pill, even a bread pill, for frequently social disturbances can be as easily cured by suggestion as bodily ones, for the origins of both, as often as not, are imaginary. Our difficulty is not one of skill but of distance, of time taken in our numerous and periodical visits, for, as the greater number of our patients are of barbarous predilections, they live in most inaccessible places.

To-day our lack of military mobility stands out in truly remarkable contrast against the present-day enormous powers of civil means of movement. Some day roads and railways will be built throughout the Empire, but only after the countries concerned are worthy of their construction. What then are we to do? We must maintain law and order so that stability of government may foster prosperity and contentment. We can do this either by maintaining an army of a million police-soldiers, costing several hundred million pounds yearly, which to-day means conscription and bankruptcy, or we can drastically reduce the army and motorize the remainder.

In the problem of domestic peace, it is again the tank which is the main factor in its solution. We may not be able to design a machine which will scale hill-tops, but why should we attempt to scale hill-tops if in an armoured box on tracks we can advance securely along the valleys, and when this progress is impossible, walking can always be resorted to. The doctor may, on occasion, have to leave his car at the garden gate and walk from there to the front door of his patient's house. Because of this his

The Problem of Imperial Defence

car is not rendered permanently useless; in internal security our problem is very similar.

And when he enters the house what does he do ? He hears that the patient is suffering from delirium tremens or Ghandiitis. Does he creep towards the bed and, when the maniac is not looking, hit him over the head with an axe ? On the contrary, he tries to pacify him, and, if necessary, straps the sick man down or injects a does of morphia, so that he may not injure himself and others. In fact, he tackles the case on the spot and uses common-sense.

Normally, the above work is carried out by a police force proper, that is a force which is *of* the people it controls, and which moves among them and which maintains a state of peacefulness more by organizing harmony and suggesting the folly of discord than by open or violent compulsion. The strength of a police force lies not in its armament but in the " human touch " it maintains with the people generally, both with those who conduct themselves peacefully and those who do not; in its social utility, its ubiquity and constant presence is its power based.

In its essential nature, military force is the antithesis of police force; consequently, when it is necessary to reinforce the police, it is equally necessary to reduce the soldier to the footing of an armed constable before employing him as a fighting man, and it must be remembered that a constable is not a fighting man but a man *who prevents others fighting* Like the Grecian heralds, the police do not apply the sword, but, when two swords are drawn, they strike them apart.

The question now arises, realizing what police work entails, is it possible for an air force to police a country, and if the answer is in the negative, then of what assistance is such a force to the existing police and military garrisons ?

To begin with, I believe that the very nature of aircraft is such as to preclude the first suggestion, because mankind lives on the earth and not in the air; consequently, in the air human-touch is lacking. For example, we really cannot say :

The Reformation of War

" Mosul is a turbulent city; very well then, send fifty bombing machines there and blot it out, obliterate it like Carthage—man, woman and child." We cannot do this, as it is really too easy to be practical; further, we cannot do it as we are no longer living in the days of Nebuchadnezzar or Ghengis Khan; and further still, because the British Empire has not been built upon obliteration but upon pacification. And yet, it is obliteration which air force officers are so frequently recommending. Thus a well-known Wing Commander writes:

> "One object must be selected—preferably the most inaccessible village of the most prominent tribe which it is desired to punish . . . the attack with bombs and machine guns must be relentless and unremitting and carried on continuously by day and night, on horses, inhabitants, crops and cattle."

In fact, an Assyrian scourge is to descend upon the land which completely puts to blush the German atrocities of 1914.

For unimaginative people it is so easy to be brutal in the air, for they are out of touch with the burning homesteads, the terror-stricken women and the maimed children below them. I do not believe that our airmen realize this, for otherwise they would not suggest it. Would the above eminent officer walk into an oriental harem and rip the women and children up with a kukri? He would not, and yet he suggests burning them alive or blowing them to pieces. Why does he do so? The answer is, because he talks like one in the air and not like one on the earth; he talks like an owl hooting over the city.

Is then the air force useless in maintaining law and order? Far from it, if it be used, as every police force should be used, namely, to pacify, and not to obliterate In the air it is a constant reminder that force can be applied, but I consider that it is not in this direction that its main usefulness is to be sought, but rather in its ability to transport political authorities to and from dissatisfied areas so that they may gain human-touch with the causes of dissatisfaction and nip them in the bud. An action, very similar to the one I here suggest, was carried out during the final stages of the recent Somaliland operations.

The Problem of Imperial Defence

Within forty-eight hours of the fall of the Mullah's stronghold, the Governor of Somaliland travelled three hundred miles in one day and visited the local chiefs, with the most satisfactory results. Had he been able to do so before the outbreak, it is quite conceivable that this particular small war might have been prevented. Further uses naturally suggest themselves, such as the transportation of small parties of policemen, the withdrawal of loyal subjects from dangerous areas, the observation of disturbed localities and the breaking up of hostile meetings by spraying the crowds below with non-lethal chemicals.

In the policing of the Empire the fleet can also play its part and an important one too, if certain minor changes are introduced. Ships in foreign stations are always " mobilized " for war, and, though they can bombard almost any stretch of coast-line at short notice, it is not through blowing towns and villages to atoms that law and order is maintained. The sailor's weakness in police work lies in the fact that he is not well equipped for land fighting. Armed with a rifle and bayonet and a few machine guns, when on land his great idea is to trundle about a funny little field-piece. The twelve-pounder has its values, but they are incomparably inferior to those of a small amphibious tank. All ships on outpost work should carry at least four of these machines; then, for police work, they can emit from them non-toxic chemicals, and for war work, if required, bullets and shells. Suppose that a rebellion threatening the lives of British citizens broke out at Hong-Kong and there were no troops there, the crew of our present-day cruiser could render small assistance on land, but, equipped with four tanks, it could make its presence felt, and felt in such a manner that the rebellion might well be quashed in a few hours.

To conclude, in the many sub-problems of the great problem of Imperial defence, the crucial factor is that " unity is strength." At present we have three separate defence forces and one objective. We have an army, a navy and an air force all striving to maintain the integrity of the Empire. Surely it is but a matter of common-sense to suggest that if, for purpose of direction and control, these three forces could be amalgamated into one force our many problems would be simplified. " Simplicity,' Napoleon once said, " is the soul of war." Unity is simplicity and triplicity is complexity ; consequently, "*Tria juncta in uno*" would appear to be the true objective of administrative reformation.

XI

THE MEANING OF GRAND STRATEGY

THE world as we know it is a conglomerate mass of relationships and not a mixture of absolute quantities; hence the impossibility of defining its terminals, which lie beyond the grasp of man's three dimensional mind. Without the conception of space, time becomes incomprehensible and *vice versa* Equally is good incomprehensible without evil, and so also is peace without war. Man cannot, in the absolute sense, destroy or create, for all that he can do is to work and think by analogy and evolve by integration

When we talk of abolishing war, we state an absurdity, for nothing can be abolished, and if man possessed so supernatural a power, the universal harmony, which is the balance between apparent opposites, would be destroyed, and the world as we know it would vanish. As well attempt to abolish the centrifugal force of a whirling planet and seek to maintain its centripetal energy as to maintain a state of peacefulness without war, for such a peace would surpass understanding.

The weakness of the human mind is due to the complexity of its surroundings. They are so mysterious that, in order to understand them at all, man thinks of things in compartments. Over the map of knowledge he draws dividing lines and says this is black and that is white. This procedure conventionally is useful, but it in no way permits us to imagine that we can destroy the absorption of light and maintain its reflection, without abolishing light itself. So with war, to maintain peace and abolish war is to destroy life.

The Reformation of War

In the preceding Chapters I have discussed in general terms a few of the phases of war, though it must be realized that its varieties are apparently infinite : Wars of mind, of thought, of instinct, of impulse, of sentiment, of words and of action, each possessing a dual motion, a forward one engendered by the differences of the extremes in its nature, and a recoil or backward movement resulting from friction between the forward movement and its surroundings This recoil, in its turn, possesses a reaction, and between action and reaction is begotten reformation, a digestion of opposites which absorbs what existing circumstances deem profitable and evacuates the dogmas of conditions which are dead.

The soldier does not only think of war as a compartment of human activity, but as a nest of pigeon-holes : strategy, tactics, organization, administration, etc , etc., each nest being crammed with pill-boxes—infantry tactics, cavalry tactics, artillery tactics, etc., etc. The danger underlying these uncorrelated values is to be sought in the temptation to invest them with individual, that is separate, existences, and then, when combined action is demanded, to produce a mixture of values in place of a compound.

This process of separation leads to a complete misunderstanding of the purpose of analysis, which should aim at separating components so that their differences may be harmonized and not merely arranged in various orders. By analysis we obtain facts, but it is not by mixing these but by an integration of them that we obtain harmony Two molecules of Hydrogen and one of Oxygen do not appear as water until they are combined, and though analysis enables us to discover the elements of water, synthesis alone enables us to unite these elements so that they form water, which, in nature, is totally different from Hydrogen or Oxygen.

With ideas and actions this synthesis is accomplished through the combustion of the intellect, which can produce a new " substance " out of a variety of old " substances " In Chapter II., I showed that there is a science of war possessing certain

The Meaning of Grand Strategy

elements and principles, and that this science is applicable to all forms of war, since war cannot exist without the elements of will, weapons, movement and protection. In that same Chapter I also showed that there is an art of war, and that this art is ever changing. I do not propose here to examine the changes which gas, tanks, aeroplanes, etc., will demand in this art; all I will state is that these changes must follow well definable lines, those of increased moral, increased hitting power, increased mobility and increased protection. I will leave it to the reader to equate the powers of a mechanical army with those of a muscular one; the changes consequent in the art of war will then become apparent. In place, I intend mounting as high as I am able the pinnacle of war and looking down upon its sides in order to gain universal perspective.

War may be compared to a pyramid possessing a base and three surfaces. Its base is represented by civil moral and resources, and its three surfaces, or sides, by the land, sea and air forces. Our great work is to build this pyramid.

In the past there existed a base and two sides, an oar-propelled navy and a leg-propelled army; then oars gave way to sails, and later on, sails to steam, and the edifice of war became a very ramshackle affair since the divergence between the two fighting sides grew to extremes. Then the air was conquered and a completed pyramid became possible.

To-day, when we attempt to join up an army, navy and air force, we arrive at a very complex and unstable organization, for the means of movement of each force is different. In place of these different means of movement—muscle, steam and petrol—I will suppose that these means are oil, petrol and petrol, then the differences will be considerably reduced. As man lives on land, I will call the three sides when built together a mechanical defence force, a force possessing no separate and distinct land, air and sea force, but a force resulting from the integration of these three. At the base of the pyramid these three forces are at their maximum divergence, at its apex they are completely united. Whether an apex will be reached I cannot say, the top of the

214 The Reformation of War

pyramid, for all I know, may be truncated; nevertheless, I will suppose that an apex does exist, then it follows that the nearer we approach this apex the more closely will the natures of the three forces coincide, until eventually they merge into one.

Whatever period of war we may examine, the base of this pyramid is, from its military aspect, the moral of the civil population and the commercial and industrial resources at their disposal. This base gives stability to the whole figure, it forms the fourth surface uniting the three above it. If we compare the three military surfaces to earth, water and air, then the civil will may be likened to fire, the extinguishment of which in war is the object of the three military elements. When these four elements are compounded, a fifth element emanates from the compound, the element of spirit or the national will to exist; it is the driving force of all warlike activities. During peace time this spirit is ever present, and though its nature, during war, does not change, the resistance offered to its progress is greater, and the relationship between this resistance and the will to win gives to any particular war its specific character.

During peace or war, our object is to conserve and control this spirit; consequently, we must understand the probable resistance to be met with, for otherwise we shall not be able to gauge the character of war, and not being able to gauge the character we shall not know what type of warfare will prove the most efficient and economical. This control and direction of the will to win and all the means whereby this will may be expressed I will call grand strategy.

Once we have obtained the differences between force and resistance we can evolve a plan of action; this is our grand tactics. The putting of this plan into motion is called strategy, of which there are two categories: major strategy, or the movement of masses outside the battlefield, and minor strategy, or the movement of units and individuals on it. From movement springs action or tactics, major tactics dealing with the actions of masses and minor tactics with those of units and individuals.

From the above it will be seen that there are no absolute

The Meaning of Grand Strategy

compartments of war in either the science or art of warfare. Analysis enables us to discover the elements of war, inference the principles of war, and observation the conditions of war. Synthesis compounds all these parts into one whole, and the nearer we arrive at a perfect compound the simpler becomes our task.

Preparation for war or against war, from the grand strategical aspect, is the main problem of peace, just as the accomplishment of peaceful prosperity is the main problem of war. I have already defined more than once what I mean by the objective in war, and I have shown that lessons learnt from the recent war would lead us to suppose that the main purpose of a fleet is in nature economic, the main purpose of an army military and the man purpose of an air force moral. Consequently, it stands to reason, even if the traditional theory of war prevail, that if, in the next great war, these three purposes can be brought to coincide in the objective, that is meet in a point, in place of, as heretofore, running on courses parallel to each other, the united strength of the defence forces will be enormously enhanced. There will then no longer be a naval campaign, a military campaign and possibly also an aerial campaign, all fought more or less independently of each other, but one single campaign, in which the various operations will be coincidental.

I have already examined the limitations of the three fighting forces and have shown that by mechanicalizing an army not only can the tactics of these three forces be more closely correlated but also their strategy, that is the interrelated movements between them. The question now arises, if in the art of war similarity of movement can be established and, consequently, its categories synchronized, is it equally feasible to unify military science and so develop one science of war which will be equally applicable to warfare on land, at sea and in the air. This may seem an irrelevant question to ask, since it is well known, or at least should be, that the principles of war are fundamental and, consequently, are applicable to all modes of warfare. In fact, however, it is not irrelevant, for, heretofore, the minor differences in the art of war, arising from the limitations and individual characteristics of the forces employed, have appeared so opposite in nature, that, during the last 400 years, a complete separation has arisen between the army and the navy, a separation which has produced innumerable complexities which, during the last ten years, have been further confounded by the introduction of a new mode of war—air warfare.

Though it is a truism to state that the basic factor in war is man, it is not generally recognized that whether man fights on the land, or on the sea, or in the air, the elements of war are the same, namely: moral, weapons, movement and protection; consequently, whatever mode of war is to be examined, in these elements we find a common denominator to all three forces. If this be accepted as correct, then I see no reason why warfare as a whole should not be treated as *one* subject.

Personally I am of opinion that the principles of war, enumerated in Chapter II., are as applicable to sea warfare and to air warfare as to land warfare, irrespective of the differences in the three spheres of action in which these three modes of warfare take place, the spheres of sea, air and land. The ultimate objective is the same, namely, the maintenance of policy. The two great means are the same—offensive and defensive action, whether material, physical, or moral. The methods of potentiating these means are identical—concentration and economy, movement and surprise, and the ultimate co-ordination is the same—co-operation within fleets, armies and air forces and co-operation between them as parts of one single defence force. It is this co-operation which, I consider, forms the foundation of grand tactics, not as heretofore interpreted—the major battle plan of an army, or of a navy, or of an air force, but of an army, a navy and an air force intimately co-operating in order to attain a common objective—the maintenance of policy.

In minor tactics, the one supreme problem which faces the fighting man, irrespective of the service to which he belongs, is, as I have already pointed out, " to give blows without receiving them." This I will call the compound of " secure hitting." In minor strategy the basic compound is " secure movement."

The Meaning of Grand Strategy

Upon these two compounds, which are derived from the three elements of war—weapons, movement and protection—is the whole art of battle founded, and according to their perfection is the remaining element, the moral of the fighting men, maintained. We thus see that, while the army, navy and air force are the protectors of the national moral, equally are weapons, movement and protection the shield of the moral of the fighting men. Ultimately, in war, the whole question of success may be whittled down to one of security of moral, which, of all the elements of war, is the most unstable, for a new weapon, a new means of movement, or a new method of protection, if introduced as a complete surprise, may effect a *déroute* among the staunchest of fighting forces.

To return to the compound of secure hitting, which forms the corner-stone of minor tactics, the question now arises : how is this hitting power to be applied ? In an army, navy, or air force individually, security of hitting demands a close co-operation of all arms in order to attain the grand tactical objective—the destruction of the enemy's fighting strength. When these forces are combined in one plan, then, to the above co-operation must be added a mutual co-operation between the three forces themselves. This co-operation, whether within one force or between two or three forces, is virtually the execution of the grand tactical plan of battle or campaign ; and it is important to remember that a plan is as necessary for a campaign as for a battle, and that, consequently, every battle plan must form an economic part of the general plan of campaign. In Chapter II., I have explained that in this plan there are four grand tactical acts which may be carried out either separately or in combination, namely, surprise, attrition, envelopment and penetration. Visibly these acts are equally applicable to all modes of warfare—sea, land, or air, and whether made use of separately or combined, these acts constitute the common denominator of the plan or idea of campaign.

The setting in motion of this plan is usually called strategy, that is the secure movement of troops to that point of decision at which it is hoped to defeat the enemy. In the past, in spite of the universal nature of the principles of war, there has been a land strategy, a sea strategy, and the future may possibly see added to these two, an air strategy. This process of separating strategy into three compartments I believe to be fundamentally uneconomical and a direct violation of the principle of economy of forces as applied to a united army, navy and air force, and hence a weakening of the principle of the objective. This separation is faulty, consequently I will now consider the strategy of all three forces as combined

The importance of grand strategy and all that it includes cannot be over-estimated at the present time, for in the whole course of history the necessity for economy has never been more vital; further, in its true meaning, efficiency cannot exist without it. At any time and irrespective of prosperity, a nation can only afford to spend a certain sum of money as an insurance against war and ultimately, when war occurs, as a safeguard against defeat For this sum to be economically spent, not only must all obsolescence be weeded out of the defence forces, but no overlapping can be tolerated. During war, nothing is so uneconomical as improvization; consequently, our peace strategy must formulate our war strategy, by which I mean that there cannot be two forms of strategy, one for peace and one for war, without wastage —moral, physical and material, when war breaks out. The first duty of the grand strategist is, therefore, to appreciate the commercial and financial position of his country; to discover what its resources and liabilities are. Secondly, he must understand the moral characteristics of his countrymen, their history, peculiarities, social customs and system of government, for all these quantities and qualities form the pillars of the military arch which it is his duty to construct. Unlike the strategist of the past, the grand strategist of to-day must no longer be a mere servant of his ever-changing government, but a student of the permanent characteristics and slowly changing institutions of the nation to which he belongs, and which he is called upon to secure against war and defeat. He must, in fact, be a learned historian and a far-seeing philosopher, as well as a skilful strategist and tactician. To-day such men are rare to come by, because

The Meaning of Grand Strategy

nations understand practically nothing of the science of war. Understanding nothing, there is no incentive without or within an army to produce a breed of strategists who may be classed as men of science. In this respect the Germans went further than all other nations, and, during the Great War, it was the firmness of their grand strategy which formed the foundation of their magnificent endurance.

The transmission of power in all its forms, in order to maintain policy, is the aim of grand strategy, its actual employment being the domain of grand tactics. While strategy is more particularly concerned with the movement of armed masses, grand strategy, including these movements, embraces the motive forces which lie behind them both—material and psychological. From the grand strategical point of view, it is just as important to realize the quality of the moral power of a nation, as the quantity of its man-power, or to establish moral communication by instituting a common thought—the will to win throughout the nation and the fighting services. The grand strategist we see is, consequently, also a politician and a diplomatist.

While, in times of peace, one of the main duties of the grand strategist is the movement of ideas and the accumulation of moral energies, his reserves for war, in times of war an equally important duty is economically to release these terrific forces, which constitute the true capital of the nation, so that in the form of a moral explosive they may impel forward, like projectiles, the fighting services. To do so economically he must be in possession of a plan of action, which cannot be outlined unless the powers of all foreign countries and their influence on his own are known, for otherwise he will not be in a position, grand tactically, to direct the forces at his disposal along the economic and military lines of least resistance leading towards the moral reserve of his antagonist, the bulk of which lies in the moral of the civil population. On his grand tactics, it is for his subordinates, under his guidance, to formulate the minor or battle tactics of the three fighting forces which will be used to attack the enemy's forces physically, economically and morally. Without a plan, none of these things can be economically accomplished; consequently, we see that, of all the principles of war, the principle of the objective is the first.

Paradoxical as it may seem, the resting time of the grand strategist is during war, for it is during peace that he works and labours. During peace time he not only calculates the resources in men, supplies and moral forces of all possible enemies, but, having weighed them, he, unsuspected by the enemy, undermines them by a plan. He attacks the enemy's man and weapon power by advising his government, (i.) to enter into alliance with other nations, (ii.) to limit his material resources by gaining actual or fiscal control over commodities the enemy's country cannot produce; and, according to their ethics, his government attacks the enemy morally either by fostering sedition in his country or by winning over the approval of the world by the integrity of its actions.

To war plans there can be no finality, for every nation is a potential enemy, and, as the policy of each nation changes, so must the plan change with it, and whatever the plan may be, the commercial and moral powers of the nation should not be squandered or degraded when it is put into force. Finally, the plan or plans having been agreed upon, the fighting forces should unitedly be trained to carry them out.

From the above, the reader will have gauged that the grand strategist is the unifier of military action in all its forms, and that, consequently, unity of command is the keystone of the military arch, which is supported on the civil abutments of prosperity and national character. For one man to carry out the multifarious duties of the grand strategist is manifestly impossible, but for more than one man to attempt to give direction to these duties, when combined in a plan of war, is manifestly absurd. Ultimately, however vast and stupendous are the forces to be employed, one man must direct them, just as the brain of man directs the far more intricate mechanism of the human body, and directs it so perfectly that the majority of its functions are unconscious. To attempt to direct an army by means of a council or committee is to seek order through anarchy. Many-headed

The Meaning of Grand Strategy

monsters cannot direct, and, like Cerberus or the Hydra, they fall victims to individual initiative.

Though in war, whether of hundreds or millions, whether of a united nation or of allied powers, whether solely on land or simultaneously on the sea and in the air, *one man must direct*. This in no way prohibits every able man in the country, if needs be, participating in the development of the plan.

Though, throughout this book, I have attempted in the main to examine the problems of the future tendencies of war from a general aspect, I now intend to examine national direction in war from the British standpoint, because I am better acquainted with this point of view than with any other, and have not the space at my disposal to inquire into the military organization of each nation in turn.

The present direction is as follows: The British Empire is virtually a commonwealth of free nations united ethically under a constitutional monarchy. At home its peoples are ruled by a representative government, which is directed by one man, the Prime Minister, assisted by a cabinet composed, for the most part, of heads of government departments. As this cabinet possesses no military member, it, at times, seeks strategical advice from the Committee of Imperial Defence, which, theoretically, can place before it three unco-ordinated military opinions—that of the army, navy and air force. These three forces have no directing head or heads, each being controlled by a council composed of heads of military, naval, or air force departments.

If we now turn from the purely British aspect of Imperial defence to that of the whole Empire, we shall find that no real system exists whereby defence can be co-ordinated in peace time and directed in war. The Committee of Imperial Defence cannot possibly accomplish this co-ordination since it is in no sense an Imperial committee, but merely a defence secretariat of the British Cabinet, and an indifferent one at that, since its members are politicians and are not even permanently appointed. In order to make good, to some extent, its lack of power, from time to time, in the past, Imperial Conferences have been assembled in London at which questions of defence have been discussed As these Conferences are in the main political assemblies, and as they only meet at several years' interval, they can scarcely be considered as a sufficient means of co-ordinating the security of the Empire ; further they offer no means whatever in directing Imperial strategy during war time.

In considering any system of reformation, the first fact to bear in mind is that the Dominions are free nations and, being young communities, are rightly very jealous of their independence ; secondly, that every Imperial war has not only accentuated this independence but has increased their military responsibilities. Their security is, consequently, becoming more and more their paramount political question ; nevertheless, this question can only be solved by a close yet free co-operation between them and the Mother Country. Our problem is, therefore, not one of amalgamation but of combination. We cannot possibly hope to create one Imperial defence force under British control, but what we can hope to do is to agree to a general reformation of each existing force so that, when war breaks out, each force may be, if necessary, like the pieces of a puzzle, rapidly fitted together to form one picture. In order that this may be accomplished, I suggest the following reformation .

- (i.) The creation of a permanent Imperial Council divided into three great departments
    - (a) An economic department to consider the resources, commerce, finance, trade and industry of the Empire as a whole.
    - (b) An ethical department to consider the psychology of the various Dominions, India and the Colonies, their customs, traditions and legislation.
    - (c) A defence department to consider the security of the Empire as a whole and to suggest the military policy for each part.

The Meaning of Grand Strategy

As this Imperial Council will represent a League of British Nations its powers can only be advisory, nevertheless its knowledge and prestige will be so great that each separate government in the Empire will be compelled not only to listen to its advice but to think twice before rejecting it.

As the problem before me is a military one, I will only consider the third of the above departments, which I will call the Imperial general staff. This staff should consist of a body of experts drawn from the defence forces of the whole Empire, and their duty should be to elaborate a policy of Imperial defence to fit the ethical and economic conditions as submitted to them by departments (a) and (b).

(ii.) The next problem is the execution of this policy. To-day, without considering the Colonies and the Mandatory territories, we have three separate defence forces at home and three in India, and each of the self-governing Dominions has three, though in come cases they are partially combined. Virtually the Empire possesses six armies, six navies and six air forces, or in the future will possess them. To co-ordinate and direct eighteen separate forces, all of which overlap, is indeed a complex problem. I suggest, therefore, that each government should establish one combined defence force under a Ministry of Defence and place this defence force under the direction of one man—a generalissimo or grand strategist who will carry out the policy of the Imperial general staff if this policy be accepted by his government.

(iii.) In order to assist the generalissimo in converting the policy into a grand strategical plan, I suggest the creation of a combined general staff, that is a staff the members of which are drawn from the army, navy and air force

(iv) In order that this plan may be put into rapid execution and its direction be controlled, I am of opinion that each army, navy and air force should come under the direct

The Reformation of War

orders of a commander-in-chief who will be in constant touch with the generalissimo.

(v.) In order to assist these commanders-in-chief, three general staffs should be established, the duty of which will be to work out, in accordance with the grand strategical plan, the grand tactical operations of their respective forces.

(vi.) Lastly, the establishment of a group of departments under each general staff is necessary in order to carry out the plans of the commander-in-chief and to administer to the needs of the services concerned.

I will now consider, as briefly as possible, first the political position of the grand strategist and, secondly, the main duties of a combined general staff, and, in the next Chapter, among other things, the organization and duties of the general staff of an army.

The grand strategist or generalissimo can either be placed under a minister of defence or he may become an ex-party war minister himself, his position in the cabinet not being affected by changes of government but by tenure of appointment, which, however, should be elastic enough to permit of an able man holding the appointment for a number of years, as von Moltke did in Germany, for rapid changes of appointment carry with them changes of administration.

As a cabinet minister, the generalissimo will be able to keep himself in close touch with the policy of the government. The main danger of such an appointment is that he may be persuaded to meddle with politics, but this could be guarded against by restricting his executive powers to military subjects alone. As a cabinet minister his object should be to understand the policy of the government rather than to influence it, so that he may be in a position to outline to the combined general staff the leading political factors which must inevitably influence national defence, for without this knowledge no true economy can be effected.

The Meaning of Grand Strategy

The combined general staff itself should consist of a chief supported by a small group of officers drawn from the army, navy and air force, the duty of this staff being to think and to plan. In order to assist it in its work, two departments, namely, an intelligence and a finance department should be established under it, as well as such routine departments as its duties may require. The intelligence department should be divided into a civil branch and a military branch · the first comprising legal, commercial, industrial and scientific sub-departments; and the second, military, naval, aeronautical and geographical sub-departments. The finance department should consist of costing and auditing branches for all three forces.

I do not propose here to enter into the detail of the internal organization of this office of national defence, but instead I will merely outline what I believe to be the main duties of the combined general staff and its subordinate departments.

The generalissimo will place before the combined general staff three quantities: the policy of the government, the sum of money voted by Parliament for the defence forces and the direction the military plan is to take in order to secure the policy by means of the money voted.

The combined general staff will then analyse the problems involved, obtaining all information required from the intelligence branch. From this information this staff will first evolve a grand strategical plan, then one or more grand tactical plans, and lastly a series of instructions based upon this work. These, on completion, will be handed over to the finance department to be costed, and will be modified if money is insufficient to meet them.

The grand strategical plan is the most important, for on it will depend the respective strengths of the army, navy and air force and their geographical distribution, in accordance with which the grand tactical plans will be formulated. Once agreed to, the various grand tactical plans, with the instructions appertaining to them, will be passed to the three commanders-in-chief, and, in order of priority, will be worked out in detail by their

226 The Reformation of War

general staffs, bulk sums of money being credited to the commanders-in-chief to pay for the maintenance of the troops, ships, etc., required to carry out the plans. Once the grand strategy of the Empire has been settled, the plan should yearly be amended according to any changes in policy or finance, and according to the innumerable changes in industry, commerce and science, at home and in foreign nations and armies ; all these changes being carefully codified by the intelligence department and notified to the combined general staff.

The bulk economy which would be effected by unifying all military effort and directing it towards the solution of one problem must be apparent to all who possess any knowledge of the internal friction, waste of time, effort and money of ministries. These great spending departments, through no fault of their own, are forced into mutual financial competition without reference to strategy ; consequently, enormous overlapping of effort takes place, such as in the provision of supplies, the acquisition of information and the training of personnel. This is largely due to a lack of unified direction, which is the foundation of all concentration of power, efficiency and economy. In the new organization proposed, all these great spending departments could be enormously reduced in size, and this reduction would not only mean a financial saving, but would result in an economy of time, and, consequently, would lead to a greater output of military efficiency ; for the smaller the human plant the quicker is the output of effort. It is for this reason that every efficient organization must ultimately be directed by one man.

The question now arises, how is this director—the generalissimo, who will possess an unchallenged power of " Yes " or " No," to be discovered. It is quite possible, even probable, that to-day in no single nation does such a man exist. Then the solution to this problem is that he must be created, just as the queen bee is developed from one of the humble workers of the hive. On mental food must he and his staff be reared, and this food must be provided at a War College of a type which to-day does not exist in any country ; for up to the present no country, however

The Meaning of Grand Strategy

military it may be, has evolved a science of war—a true science and not a collection of maxims, shibboleths and dogmas. If this is doubted, then let the student re-peruse the various Field Service Regulations of 1914 and ponder over the events of the Great War.

From this university of war, as years pass by, will be turned out a body of officers who are capable of understanding warfare as a whole, and from whom may be selected the future generalissimo—the grand strategist, the military director in peace, and its military dictator next time the nation is called upon to fight for its existence.

Napoleons are not born, Napoleons are manufactured from able men. Napoleon, possessing all the genius he did, would have been but a good general had he not simultaneously possessed liberty of action in order to direct his genius according to the necessities of war.

We want no Napoleons in peace time, no military controllers of the nation's policy; the nation must settle this itself, for it is, in the light of our present-day civilization, the right and might of the people to do so. But in war, when Cosmos is dethroned by Chaos, when whole nations grow demented, when the crowd mind sways the multitude,. a nation requires THE MAN, because a study of the history of war, from Cyrus to Marshal Foch, has proved to us, by many a bloody lesson, that the free untrammelled director in war is the dictator of victory.

Here then is an immense problem which faces the civilized world to-day—the problem of grand strategy, or the economy of military forces. Whether the last war is the last of wars, a condition which has never existed on earth, we cannot say for certain, but we can hazard that it is not. Supposing that this hazard be correct, is any great nation to-day, after the appalling lessons of the last war, a war which cost the world millions of dead and thousands of millions of money, and the gloomy repercussions of which surround us and are likely to continue surrounding us for half a century yet to come, merely going to slide back into the complacency of 1914 ? A year which has long become a military mummy, a thing dead and wound up in an archaic past. Should we not instead think big and bigger still, never being content with our thoughts, never being content with our theories or with our practices, ever weeding them through and costing their values in terms of grand strategy ? We should, for discontent with custom and prejudice is the quintessence of mental youth.

XII

THE REFORMATION OF THE ARMY

HAVING in the last Chapter fashioned a mould, rough though it be, wherein may be modelled the grand strategical brain of the combined defence forces, it is my intention, in the present Chapter, to attempt to fashion yet another mould wherein may be cast a new army. As a soldier, educated and trained solely for war on land, I realize that it would, under existing conditions, be considered an impertinence if I attempted to create a mould for the navy and air force as well. That I should be able to do so is too rational to be questioned; consequently, there can be little doubt that my deficiencies in this respect point to a serious lacuna in the existing scheme of military education.*

Granted a grand strategical brain, the first question which arises is the economical expenditure of its energy. Energy means action, and as misdirected action means loss of power, I will first make certain of the premises upon which I intend to base my military reformation.

The Great War of 1914-1918, as I hope I have clearly shown, opened a new epoch in military history, the epoch of scientific warfare, the two leading inventions being gas and tanks.

There can be no disputing it that this war proved

(i) That large conscript armies, based on muscle-power, have two fundamental defects: extreme vulnerability due to superficial area; extreme immobility due to bulk. The first necessitates the seeking of underground protection, which increases the

* In my opinion the reformation of the navy and air force can be carried out on approximately the same lines as laid down in this Chapter; consequently, a combination of certain training establishments, etc., is possible. This alone demands the establishment of a combined general staff to carry it out.

second, which is further accentuated by armies being tied down to roads and railways for their supply.

(ii.) That the petrol engine has not only reduced the human target by enabling few men to do what many were required for, and by enabling above-ground and mobile direct protection to be introduced (with the result that wastage of man-power is lessened), but that roads may be dispensed with and mobility of manœuvre and supply increased.

The fundamental fact to be deduced from these premises is that *mobility*, carrying with it enhanced offensive and defensive power, and not *numbers*, is the line of economic direction along which future preparation, that is the remodelling of the army, should proceed.

The object of the military forces of the Empire, as I have repeated again and again, is to secure Imperial stability, consequently the army must not be looked upon simply as a means of limiting the ravages of war, *but as an instrument which will prevent war occurring*

Based on this objective, the remodelling of the existing forces should create, within the limits of the money available, a military organization of the highest efficiency and with powers of efficient development along the economic line. Under existing conditions the purposes of the army, in order of precedence, are

(i) The maintenance of the integrity of the Empire from internal disruption.

(ii.) The security of the Empire from external policy and foreign invasion.

(iii.) The power of producing in a great war the most potent scientific weapon, within the limits of money, that it is possible to create.

The means at our disposal are our existing forces, which form a conglomerate and incoherent mass, not only of separate arms, but also of similar arms in various categories of efficiency. Our present army is a monster carrying with it all kinds of rudimentary organs and ever sprouting new horns.

To refashion this Hydra, rational military thought is required;

The Reformation of the Army

consequently, however perfect may be the grand strategical brain, the military spinal cord must also be efficient. I will now consider this sub-brain or ganglion

The most perfect organization which exists in this world is the body of man, at the summit of which is to be found a directing organ—the brains, securely ensconced in a bone box and kept warm by a mat of hair. In an army, this organ is represented by the commander (the deciding will) and his staff (the assisting faculties) Before the Great War, our general staff officers worked but did not think scientifically. They were slaves of the past in place of being masters of the future. Had the general staff, in 1913, been a true brain, they could not have argued for a whole year about the trajectory of a rifle and failed to equip infantry battalions with more than two machine guns * Had they thought deeply on the most important tactical problem in war " how to give blows without receiving them," we should have had tanks twenty or more years ago. Had they even been liberal in judgment and open-minded, they would not have paid such little consideration to so many of the new inventions the war eventually proved essential. The general staff were and, in many respects, still are monastic in mind. They accept dogmas which bear but an antiquated relationship to truth and repeat rituals which belong to a dead epoch. They do so not because they lack ability and brain-power, but because their ability and brain-power are swamped by routine and lack the direction of a commander-in-chief, a thinking head who, working under the generalissimo of the combined general staff, will be in a position to vivify the whole nervous system of the army.

Granted an efficient commander-in-chief, the next question which arises is : how should his staff be organized ?

What has it to administer ? An army ! An army, as I

---

* In the autumn of 1913, as a brigade machine-gun officer, I was so convinced that an increase in machine guns was necessary that I suggested officially that each battalion should be provided with eight, and that each infantry brigade should possess a company of eight guns I was informed that this was impossible as it would mean " a reduction in the number of bayonets."

have shown in Chapter II, is a compound of certain elements; therefore I will think in terms of these.

He and his staff must think in terms of men, protection, weapons and movement. This gives us four departments of the staff.

Department A (Men) to deal with recruiting, moral, discipline (rewards and punishments), health and mobilization.

Department B (Protection) to deal with housing, feeding, clothing, ammunition and lands.

Department C (Weapons) to deal with research, design, experiment, production and repairs.

Department D (Movement) to deal with the organization of road, rail, water, cross-country and air movement.

As protection is a tactical word, I will substitute for it "supply," and in this there is nothing illogical, supply being the stable, that is protective, base of all military organization.

As the elements have to be compounded before they become of practical value, and as this compound has to be paid for, to the above departments must be added two others:

Department E (Operations) to deal with intelligence, planning, organization and training.

Department F (Finance) to deal with costing, auditing and accounting.

Such are the six great departments of the staff, and, outwardly, they do not differ very much from the present Adjutant-General's, Quartermaster-General's, Master-General of the Ordnance's, General Staff and Financial Departments, except that a separate department for Movement has been added. Now I come to the keystone which is at present lacking in the military arch. All these branches of the staff are separate unities unless a co-ordinating body is placed over them. This body I will call the general staff, because it is general and not, as at present, special and particular; it should be placed under a chief general staff officer, the right-hand man of the commander-in-chief Before examining its duties, I will first outline the general organization of the departments of the staff which it controls.

The Reformation of the Army

Each department should be organized in three sections :

(i.) A thinking section.
(ii.) A liaison section.
(iii.) A routine section.

The thinking section should form the brains of its department, and, working on the orders of the general staff, should apply the policy (principles) received according to existing circumstances (conditions). The liaison section (senses) should watch the application of this policy, criticize the work of the army (muscles) and keep the thinking section alive to local and changing conditions. The routine section (nerves and system of circulation) should deal with all matters of routine, renovate and clear the whole department of waste products and constitute the channel of correspondence.

In order that logical thought may be established, each thinking section should be organized in three sub-sections :

(i.) A historical sub-section to draw deductions from the past.
(ii.) An economic sub-section to evaluate the present.
(iii.) A planning sub-section to shape these deductions and values to the future.

Now I will return to the general staff, which should be similarly organized. Its duties are to convert the policy received from the combined general staff into a military plan ; it, consequently, must be in the closest touch with the combined general staff, and, in order to co-ordinate and systematize its work, it must also be in close touch with the various thinking sections of the departments of the staff. It should look at the army as a whole and, when necessary, reduce the thought of the various thinking sections to book form for the instruction of the army. The present system of producing manuals written by specialists, soused in one idea, does not tend towards efficient co-operation between the arms, and is apt to lead to military pedantry and tactical bunions.

The Reformation of War

A question of the highest present importance is the organization of Department C, for it constitutes the weapon-producing department of the New Model Army. The personnel will have to be a mixture of civilians and soldiers, and these will have to work in the closest liaison with civil scientists. Besides the general organization outlined above, its creative duties should be subdivided as in the diagram.

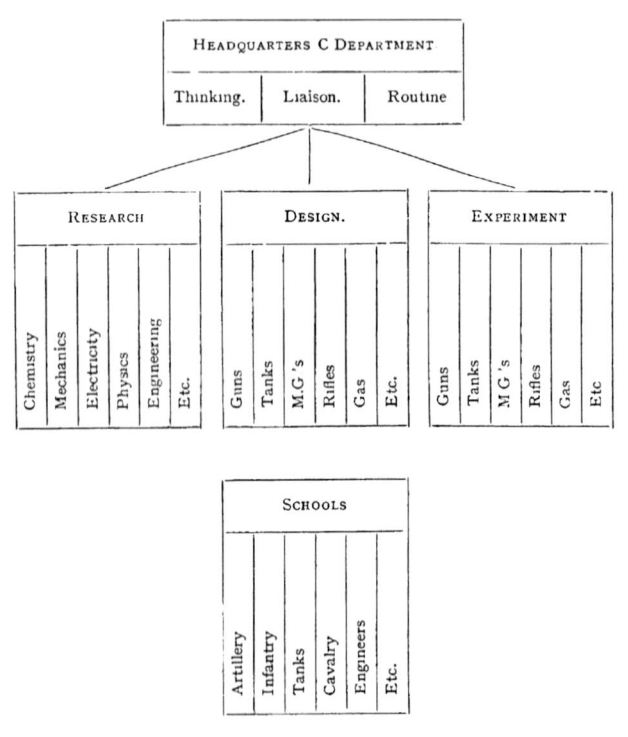

```
                    HEADQUARTERS C DEPARTMENT
                    Thinking. | Liaison. | Routine

    RESEARCH                    DESIGN.                    EXPERIMENT
Chemistry | Mechanics |    Guns | Tanks | M.G.'s |    Guns | Tanks | M G's |
Electricity | Physics |    Rifles | Gas | Etc.        Rifles | Gas | Etc.
Engineering | Etc.

                            SCHOOLS
            Artillery | Infantry | Tanks | Cavalry | Engineers | Etc.
```

The general scheme of its duties should be as follows.

Under its Headquarters should be established three sub-

The Reformation of the Army

departments—Research, Design and Experiment, which can either deal with their respective subjects directly or through civil firms. The research sub-department should be divided according to the sciences, and the remaining two according to the weapons, machines, etc., the army will require. For example, the general staff considers that a Mark X machine gun is needed. It forwards these requirements to Headquarters C Department, which consults Research, if research work is required, and eventually passes them on to Design. Design reduces these requirements to specifications and drawings and forwards these to Experiment. Experiment produces Mark X up to specification or refers it back to Design if it cannot do so. Once the new weapon is produced, the next step is to test it out, i.e., the weapon must be made "fool-proof" and "campaign worthy." Experts are too skilled to carry out this work, consequently, Mark X is sent to the school dealing with machine guns and put through exhaustive trials. This school reports on its suitability through Department E to the general staff, which accepts Mark X or refers it to Department C for improvement or alteration.

Though, in practice, the procedure cannot be so completely cut and dried as the above, and in many cases civil firms will have to carry out the work, the process outlined guarantees that all new weapons are attuned to the limitations of the private soldier and that their inter-relationship is co-ordinated, as they all originate from one brain—the general staff.

From the above it will be seen that the responsibilities of the general staff are considerable, and, in my own opinion, the type of officer required for this work scarcely exists to-day. In the past the general staff have dealt chiefly with military metaphysics, and if the nature of future warfare as outlined in this book is considered probable, then the general staff officer will have to deal very largely with military mechanics. He will have to study modern engineering journals and the old prints of hundreds of years ago depicting flame-projectors and gas bombs; these will set vibrating "brain-waves," which will awaken new design. He will have to study the evolution of weapons from the sarissa

236 The Reformation of War

to the aerial torpedo. In fact, he must become an adept in war-tool biology.

The present Staff Colleges do not permit of the training of such officers. In 1914 their teaching was, from the point of view of scientific warfare, antiquated. They were routine schools looking back on past wars, with scarcely a glance at the future. What is required is a total revision of their military outlook. They must be brought to visualize that the past is only a road to the future, that to-day the epoch of all former wars, an epoch based on muscular force, is rapidly closing down, and that a new epoch, based on mechanical energy, is rapidly opening up. Consequently, that, in a few years time, the army of 1914 will be as obsolete as the army of 1814 and far more expensive.

Unless we have commanders and staff officers who can grasp this and all that it portends, we, a generation hence, shall be fighting battles with an army of three-deckers in place of an army of battle cruisers; meanwhile the commercial loss will be appalling and our political stability the weathercock of every international breeze.

In order to establish a new creed of war we require a new military testament. I ask the reader to look back and examine our pre-war training manuals. What will he see? A tangle of valuable information wanting in logical reference or simplicity of relationship and dull beyond belief. On what central idea should the new testament of war be written? On the idea of men and not on that of weapons, for it is men who read books and not guns and rifles, and men, being living beings, require " live " books, not compendiums of uncompromising dullness and polished platitudes.

As regards men, as soldiers, there are four main types: commanders, leaders, led and administrators; consequently, the new testament of military knowledge must follow suit.

(i.) *Books for Commanders.* A manual on " The Science and Art of War," deduced from an analytical study of the

The Reformation of the Army

history of war, and a manual on " The Science and Art of Military Training," based on the principles laid down in the first manual.

(ii.) *Books for Leaders.* A manual on " Combined Tactics," and another on " Combined Training," based on the two former works for commanders.

(iii.) *Books for the Led.* On the general knowledge contained in " Combined Tactics" and " Combined Training," a " Battle and Training Manual " should be written for each arm.

(iv.) *Books for the Staff.* A manual on the " Economics of Administration " and another on the " Psychology of Administration." In these two books should be included all staff duties from those of an adjutant upwards.

The above list is not formidable, but once again it is quality and not quantity which is required—quality set forth logically and humanly, for man, being human, will not read dull books when instead he can read " live " newspapers.

Having now provided a mould for the remodelling of the spinal cord of the army, I will turn to the muscles of the new military organization. I have written enough to render it needless to prove again that the entire tendencies of military evolution are directed towards the replacement of muscle-power by machine-power. Mechanical movement, consequently, is our pivot of reformation.

This reformation must of necessity be a slow one and, before it can be begun, a period of experimental work will have to be undergone ; consequently, every army to-day requires a military laboratory, an experimental formation large enough to include all existing arms.

In 1803, through the wisdom of the Duke of York, an experimental brigade was established at Shorncliffe under the command of one of the most able and humane officers in the British Army —Major-General Sir John Moore. The work carried out at this camp had a stupendous influence on the Napoleonic wars, for

238   The Reformation of War

by degrees the tactics evolved were adopted by Wellington, and by means of these tactics did he beat the French wherever he met them. On the fifty-third anniversary of the battle of Waterloo, Colonel Gawler (52nd Light Infantry), who had seen in the field, between 1810 and 1815, the practical working of the Shorncliffe training, wrote to his son:

> "With this system (Sir John Moore's), the old Duke out-manœuvred every army opposed to him, and never lost a battle To the very end of the day (Waterloo), we manœuvred by well-formed battalions, as smoothly and as rapidly as we should have done on Southsea Common. While from the beginning of the day French *élan*, like soda water, had to be corked up in masses. The moment the density was rudely broken, all went off in smoke and confusion."[*]

To-day every civilized army requires such a brigade as Sir John Moore's, a military laboratory wherein to test the new against the old; but as a laboratory, however well equipped, is useless without a skilled chemist, so also is an experimental brigade useless without a John Moore. Further, as the chemist within certain financial limitations, must be given a free hand to carry out his experiments, and as he cannot do so if the whole of his appliances are changed at short intervals, so must the commander of the experimental brigade be given a free hand, and so also must his brigade be a permanent one, his men and means changing as little as possible.

Granted the above mechanism of research and granted that reformation is to pivot on the internal combustion engine, then the object of an experimental brigade is in nature a dual one:

(i.) To test out the existing organization.
(ii.) To test out the theories of cross-country movement.

This work will enable us:

(i.) To discover the tactical and administrative influences of the new arms on the old.

[*] "The Oxfordshire Light Infantry Chronicle," 1901, p. 162.

The Reformation of the Army

(ii) To work out the proportions of the new arms to the old.
(iii) To set together these proportions in a definite organization.
(iv.) To discover the time necessary wherein to train the new organization.
(v.) To enable us to estimate the cost of the new organization, not only in terms of money but in terms of increased efficiency.

In my opinion it is very necessary to separate idea from action, that is theory from practice, for idea should be the product of the study and not of the laboratory. Consequently, idea should be evolved outside the brigade, and, as ideas will affect the whole of the defence forces, they should of necessity be originated by the combined general staff. Once originated, ideas should, as far as the army is concerned, filter through three examining bodies First, the War College, where they will be considered from the aspect of the three defence forces combined; secondly, the Tactical University (which I will explain later), where they will theoretically be compared with the existing values of all arms separately and combined; thirdly, the Staff College, where the changes in tactics suggested will be organized and administration shaped to meet them. When these three processes have been completed, the refined idea should then be handed over to the experimental unit to test out, and the staff and students of the Staff College and Tactical University should be kept in close touch with the experiments—the action resulting. Directly the new idea has been satisfactorily tested out, it should be adopted by the general staff and the army modified accordingly.

As the whole existing military organization will have to be reformed, the work to be carried out is enormous; consequently, some logical plan of procedure must be established, for otherwise time and effort, let alone money, will be squandered. At what end or part of the army are we to begin our demolition and reconstruction? This question is a very easy one to answer if we write down the main needs of the soldier in order of importance They are :

(i.) The first requirement of the soldier is to live—he requires food and lodging.
(ii.) The second requirement is protection while he approaches the enemy.
(iii.) The third requirement is fighting power, in order to defeat the enemy.

We should, therefore, begin by mechanicalizing our transport. This is the simplest problem, being purely administrative and not tactical; meanwhile our existing artillery and infantry can remain much as they are.

Secondly, we should mechanicalize our artillery—our main protective weapon, and a simpler arm to deal with than infantry, who can still continue to remain somewhat as they are.

Thirdly, we should mechanicalize our infantry by placing some in tanks—the attackers of positions, and some in cross-country " buses "—the holders of positions.

Surely this evolution is an economical one, for we cannot expect our present army to adapt itself to a new means of movement in two or three years; in my opinion, accepting man as he is, a very conservative animal, the whole process will take about a military generation—say twenty years.

Having now arrived at a logical plan of action, the next question is the size of the army we wish to create. Hitherto the size of the army has borne little relationship to national needs, because defence policy has been built upon expedients and not on principles. Before the recent war, why did the Home Army consist of six divisions, why not four or five or seven or eight or eighty ? The late Field-Marshal Sir Henry Wilson was never tired of repeating that there was no military reason for six divisions—none ! In fact the reason had nothing to do with military requirements, for it was based on unemployment in the civil labour markets. Before the war it was found possible to recruit on an average 30,000 to 35,000 unemployed

The Reformation of the Army

or unemployable men yearly. Such numbers would enable six divisions at home to train reinforcements for a certain number of units abroad, consequently six divisions were considered sufficient. There was no military reason—none !

The Great War eventually required between seventy and eighty divisions. To suggest such a number to-day would be foolish, because we are not faced by a great war problem ; our problem is not to fight another World War but to maintain the integrity of the Empire. What does the maintenance of this integrity entail ? I will repeat the answer yet again :

(i.) First, domestic peace.
(ii.) Secondly, power to win small wars.
(iii.) Thirdly, power to prevent or win great wars.

I will, therefore, from the point of view of reformation deal with these three problems in turn

As I have already pointed out, the problem of internal defence is a fairly simple one, as rioters and rebels are usually badly armed. Police work presupposes the rapid movement of small bodies of men so armed that they can break up hostile assemblies, and, consequently, prevent them from solidifying into organized form ; for the first step, in order to quell a revolution, is to keep it fluid or mobile—in other words to deny it stability, without which it cannot for long exist.

The only satisfactory way to carry this out is to organize dispersion of force prior to the emergency, and this is best accomplished by establishing over the country in question a series of police posts which are sufficiently stable to withstand attack and sufficiently mobile to assist each other.

Having no firm precedent to work on, I will start with a theoretical example I will take an area of country six hundred miles long and three hundred miles wide which is in a disturbed condition, and will then ask myself this question : " What will be the most economical and efficient method of policing it ? " To begin with I will split this rectangle up into two primary squares, A B E F and B C D E, and each of these squares into four

242   The Reformation of War

major squares and each major square into four minor squares ; each minor square will then have a side of seventy-five miles.

In the centre of each minor square I place a mobile group, shown by a black dot, or I run two or four minor squares together and place a dot in their centre. At K and M, I place a stable reserve, shown by a small square. In order to arrive at some basis of calculation, I suggest a force of fifty mounted men as sufficient to patrol each minor square, and for a rectangle twice this number, and for a square four times the size of the minor square (e.g. square n r s o) four times this number. It then will

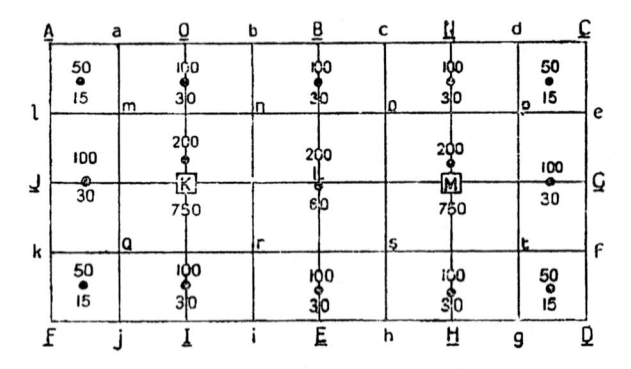

be found that the whole area A C D F is divided into three rectilineal figures, namely A C e l, l e f k and k f D F. These figures contain the following mobile forces : 400, 800 and 400 mounted men, which in principle is sound, because this organization permits of a strong backbone of police running through the centre of the country.

The above comprises the mobile element, but as mobility should always operate from stability, I will add two armoured cars (crews 15 men), preferably of a cross-country type, to every 50 mounted men. This will enable these men to be supported by 48 armoured cars.

At K and M, I place two mechanical striking forces, the

The Reformation of the Army 243

object of which is to supply stability to the mobile outpost organization These forces I suggest should be organized as follows :

- (i.) One company of tanks—12 machines, 140 personnel.
- (ii.) One company of armoured cars—12 machines, 140 personnel.
- (iii.) One battery of mechanical gun carriers—6 guns, 90 personnel.
- (iv) One flight of aeroplanes, 6 machines, 80 personnel.
- (v.) One company of cross-country tractors, 12 machines, 80 personnel.
- (vi.) One machine-gun company, 12 guns, 100 personnel.
- (vii.) Signallers and sappers—120 personnel.

The total fighting personnel will then be 750.

The combatant personnel of the entire police force will then consist of the following :

- (a) 1,600 mounted men.
- (b) 1,860 mechanical troops.

The latter being equipped with 24 tanks, 72 armoured cars, 12 field guns, 12 aeroplanes, 24 cross-country tractors and 24 machine guns.

In normal conditions, the mechanical columns will remain stationary, and the whole of the area A C D F will be patrolled by the mounted men. Should rebellion break out, which any one or more of the mobile groups is unable to suppress, these would at once stabilize themselves in their defended posts and the mechanical columns would move out and become the mobile element of the police organization. As the rebels are unlikely to possess weapons which will impede the movement of these armoured forces, their effect should prove decisive.

I fully realize that, in practice, the policing of an unsettled country is not so simple as depicted above ; that countries are not rectangles, and that forces of men cannot sit in the middle of hypothetical squares. Nevertheless, I now intend

244 The Reformation of War

to apply my theory to the actual problem of Imperial security in order to show that the principle of movement underlying it is, as I believe, sound. If I am right, the adjustment of detail to local circumstances becomes simply a matter of elementary common-sense. As a datum point I will start with India, for the security of India is our greatest military liability.

In 1913 the garrison of India was approximately as follows :

(i.) 76,000 British troops
(ii.) 160,000 Indian troops (less reserves).
(iii.) 21,000 Imperial Service troops.
(iv.) 39,000 Volunteers.

In all some 300,000 men, of which the British and Indian Armies cost about £21,000,000 yearly.

I will suppose that a tank exists which has a speed of 20 miles per hour on the flat, a radius of action of 400 miles, and that it will run 3,000 miles before requiring to be overhauled.

India consists of some 1,800,000 square miles of land, of which about 400,000 square miles may be deducted as sparsely inhabited mountain and desert country. I will now apply my grid theory, and divide 1,400,000 miles of country into squares of the side of 300 miles. The quotient is approximately 16. I will call the forces required to hold each of these squares—a mounted regiment (800 men) and a mechanical battalion (930 men), then for police work we shall require 16 regiments and 16 battalions It should be noted here that I am treating India as a thoroughly unsettled country and so am assuming the worst case possible

The next question is what is to happen if a small war breaks out ? As it would be dangerous to withdraw the police force, a central reserve must be established to meet such an eventuality. The strength of this reserve army, I suggest, should be sixteen mechanical units of say 930 strong each, these to be equipped with the three main types of tanks which, in Chapter VIII , I visualized future warfare would demand, namely, an artillery tank, an infantry tank and a cavalry tank. As these units are

The Reformation of the Army

not generally suitable for garrison work or for all phases of mountain warfare, a second line army must be maintained. For this I suggest a force of four divisions of about 12,000 men each. I will call this force the Garrison Army in order to distinguish it from the Mechanical Army, the units of which might be organized as follows: One regiment to consist of two battalions, one brigade of two regiments and one division of two brigades. The strength of a mechanical division will then be 7,440 men. For purposes of administration I will add forty per cent. to the total combatant strength.

The military forces required in India will then be:

(i.) 16 mounted police regiments (12,800 British and Indian).
(ii.) 2 mechanical police divisions (14,880 British).
(iii.) 2 mechanical reserve divisions (14,880 British).
(iv.) 4 garrison divisions (48,000 British and Indian).
(v.) Administrative personnel (36,224 British and Indian).

A total of 126,784 British and Indian soldiers, and not 236,000, as was the case in 1913.

Outside India our main military responsibilities lie in Iraq and Egypt; one mechanical police division and eight mounted police regiments should be sufficient for these countries, and, if a small war breaks out and reinforcements are required, they can be sent out either from India or from home.

The last question is that of a great war. Great wars do not suddenly shake the world like an earthquake; they occur about once every fifty years and normally give a prolonged notice of their advent. In preparing to meet them we require three things.

(i.) A body of men who can appreciate their growth and predict the probable date of their outbreak.
(ii.) A thoroughly good foundation whereon to expand our defence forces when the above body of men issue their warning.
(iii.) Power of the most rapid expansion when the warning is issued.

As regards the first, this is the duty of the generalissimo and the combined general staff. The second and third I will now consider.

As the foundation I suggest the following force :

(i.) 5 mechanical reserve divisions (37,200 men).
(ii.) 3 garrison divisions (36,000 men).
(iii.) Administrative personnel (29,280 men).

A total force of 102,480 men. The garrison divisions should be so organized and trained that they can rapidly expand into nine mechanical reserve divisions ; consequently, they should be partly mechanicalized during peace time.

If the self-governing Dominions also mechanicalize part of their military forces, there would appear to be no reason why Canada should not raise two divisions (one possibly in cadre), Australia one, and New Zealand and South Africa one between them.

For a great war we then arrive at a total of twenty mechanical reserve divisions the power of which when compared to that of existing divisions can only be thought of in terms of Dreadnoughts and three-deckers.

The above suggestions are admittedly crude. I have not aimed at exactness in any form, but solely at illustrating a principle of reformation—a foundation and a line of direction ; that is all. I will now turn to my third requirement, power of expansion to frustrate or limit a great war.

In the past, power of expansion has been viewed almost entirely from a physical and numerical standpoint—reserves of men and matériel. This is, however, but one aspect of the subject and not the chief one. Preparation to be scientific, in my opinion, includes the following :

(1.) *Military foresight.* To any student of European history between the years 1864 and 1914, it must be apparent that Germany was organizing herself to upset the balance of world power, and that all the causes of the recent war were sown prior to the year 1900 ; further, that, between 1901 and 1914, pretexts to declare war were constantly sought for by Germany. In England,

The Reformation of the Army

Lord Roberts and others saw this quite clearly; yet as late as 1912, when this eminent soldier proposed the creation of a national army, he was openly flouted by the general staff.* Worse still, he was derided in the House of Commons, and still worse, when, in 1912, Lord Haldane visited Berlin at the request of the Kaiser, "the Kaiser demanded a free hand for European conquests at the price of a friendly understanding with England. England was asked to pledge herself to absolute neutrality in the event of Germany being engaged in a war." On his return what did he do? In place of taking the nation into his confidence, he hoodwinked the people, who only learnt the truth of the situation in 1912 shortly after the battle of the Marne in 1914!

I maintain that these things must never be again, for unpreparedness for war is a greater incentive to its outbreak than over-preparation. Had we had, let us suppose, in 1908, a highly trained combined general staff and a generalissimo of moral courage, I imagine this is what he would have suggested to the Prime Minister: "The balance of power is being upset because Germany is adding to her immense army a formidable fleet, and any nation which controls the sea as well as the land controls the world. We rightly have not introduced conscription, for had we done so the identical accusation I am now levelling against Germany would have been levelled against us. Nevertheless, the situation is becoming so critical that, in my opinion, you should take the nation into your confidence and then say to Germany: 'We have tolerated your immense army long enough; we do not, however, intend to tolerate an immense German navy as well, for we know that this must lead to a world war. We do not want a world war, and, to prevent its outbreak or to shorten its duration, we intend, while we are still strong enough at sea to drive you off it and to occupy your colonies and capture your trade, not only to lay down two keels to every one of yours, but to raise an army of 1,000,000 men and to support whatever

* See "Our Requirements for Home Defence," *The Army Review*, Vol. III., July, 1912.

country you attack. But directly you reduce your fleet to its 1900 footing and cease increasing your army we will reduce our army of 1,000,000 to its present numerical strength.' "

Such a jaw blow might have led to immediate war, which could scarcely have been worse than the war of 1914-1918. It might, however, have knocked the German project out of the German head. But, it may be urged, our party political system does not permit of such frank action , then all I can say is that our political system needs a thorough spring cleaning. The outbreak of the Great War, in 1914, was due not only to German militarism *but to British pacifism.* Both were *equally* to blame, one was flint and the other was steel.

(ii.) *National Registration* The whole of the civil population should be registered for war according to their vocations, so that when war breaks out a man who knows eleven languages is not sent to St. Nazaire as a R.T.O. and a professor of English history turned into a sanitary fatigue man. Each class should have its mobilization centre and should come on to war pay on the outbreak of hostilities

(iii) *Calculation of Resources.* The entire resources of the Empire should be scheduled for war, so that it may be known exactly what these resources are and how deficits may be made good, not only in order to assist military operations but to lessen the unhinging of industry and commerce.

(iv.) *Standardization of Factories.* All factories, laboratories, etc , should, within the limits of peace economy, be standardized for war, so that, when war breaks out, they can easily be changed from a peace footing to a war footing. The same process should also be applied to means of movement by road, rail, sea and canal.

The above I consider to be the main national preparations for war, and in order to guarantee expansion of national force before and after war has been declared. I will now turn to what I believe to be the primary military preparative, namely, training, and the power of accelerating training when war becomes imminent or after its outbreak.

The Reformation of the Army

Training in an army may be divided into two main categories :

(i.) Unit training (the training of individuals and units).
(ii.) School instruction (the education of instructors).

The first should be based on the following rule : *No individual, once he has finished his individual training, should be considered fully trained until he can take the place of his immediate superior.* Thus in a section of eight infantry men, there is one section commander and seven followers. This section should not be considered trained until the section commander can command a platoon and each of the seven men can command a section. To the private soldier, thinking of the future is thinking of the next grade. With a unit it is very much the same , no unit should be considered fully trained until it can co-operate with all other units in the formation to which it belongs. This rule carries with it the main power of military expansion, for every officer and man right down to the private soldier will, when expansion is ordered, be in the position to fill a grade above the one he actually holds and instruct the grade below the one to which he is promoted.

The second should strive at the attainment of the following objective : the object of school instruction is first, to teach men *how to teach men*, and secondly, to teach men what to teach men. Every school, no matter what subject is taught in it, should pay the greatest attention to human psychology

I have already accentuated the vital importance of the creation of a War College and a reformation of the Staff College. I now will consider, not all necessary schools, but the co-ordination of one large group of schools—the weapon schools.

In most armies a separate school exists for instruction in each weapon or branch of the service. Thus we find . Rifle, Machine Gun, Cavalry, Field Gun, Gas and Sapper Schools, etc. This is as it should be, as it enables the technique of each arm to be acquired, but it is not sufficient, as technique is subordinate to tactics, and the various parts of an army—infantry, cavalry, artillery, etc., seldom fight as separated units. In order to co-ordinate the instruction gained in the Weapon Schools, a Tactical University is required, the duty of which is to set together the elements of war in a coherent tactical scheme. Dealing with men as well as with weapons, movement and protection, in it must be taught the *psychology of leadership* as well as the mechanism of tactics and the organization of contentment To-day such a school does not exist in any army, which fact only accentuates its importance.

I have now dealt with the reformation of the brain and body of the army, and, in the remaining pages of this Chapter, I intend, very briefly, to consider the reformation of its soul, which, curious as it may seem, is very closely related to money—the sinews of administration

Economically, management revolves between two poles—centralization and decentralization. The one cannot exist without the other, but, in non-competitive organizations, the first is always apt to become obese. I have already, in Chapter III., dealt with the organization of government departments, and have shown that ministries are virtually monasteries in which the law of the survival of the fittest ceasing to operate results in the creation of a body of administrators who, having lost all human touch, have become soulless shells of men.

The following are, I believe, the main causes of this spiritual decrepitude :

(i) *Lack of an economic objective.* The economic objective of army administration is to transmute money into military efficiency and not to spend money according to regulations which may be totally inapplicable to existing circumstances. This is common-sense ; nevertheless our present Treasury System (last reformed in 1689) seldom enables this virtue to be exercised.

To the soldier, there can be no doubt that the duty of a battalion commander is to obtain in his battalion the highest possible standard of fighting efficiency. I will suppose that this efficiency is represented by a, b, c, d, . . . n ; that " a " is musketry, " b " bayonet fighting, " c " recreation and " d " physical health.

The Reformation of the Army

Suppose now that the central management has laid down that £100 is allotted for training in musketry; but, as it happens, this battalion does not require it for musketry, being highly efficient in this subject, and, the battalion being quartered in the centre of a large town, its commander would like to expend this money on the hire of a neighbouring field, which will enable him to train his men in bayonet fighting, for which he has no facilities, and, incidentally, will enable them to play football every afternoon. Should permission be granted to him, not only will his men become more efficient but more physically fit and more contented, all very valuable assets. But, alas! as every soldier knows, it is very seldom granted, because, if a battalion costs, I will suppose, £200,000 a year, this sum is divided up into " watertight " compartments ; so much for food, so much for pay, so much for clothing, so much for musketry, etc., etc. In fact the object of finance is not to obtain the maximum efficiency at a minimum cost, but the maximum observation of routine regulations out of a fixed sum of money. Such a procedure can bear no relationship to changing circumstances, consequently it is contrary to common-sense, and not only destroys the desire to attain efficiency but stimulates dishonesty if this desire refuses to die.

Suppose now, for example, that a complete decentralization be agreed to and that the whole of the £200,000 be handed over to the battalion commander, and that a standard of efficiency be laid down for all objects of expenditure, and that, directly any one standard is attained, any surplus money be allocated to assist in the attainment of the remainder, and that at the completion of each year a comparative table be made out for all units in the army showing :

(a) The standard of efficiency reached.
(b) The expenditure in attaining this efficiency.
(c) The balance of money left over after attaining it.

Then it will be possible to see at a glance which are the most economical battalions and who are the most efficient commanders, and according to their degree of efficiency should they be rewarded by promotion or extra pay, and according to their degree of failure either dismissed or their pay reduced.

By this system the unit commander would control his own accounts, and the present accountants and auditors would cease to be the *dictators* of his accounts.

I fully realize that so complete a decentralization cannot and should not be attempted; nevertheless, steps should be taken as far as it is possible, and certainly as regards training, to decentralize the present soul-destroying system. Some cases of individual dishonesty may result (as they do to-day), but I doubt whether any dishonesty could possibly be as expensive as the safeguardings of the present Treasury restrictions, for corruption is not safeguarded against by refusing to declare a dividend—efficiency, but by a constant inspection of the executive (human not paper) side of the business.

(ii.) *Lack of application of economic principles.* I do not here propose to enter into an analysis of the principles of " supply and demand," " profit and loss " and the law of " decreasing returns," but in place to lay down four economic principles which are not observed by the financial management of the army. They are as follows:

(a) The balancing of accounts is not in itself equivalent to efficiency in training.*

(b) Training, to be economical, depends on the acceptance of a policy which will influence with the least detriment commercial prosperity.

(c) The cost of an army can only be considered economical when the army attains a higher efficiency than the depreciation of capital consequent on its attainment.†

(d) Unremunerative expenditure by decreasing the value of a soldier as a citizen is as grave an injustice to the nation as in-

* Conversely, if efficiency in training does not result, however carefully the accounts may have been balanced, the money spent will have been squandered.

† I e, as the civil capital value of a soldier may be taken at £6,000 and his yearly depreciation at £300, his military efficiency must be worth to the nation more than £300 a year.

The Reformation of the Army

adequate expenditure which reduces his capacity as a fighting man.*

The non-observance of these principles by the army, on account of the existing Treasury restrictions, results in a yearly wastage of many millions of pounds, let alone an incalculable loss of efficiency.

(iii.) *Lack of appreciation of economic conditions.* In economics, as in war, conditions either assist or resist the economist, who, consequently, must possess dynamic force, that is—POWER TO CHANGE. The struggle for existence applies to him as to all other human activities; it constitutes an impeccable sorting machine, for without competition there can be no economic growth. To vegetate is not to economize, and yet this is precisely what most armies in the past have done; they have, in fact, remained static absorbers of money—bun-swallowing bears which, when well caged by Treasury restrictions, are kept to amuse the populace. There is as much difference between a growing army and a subsisting army as there is between a growing tree and a branch in a jug of water.

Sir John Keane writes " The manager of a department in a business is given a free hand and judged by results. If the results are bad, he probably gets the sack; if good, he is probably promoted. But the essential point is that power for good or bad lies with the individual."† In an over-centralized organization what do we find ? We find that the permanent officials are tied down to fixed rules and regulations, and that the executive personnel administered by them are tied down by these officials, whose rules and regulations, normally, bear not the faintest relationship to existing requirements, their utility having years before grown impotent.

In order to amend these " Chinese writings " the conditions of military management must be placed on a level with those to be

---

* I have adapted the above principles from a paper on " Military Economics " written by my friend Brigadier-General W G Ramsey Fairfax, D S O

† " Government Extravagance and its Remedy," *National Review,* July, 1920 Also see " The Zealots," by the same author.

found in any well-conducted business. The object must be laid down as well as the requirements requisite to attain it, and then, as Sir John Keane says :

" . . . the Treasury should fix the sum and the executive officers should decide how it is to be spent. Those who know the facts must be allowed a free hand. Those who do not know the facts, like the Treasury, and try to control in detail, will be humbugged every time. . . In business a proper system of cost accounts enables an employee to be placed in a position of responsibility with sufficient working capital, and to be judged by results "

Military efficiency, I maintain, can be evolved just as readily as its counterpart in business, if an army is endowed with a soul, and souls are born of responsibility—*free will*, and thrive through judgment—*free criticism*. To be predestined to do something is to be damned, and the damned go down to hell or to Aldershot.

I am not such a purblind pedant as to believe that the system of reformation outlined in this chapter should forthwith be adopted. Though a system, it is but an illustration of an idea, and for this idea, this acorn of thought, to sprout into an oak and grow will require years of careful thought, and before this thought can develop prejudice in things old must cease.

To-day the British Army may be compared to the owner of a stately Jacobean mansion who cannot afford to keep it in repair. It has been in his family for 300 years, and he naturally is very loath to part with it and inhabit some horrible ferro-concrete house. He cannot afford to modernize it, and, to make both ends meet, he shuts up room after room, and so " economizes " his reduced income and hopes for better times. He cannot tear himself away from its memories and traditions and family ghosts, and so the dry-rot creeps through its foundations and the rain percolates through its roof.

The passing of grandeur is always a sad sight, but what is a sadder sight still is to watch those who once were grand imagining that they can continue to be so in decrepitude. Houses are made for men and not men for houses, so also are armies created

The Reformation of the Army

to protect nations and not nations to maintain obsolete armies. Yet it is the nation which must pay for the building of the new military house, and as long as this habitation is not built the nation must not complain if its army continues to shelter itself in its tumble-down old mansion. To camp in the open, these troublesome times, is sheer folly. To build means money. What the army to-day requires, in order that military economies may be effected, is a sum of money—I will suppose £50,000,000 as a loan, and then a fixed allowance of, I will suppose, a similar sum for the next ten years. Out of this allowance, or budget, it should pay a yearly interest on the loan of five per cent. and pay back £5,000,000 at the end of each financial year. To-day, this is impossible, as the Treasury System does not permit of it; further, possessing no combined general staff, a thinking organ, no architect exists who can plan the new residence. Instead, economy is sought by each year strapping the army on to the financial operating table, and by removing bits of its arms, legs and internal organs. The result is that the army is in a perpetual state of convalescence; one day its crippled remains may be allowed to hobble along on two sticks, and this is called economizing! If economy it be, then surely must Bedlam be the Adytum of economics. Would it not be wiser to cry with King John: " Bedlam have done ! "

XIII

THE PEACE WHICH PASSETH UNDERSTANDING

IN the last two Chapters I outlined the main features of an organization which, I am of opinion, can produce the scientific military thinker, without whom warfare must continue to flounder through traditional darkness. As from the alchemist of the Middle Ages arose the chemist of to-day, so do I believe that, from the swashbuckler of the present period will arise the war-scientist of the future, who, understanding war and its purpose, will liberate the armies of civilized powers from the obsessions of bloodshed and destruction.

I have shown that the grand strategist and his combined general staff must, in order to secure policy, understand policy. To understand policy there must be a policy, and in this Chapter it is my intention to examine the machinery which produces policy, a machine which has fallen into such disrepair that, unless the theory of traditional politics is changed, there can be little hope of any radical change in the theory of traditional warfare. In order to remedy this political machine, it is necessary to understand its nature, and, as it is essentially a human machine, I, in this last Chapter, will turn back to the first, in which I examined the forces which control all human actions.

In Chapter I., I pointed out that collectivism suppresses individualism and does not express it, and that, as suppression increases, the more eagerly does the individual seek to express his individuality in the free and untrammelled exercise of the hunting spirit. I will now examine this statement from its political aspect.

Man desires rest, physical and mental, but this ideal is denied

The Peace which Passeth Understanding 257

to him, for, in order to live, he has to struggle. Further, though he desires restfulness, he fears the absolute state of rest typified in death. He is in every way a discontented animal, and the degree of his discontent, his incessant search after some unobtainable solvent, is the measure of his physical and mental virility His instinct of self-preservation, fear of death, urges him to hunt for food. In the woman, the instinct of racial-preservation urges her to mate, that is, to form with man a co-operative association which, as the family arises, establishes among human kind a purely natural form of communism. A new spirit is thus evolved and a much more tangible one, it is the spirit of the family, the restful home after hunting, and the only practical solvent man is likely to discover on earth. From the family springs creative society, that is, a community of individuals who evolve through self-sacrifice and mutual support. The simple hunting spirit has now grown into a complex, a hunt after codes and laws, ideals, morals, ethics and knowledge, which stabilize the community in a state of internal restfulness. Yet, without discontent, that haunting spirit of change, inherent in the law of survival, the community cannot for long endure.

From the family, eventually, evolves the nation, the head and councillors of which constitute its masculine and the people its feminine elements. Imbued with the hunting spirit, the king or chieftain aims, through his own activities, to produce a condition of restfulness among his subjects. The stimulus is fear, fear arising from his instinct of self-preservation, fear that, unless his people are well supplied with material and mental food, they will destroy him; in other words, that they will hunt him off his throne. On this fear he forms two managerial or stabilizing bureaucracies · an army to stand behind his will and, by enforcing it, control the hunting spirit of the community; and a church to stand behind the ideal of restfulness and control the mind of man by denying or promising it this ideal. Later, when customs stabilize into rights, a judicial bureaucracy is formed to administer these rights or laws, and, eventually, the modern state evolves with its numerous ministries, offices and departments, all of which should be feminine in nature; that is, fertilized by the king and his councillors, they should produce a state of national passivity in which the dynamic force in life and its static inclination are balanced by law and order.

As governments grow more and more complex, we find that individual rule—kingship, is replaced by a collective sway—proletarianism. Nations are then governed by small crowds of politicians elected to represent their interests. These interests, in a healthy society, are closely connected with the hunting spirit in all its forms, the object of which is not only to preserve individuals and families but to render them contented, that is, to supply them with rest (leisure) as well as labour. Thus, if we examine English political history, we find that formerly Parliamentary representation was largely based on agriculture; each agricultural district, normally, returning as its member its most influential landlord, because, of all men in the district, he was the best suited to express a common opinion in the interests of the staple occupation, the form taken by the hunting spirit in his area.

To-day we find that these political districts or constituencies are very similar to those which existed a hundred and fifty years ago, in spite of the fact that that portion of the dynamic force of life which constitutes the hunting spirit no longer seeks its freedom in ploughing, sowing and reaping, but in casting, tooling and machining. In brief, the form which the hunting spirit to-day takes is industrial and not agricultural production and acquisition. What does this mean? It means that, in theory, representation is no longer based on the interests of the constituencies, but on the *number* of people within them who can be induced to vote. It is theoretically a numerical representation based on brute force and frequently the brute stupidity of *numbers*. It is, consequently, closely related to the brute force theory of traditional warfare. Practically it is, however, a great deal more, for the candidates have to struggle between themselves for election, and are, consequently, driven to every subterfuge in order to acquire power; not for the purpose of fostering national pros-

The Peace which Passeth Understanding

perity but as a weapon to enable them to defeat their opposite numbers.

The question now arises, where does this power reside ? Theoretically it resides in the people, but, as most of these have daily to struggle for their existence, they have little time to accumulate it in its modern form of money. Practically, we find, therefore, that this power is to be sought for among those who, possessing money, are to a greater extent freed from the above struggle. From this we may assume that their hunting spirit has become subservient to their inclination to rest, and, consequently, their power is psychologically antipathetic to the interests of the multitude upon whom virtually they are resting, and on whose passivity the stability of this rest depends. We find, therefore, that, to-day, instead of representing the interests of the nation, our Members of Parliament represent the prejudices of small sections of the nation. These sections are deeply imbued with bureaucratic (traditional) tendencies, consequently their object is to maintain the *status quo* upon which the existence of these prejudices is based. This *status quo* is founded on a fear of change, and here we arrive at that dangerous social condition in which the irresistible force—the hunting spirit, is restricted and tamped by the all but immovable substance—the inertia of the governing classes.

We see, therefore, that to-day representation is ultimately based on fear, fear of a free expression of the hunting spirit, and that, consequently, Members of Parliament are the mere needles and sound-box of the national gramophone, the records of which are prepared by the various contending parties. All of these are controlled by small self-seeking bureaucracies, none of which are more bureaucratic than those obsessed by socialistic and communistic doctrines. In fact, communism is bureaucracy standing on its head, for communism expects a community to live like one family : in theory a beautiful ideal, but in practice an attempt to balance a pyramid upon its apex.

The growth of industry, due to the general use of steam-power during the last century, carried with it a stupendous social revolution. Among civilized nations, manual labour was replaced rapidly by machine work, which, by increasing output, increased wealth and to a high degree liberated the worker from the serfdom of the soil, but only to sell him into bondage in the workshop. In the manufactories he was completely cut off from his natural activities ; the changing phases of nature which once surrounded him in the fields being replaced by a grim monotonous routine which enslaved him to the machines the brain of man had designed. The result of this suppression of his natural instincts by machine-power tamped down his hunting spirit, until, towards the middle of the nineteenth century, a series of social explosions occurred and have never ceased their repercussion. When internal vents could not be found, if we examine the history of this period, we shall find a steady growth of warlike fervour in the nations which had benefited most from industry. From the Crimea onwards, Great Britain is engaged in a series of small wars ; France builds up a great colonial empire, and Germany rapidly grows intoxicated on the dream of world dominion. Though many causes were at work, in my opinion, the leading cause of this activity was the suppression of the hunting instinct in man due to the tamping down of the social revolution created by the general adoption of steam as a motive power.

The social and political recoil of this commercial and warlike fervour, generically may be termed " pacifism." The commercial pacifist dreaded social disturbance as it would affect his personal wealth, and the political pacifist dreaded foreign wars as they would upset the stability of his political prejudices. From this fervour and its recoil developed two great political schools of thought—the war-lovers and the peace-lovers, which in all civilized countries, during the last fifty years, have formed the centrifugal and centripetal forces in politics. One quantity they held in common, namely, their power was based on wealth.

Out of the friction engendered by these two opposite schools, emerged a new political group—the under-dog, the eventual Socialist party. Outwardly its policy is pacific ; but why, since without struggling it cannot survive ? Because, by proclaiming foreign wars evil, it aspires not only to weaken military power and so undermine the stability of domestic peace, but also simultaneously to dam up within the country itself the hunting spirit of the people, which, finding no escape for its activities in foreign wars, will explode into wars of purgation and destroy all traditional government. In other words, the aim of the socialist is to do away with ordered force so that he may employ disorder as a force for his own immediate benefit. In character, socialism is atavistic, for it does not so much attempt to reform as to deform, it does not attempt to progress to a condition in advance of the existing one, but to retrogress to a condition so far behind it that it appears totally different from it in character. Socialism is not creative ; it is imitative, it is a social throw-back. To the socialist the past is far distant, consequently simple and beautiful, for its jagged edges cannot be seen and its form glows pink through the rays of the setting sun of history. Yet, in spite of this predilection for the mythology of Eden, socialism being primitive is intensely human ; consequently, within its barbarous body palpitates a sentient heart. Though impelled to use brute force in order to reinstate the baboon, the socialist dreams of an eventual Paradise, wherein there is neither labour nor competition, and where love, meat and drink are free and the sky is ever blue, and the benches soft to lie upon—a veritable Fragonard picture dreamt of in a glue factory.

As the separation of the two great political parties, the Progressives and the Statists, from the instincts and interests of the people widens, the Socialist, or retrogressive party, grows in strength, and, being the recoil, or enemy of both parties, it compels both to turn from national policy to party salvation. In place of attempting to secure the nation against foreign attack—ethical, economic, or military, both parties attempt to maintain civil tranquillity, not in order to secure prosperity but to secure their own existence, which is based on the common foundation of wealth. To illustrate this I will turn to history.

The Reformation of War

From the year 1588 to 1815, English foreign policy, with few exceptions, was based on the principle of the balance of power, which formed the expression of political brute force against all would-be disturbers of the world's peace. From 1821 to 1864 the introduction and growth of railways takes place. Coincidental with the industrial development which followed is the falling off in the vigour of this policy, until, in 1864, the British Government, headed by Mr. Gladstone, tore up their treaty agreements with Denmark and so permitted Prussia to violate the balance of power in Europe.

The tigress having tasted blood and finding the inhabitants of neighbouring lands succulent meat, two years later rends Austria, and four years later France falls a victim to her lust. Meanwhile England stands still and does nothing. This results in the German Empire becoming the supreme military power in Europe; in fact Germany henceforth is dictator of continental wars. What has really happened? The German hunting spirit has found a vent, and rushing outwards, seeks to secure internal peace by the search after unattackable frontiers. As within the country domestic tranquillity stabilizes, prosperity increases and commerce demands economic frontiers. To be secure, they must be made unattackable, consequently Germany dreams of the command of the seas. She must create a supreme navy to add it to her supreme army. The child begotten of these two monsters, as has always been the case in the past, is world dominion; and for Germany the only obstacle on her road to brigandage is British supremacy at sea.

I cannot here enter into the development of world politics between the years 1871 and 1914, for this is outside the scope of this book. All I intend doing it to summarize the means open to Germany in order to realize her dream. To reduce Great Britain to the position of a second-rate power, three lines of attack could be followed:

(i.) Economic expansion which, by degrees, would destroy the British markets.

The Peace which Passeth Understanding

(ii.) Direct naval attack which, if successful, would place Great Britain at her mercy.

(iii.) Military action on the continent which would enable her to absorb Holland, Belgium, North-Eastern France and the French Colonies, and gain economic control of Austria, the Balkans and the Turkish Empire.

The first was unlikely to prove successful unless guaranteed by supremacy at sea, besides Russia was a rapidly growing menace. The second was most difficult, for, though a great navy could be created, the geographical position of the German naval bases was unpropitious to decisive naval action on traditional lines. Had Germany, in 1900, appreciated the powers of the submarine, she might very easily have won the war *at sea* in 1914. The third was not only the traditional method employed by Germany since 1864 and, consequently, the upmost thought in the German mind, but it offered the greatest possibilities. If France could be annihilated in six or eight weeks then the war would be won, and any obstruction on the part of the British fleet arising later on would at most but present a minor problem, and, as we know to-day, would have been solved by the underwater attack on our overseas trade. The war won, twenty years of Germanic internal prosperity would have followed, which would either have enabled Germany to annihilate the British Empire by economic pressure or to have attacked it successfully by naval action. With the destruction of the British Empire, for its period, the German dream of world dominion would have been realized.

From the opening of the present century until the year 1914, only pretexts of war are to be discovered, for the causes had long since taken root. The nature of the war which followed is not to be sought in these causes but in their effects, and above all in the peace terms which followed the cessation of hostilities. In brief, what were these terms? Not the establishment of a higher prosperity than that which existed before the war, but the destruction of Germany as a civilized power, because Germany had outlawed herself in the eyes of mankind by attempting to gain dominion over the world. In place of reinstating her in a position which economically would have benefited the world, a course which would undoubtedly have been followed had the war originated solely from an economic cause, the signatories of the treaty of Versailles attempted to assassinate her, for had she not sought to steal the very souls of the nations of the world in order to dominate them by her " Kultur " and to enslave them to her will? For such a crime there can be but one fitting punishment—death. Unfortunately for the signatories, however just may have been their indignation, nations of sixty-five million souls cannot be exterminated; further, it is foolish to attempt such an action even on paper, since it is not their bodies which have offended but their spirits. The signatories were, however, acting on well-defined traditional lines. Their own power was based on wealth, consequently they attempted to murder the German nation by cutting off its economic means of existence. By so doing, they inflicted a wound on the body of the world which if unstaunched will bleed this body white.

Whatever may have been the conditions in which the belligerents were labouring during the war, one fact is certain, namely, that on November 11, 1918, they had saved their souls, consequently any succeeding attempt to impair the body of the world was an act of madness, for the world-soul has to inhabit this body. The mistake made was the Armistice itself, for a soul is attacked by a soul, and though the German body had been defeated her soul remained intact, because war was never carried into her country and her spirit purified by terror and the visible signs of complete defeat, namely, military occupation. From this mistake will originate most of the evils of the present age. I will now turn to another aspect of this subject.

The final victory of the Allies, in November, 1918, was so stupendous an event that it is apt to obscure the main issue of over four years of war, which was not the physical defeat of Germany, but the destruction of the world outlook—social,

The Peace which Passeth Understanding

political and military, as it was accepted by all civilized nations before the outbreak of the war. So all-embracing was this cataclysm that, during the years immediately following the cessation of hostilities, no other condition could have been possible save that of a world-wide revolution, the intensity of which can better be gauged from the changes which have taken place in ideas than from the quantity of blood spilt. These changes are still gaining impetus, and, in the vortex which is sucking down old institutions and belching up new ones, the political forces must take their place.

The Great War of 1914-18 was not waged to end war but to maintain the liberties of nations, so that they might continue to struggle one with another and in the process refine their respective natures. A war to end war is an absurdity, just as a peace to end peace is an absurdity; both are the cries of maniacs which end nothing except common-sense. What, however, the Great War did end was the reality of 1914; it dematerialized this condition, which, to-day, stalks the world a giant phantom palsying our minds.

The Devil took Christ into a high mountain and showed to him all the kingdoms of the world, saying : " All this power will I give you if you will fall down and worship me " ; and Christ said . " Get thee behind me, Satan." To-day the Devil of 1914 takes us up the blasted pinnacle of hope left standing by the war, and shows to us the world as it was before the war destroyed it, and he says . " All this splendour and contentedness and wealth will I return to you if you will but fall down and worship me." To this the politician answers : " Thank you very much," and then goes on hammering at Germany and Russia, one a sick and the other a demented nation; the outrage is brutal, and the Devil of 1914 rubs his hands and smiles.

Yet there is still a Christ in this world—the spirit of humanity, which is audibly whispering · " Get thee behind me, Satan . . . we will have none of these past wonders, because they are but phantoms of things dead, they are soulless and void of salvation."

The world of 1914 has been purified by fire; to-day this world is a better world than it ever was before, for it has vanquished the greatest of all evils—the spiritual enchainment of liberty. Certainly it is a poorer world, yet " Blessed be ye poor," for poverty means struggle, and struggle means self-sacrifice, and self-sacrifice means progress; the stepping forward on our dead-selves to better things, and progress, that is rational thought, is the road to Paradise.

The outstanding result of the Great War was a moral revolution. The new spirit, blind as it yet is, like a second Samson has seized the pillars of the temple of traditions, and prejudices and interests have been scattered to the ground. Those who are engulfed in this cataclysm see nothing but evil, but those who stand apart from it see nothing but good.

Much debris has fallen in Russia and many have been entombed, because, of all civilized nations, Russia was the most traditionally unprogressive and ignorant, and the ignorant always suffer most. In Russia the revolution destroyed 1914 so that it might create a better nation; in England the revolution set out to reform 1914, and the progress already made is so stupendous that, to most people, it is invisible, yet the Russian revolution has been but a miasmal zephyr compared to the invigorating hurricane which has swept the British Empire from end to end.

Say you, that discontent stalks broadly through the daylight? Then, answer I yet again, discontent is the quintessence of mental youth, it is the surest sign of health since it is the visible sign of activity. Anarchy more often than not is terrible, yet there is something worse—communism, or the slow asphyxiation of the human soul by a creeping, drivelling idiocy. Anarchy is, after all, nothing but brutal healthfulness; we do not want anarchy, but of all things precious is the force which creates it, and it is this force, to-day dancing drunkenly, which we must divert towards the reconstruction of the world.

I cannot forbear quoting one small example of this liberty abroad. We are told by the moralists of 1914 that England is a land of corruption and that virtue has passed along her way. We are told that never were the divorce courts so full and that,

The Peace which Passeth Understanding

consequently, never have morals been so low. What sophistry! I cannot vouch for the numbers of the unhappily married, but I can vouch for this, that unhappiness is not a virtue, that happiness is, and that those who cannot find happiness in wedlock show not only common-sense but virtue in seeking divorce, for marriage was instituted for man and not man for marriage. So also with each of the great changes, the seeking of liberation from 1914 ideals is, by the traditional school of thought, classed as a vice, simply because liberty will not and cannot stand still ; for if it were able to do so it would cease to be liberty, and instead would be slavery, nothing more and nothing less.

Socialism, which has been one of the great forces since 1848, has also divorced many of its pre-war preposterous traditions ; it too has been refined by war ; the lanky good has filled out and has become much more human in form, while the retrograde bad has become still more deformed, if only by comparison. It is becoming idiotic, and idiotic through dotage, which is a good sign, as this shows that it is nearing its end.

Except in Russia, socialism has, to a very considerable extent, lost its pre-war shortsightedness. Then there was much talk of maximum and minimum incomes, but since, during the war, so many socialists remained at home and amassed fortunes, this topic of conversation has been quietly dropped. The present trouble is that the bad in the old socialism is still in a state of decomposition ; consequently, it stinks, but this should not frighten us, for again it is a good sign, for a decomposing body is one which, if given fresh air above ground, will rapidly fall to dust.

One of the great backwashes of the Great War was the rapid spread of communistic theories and action. Brotherly love was the natural recoil of the horrors of traditional slaughter. For over four years men had been cutting each other's throats ; consequently, once this madness was over, the pendulum of life swung in the opposite direction, and universal kissing, a most disgusting operation, was proclaimed the goal of all progress.

Out of Russian military chaos and bureaucratic corruption stealthily crept revolution, which, in March, 1917, gathered speed as the railways broke down. It opened almost like a school rag. On March 16, one soldier said to General Knox :* " We have suffered 300 years of slavery, you cannot grudge us a single week of holiday." Then discipline gave way In June, Kerenski calls upon the army, " fortified by the strength and spirit of the Revolution, to take the offensive." The men in some units say : " We will attack, but if we fail, we will kill the Corps Staff," while others pin up on their barrack doors: " Handshaking is abolished in hot weather." Lenin issues an order to his own party which ends . " I demand, I beg, I hope that this order will be carried out," and General Knox adds · " Damned ass ! "

All sense of humour having been lost, madness supervenes, physical and material disorder create mental and moral disorder —all go mad.

> " The thieves of Moscow had a meeting outside the town, and the Chief of Police showed his human sympathy by attending It is said that a unanimous resolution was passed to refrain from stealing for two days ' in honour of the sun of freedom ! '
>
> " Similarly the deserters met in a conference at Odessa, and the Commander-in-Chief was received with acclamation !
>
> " In Petrograd, children have been seen parading with banners inscribed : ' Down with parental yoke ! ' "

Lastly, out of madness howls the beast ; a wolfish spirit of lust and cruelty sweeps over the maniacs.

At Kalusz " eye-witnesses related that forty to fifty men in turn outraged old women of seventy. . . . The retiring Germans bombarded the town, but the noise of the bombardment was literally drowned by the cries of women. . . . Soldiers stripped little girls naked . . . and one after another, there on the street, violated the children and then cut them to pieces."

Thus do we see emerge, from the green leaves of the " little holiday," the red slug of Bolshevism, which has slimed Russia with a bestiality which puts to blush the shame of Sodom and Gomorrah ; once the cities of the plain, but, in 1917, rearisen more monstrous still as Moscow and Petrograd.

* The British Military Attaché at Petrograd The following quotations are taken from his book, " With the Russian Army, 1914-1917."

The Peace which Passeth Understanding

We rub our eyes and can but mutter with Isaiah : " We grope for the wall like the blind, and we grope as if we had no eyes ; we stumble at noonday as in the night ; we are in desolate places as dead men." Yet this orgy of blood was but the curtain-raiser to a still more demented scene, for the madness of anarchy was about to be replaced by the idiocy of communism, which, in 1918 and 1919, swept over the world like a leprous plague.

First, I will examine economic communism—the theory held by Lenin ; and secondly, ethical communism—the theory held by President Wilson.

The economic communist says : Huge money capitals are an evil and are a result of competition. If every man possesses a million pounds the world is no better off than if every man possessed one penny. Lenin then says : But why should he possess a penny ; if you agree to a penny, why not to twopence, a shilling and eventually back to the million ? I shall, therefore, destroy all capital, so that, as no one will be *allowed* to possess capital, all forced competition will disappear.

The ethical communist says : Huge mental capitals are an evil and are the result of competing minds. If every man possesses high ability the world is no better off than if every man possessed a low ability. What does President Wilson say ? He says, somewhat vaguely, that every nation has a right of self-determination, or, in other words, that a highly cultured nation is of no greater value to humanity than one without any culture at all, *ergo*, culture, or mental and moral capital, should be abolished.

Darwin, some sixty years ago, did his utmost to prove that because of competition (the struggle for existence) from the ape evolved the man. If he is right, then lack of competition will mean that from man will devolve the ape. Is he right ? I, for one, do not know, but I know this : that in this world there is no equality ; in place there is incessant variety ; consequently, to talk of no one nation being allowed (which presupposes some omnipotent power) to do this or that is as absurd as the search after the philosopher's stone. Lenin has searched for it, and the result has been called " a bloody baboonery." President Wilson has searched for it, and the results up to date are none too encouraging.

The fourteen points and the League of Nations ruined the peace treaty, because they were based on sublime nonsense and not on common-sense, which includes human nature. The terms of the Armistice based on the fourteen points proclaimed the Brotherhood of Man, and were proffered to the Germans when friend and foe, the eternal brothers, were still gazing at each other through a haze of blood which proved the unreality of this amiable dream. The Germans, ever foolish in diplomacy, swallowed the fourteen points hook and all. The Allies thereupon repudiated the fourteen points and drove the gaff of the Treaty of Versailles through the German skin. "The German commentators," says Mr. Keynes, "had little difficulty in showing that the draft Treaty constituted a breach of engagements and of international morality comparable with their own offences in the invasion of Belgium."* Very true, but just as, in 1914, the Germans tore up their treaty because self-preservation demanded that their armies must advance through Belgium, so, in 1919, the Allies tore up their Armistice Terms because instinctively they felt that Germany had not as yet felt the spiritual smart of defeat and must do so. The blunder was the Armistice, the black day in European history. The fourteen points were all kisses; life is not made up of kisses alone, and if it were the world would be a very dull place to live in. This every cinema play reveals, for the hero who kisses has always got a gun in his pocket for the other kisser, the villain. The terms of the Armistice were not true to human nature, the cinema generally is. If you are out to kiss make sure you have a revolver, for kisses and revolvers are near related to the eternal forces in life —love and fear. President Wilson was all love, the Allies were all fear, and until these two wed, Europe will continue in a turmoil.

Under the influence of the fear of Germany in the future, the Allies attempted to reconstruct Europe on such lines that Germany would for years to come be rendered impotent. To

* "The Economic Consequences of the Peace," J. M. Keynes, C.B., p. 59.

The Peace which Passeth Understanding

accomplish this they employed the tool of self-determination, not because they believed in kisses, but because, for their purpose, they found it possessed a very sharp edge.

I cannot here enter into the ramifications of this reconstruction, which mediævalized a great part of Europe, splitting up nations according to weight of ignorant *numbers* irrespective of their culture and fitness for independence and sovereignty. Instead, I intend examining four great national influences—British, French, German and Slavonic, and show that from them, in all probability, will be engendered the next great European war.

In order to understand future international war tendencies, the question of security of frontiers must never be lost sight of. Frontiers in nature are not only military but also economic and sometimes ethical. In 1914, Germany's military might was based on her economic security, consequently, if Germany could, by military force, extend her economic frontiers to the sea coasts of other nations it would have endowed her with a world supremacy, for then, at will, she could either have attacked other nations militarily or forced them to economic surrender.

The British Empire stood in the way, and at the end of the war, though our Imperial resources had been bled white, the economic frontiers of the Empire remained intact. The French frontiers, which, in nature, were military, were, in 1914, overrun for the fourth time in a hundred years; consequently, once the Armistice was concluded, the first and all-important problem which confronted France was her future frontier security. Physically, Germany could not be erased from the map of Europe, but economically she could be ruined, and the instrument to accomplish her destruction was President Wilson's principle of self-determination, and, as the majority of effaced nations were of Slav blood, the economic ruin of Germany could only be accomplished by the resurrection and creation of moribund and effete Slavonic States, such as the Baltic States, Poland, Czecho-Slovakia and Jugo-Slavia.

This breaking up of German economic prosperity, as well as the general Balkanization of large tracts of Europe, was a direct blow against British trade. Depending on her overseas commerce and not being self-supporting, British policy demands a prosperous and progressive Europe which carries with it military strength. France, being a self-supporting country, demands military weakness on the part of the rest of Europe, and, consequently, economic poverty, which can best be guaranteed by social disorder. Hence the present wrangle between Great Britain and France.

The nature of this problem is, however, a more complex one than at first meets the eye. The Slavonic races are of a low culture and possess an oriental temperament. In Russia they have proved themselves quite unfit to govern. Their main power, however, is to be looked for in the probable enormous increase in their population during the next two generations. What does this mean? It means either internal disorder or foreign invasion in order to guarantee domestic tranquillity. Out of this guarantee will once again evolve that search after an unattackable frontier, which carries with it the idea of world dominion. For the time being Germany may attempt to exploit Russia, but sooner or later the hunting spirit in Russia will seek a vent, and the lines of least resistance run westwards to the Baltic, the North Sea, the Atlantic and the Mediterranean. For self-preservation the nations of Europe will coalesce against the Slav, and the most probable alliance, in order to maintain the balance of power, is that of Germany, France and Great Britain. Should war break out, Germany will receive the first shock, and if she militarily is weak France and Great Britain will have to bear the brunt of the contest. We see, therefore, that a weak Germany is but an ephemeral advantage to France, as well as being a cause of friction between France and England. The date of this next great war, in my opinion, will depend on the revival of Russia, and it is almost certain to be preceded by wars between the new " Balkan " states created by the Treaty of Versailles.

Since the ratification of this treaty, Europe has been faced by two problems—how to enforce its terms and how to wriggle out of enforcing them. The first problem is the French problem

The Peace which Passeth Understanding

and the second the British. While these problems were being wrangled over, the United States of America, scared by a phantom war with Japan and engaged on an enormous naval expansion of an obsolescent type of warship, called together a disarmament conference at Washington, the aim of which appears to have been, not to guarantee peace but to manœuvre into a good position for the next war. If the British Alliance with Japan could be severed, Japanese naval strength could be weakened ; if European naval power could be reduced, American economic prosperity could be better guaranteed.

England, with an exceptional lack of foresight, fell into the economic trap. She severed her alliance with Japan, which, in the future, might well prove a decisive requirement in a war against Russia, and, smarting from her recent trade losses, sang chorus to the United States' incantation against the submarine. France played her part with marked astuteness ; what apparently she wanted was supremacy of the air, for, though her aircraft are, at any time in the near future, unlikely to be able to attack America, with a supremely powerful air force she can enforce her policy on two thirds of Europe. She made a great fuss over the capital ship, with her tongue well in her cheek ; she made a greater fuss over the submarine, so great that the aeroplane remained undiscussed. The United States won the rubber, but France won on points and Great Britain was handed the baby.

Once again at Genoa, in the spring of 1922, the wrangle is reopened. The United States, having gained their point at Washington, very wisely take no part in the hubbub. The wrangle is purely an economic one. The problem is how to make plus and minus agree, plus being the British policy and minus the French. But they cannot possibly agree ; then one of the two will have to be abandoned, and the point now arises which ?

If a pugilist has an argument with a wealthy shopkeeper, should the point under dispute lead to blows, which of the two will win ? The answer is self-evident—the prize-fighter. To-day England possesses a smaller army than she did in 1914, a one-power navy, and an air force of thirty-five squadrons. France possesses a stronger army than she did before the war, a strong navy, and she is aiming at an air force of 220 squadrons. In the British Army there are four battalions of tanks and in the French between thirty and forty. I will now leave it to the reader to decide who is the shopkeeper and who the pugilist?

I do not for a moment accuse France of any wish to go to war with England, for the French are at heart a peace-loving nation and the French love peace so ardently that they have every intention of safeguarding themselves against war. But I cannot obscure from my mind the fact that as a pugilist can always threaten, that is morally attack, a shopkeeper, British diplomacy must suffer unless it is backed by military force.

Now that I have shown that the idea of a war to end war is pure bunkum, and that Europe to-day is seething with warlike problems, I intend to return to the question of political reform, for without this we, as a nation, shall never succeed in getting a policy, and, unless we have a policy, our fighting forces, upon which ultimately the security of our prosperity depends, will be comparable to a watch without a mainspring.

If the deductions I have now made in this Chapter are in any way correct, then it would appear that the last war, in place of being a war which will end war, will, like most other wars which have preceded it, merely have reaped one crop of contentions and simultaneously sown another. The peace which followed it has left Europe split up into truculent factions with a strong Slavonic bent, for as a few hundred years ago the Turks were outside the gates of Vienna so are the Slavs there to-day. That the League of Nations can maintain any semblance of peace between these resuscitated nations is improbable, seeing that this league possesses no political power. Some other solution must be sought, and one which is not solely concerned with preventing the decadence of peace. This solution, I believe, will be discovered in a new political outlook which will aim at the creation of spiritually healthy nations in open and equitable competition, nations which understand the meaning of peace and the power of war to enforce this meaning.

The Peace which Passeth Understanding

I have already shown that the present position of political election has outgrown its original utility and is fast becoming moribund. Further back, I described how the primitive State possessed a threefold nature in order to secure the activities and instincts of its people. To enable the people to thrive economically, the soldier protected them and enforced order, the judicature formulated laws in accordance with the will of the most able, and the Church combined all classes in a spiritual whole by endowing all with a common origin and a common end ; Adam was the primal father and heaven or hell the final goal of both rich and poor.

To-day this triple state does not exist, for government has been swallowed up by economics ; it has in fact infringed the rights of the individual and suppressed the hunting spirit, hence many troubles. Religion has lost its sting, and with the weakening of the fears of hell the blessings of heaven have become counterfeit celestial coin. Once human life was looked upon as an analogy ; to-day it is, for the masses, but a cog in a tyrannical machine. What we must reinstate is free work guaranteed by common rights, impelled forward by the liberty of labour and secured by military force. For a moment, I will consider the nature of life, which to-day is obscured under a mass of absurd idealism.

Life is a dynamic force, it is the swinging pendulum. It cannot be regulated by a fixed idea or system. No definite social architecture can be designed to meet its needs, for it is ever growing and changing its shape. Spiritually, man's sense of dignity has evolved out of his instinct of self-distinction, that instinct which impels him to excel others so that he may morally as well as physically secure himself against their competition.

From this instinct is developed pride of work, which distinguished the guilds of the Middle Ages, but which to-day has been extinguished by *quantity* production. In this age of steam-craft the worker has become slave to the engine, at most he has become but a part of the machine; consequently, his whole outlook is mechanical; not only does he see himself as a cog but the whole world as a complex series of cogs slowly grinding each other to pieces. With a loss in the love of work, he has lost his freedom.

When religion was a living, all-penetrating force, the worker beheld himself as a living part of a great dynamic scheme in which all toil was rounded off by a peace beyond understanding; to-day he appears to himself but a fragment of animated matter. Then he looks upon those who rule him, and he finds that their lives do not coincide with his life, there is a difference. He does not understand that this difference is due to leisure (love), which enables those who enjoy it to free themselves from the mechanism of toil by exercising liberty in the choice of pleasures. In place, he merely sees the difference, which, obsessed as he is by the machine his master, appears to him to be mechanical in character. Some cogs are better lubricated than others; here, then, is the source of the difference; there are two classes of cogs—the rich and the poor; destroy this distinction and the difference will be made good. How can it be destroyed? By abolishing the privileges of property, hence the tragedy of Russia.

This absurd mechanical outlook on life is the result of the *quantity* theory which is the basis of the modern capitalist system The capitalist is also the materialist, and Quantity is his god. As in military organization, quantity or numbers, as I have shown, forms the pivot of the traditional theory of war, so in economics and finance does quantity form the pivot of the present traditional theory of prosperity. To the capitalist labour is but a commodity; once man himself in the form of a slave was looked upon as a chattel, a thing to be bought and sold; now it is his ability to work which is bartered. But man is not a commodity, neither is his ability to work a commodity; it is a living force which cannot be measured with pint pot or by foot rule. Man has a right to his activities; at least he has a right to protect them, also has he a right to his leisure. The worker feels this, but he cannot express it as long as he is obsessed by the machine. Therefore, if a solution is to be sought, he must be brought to master the machine so that he may regulate his leisure and regain his lost freedom.

The Peace which Passeth Understanding

True leisure is but the free enjoyment of the hunting spirit; it is, therefore, a vent for those forces which, if suppressed, seek exercise in discontent and war. Leisure is, consequently, the foundation of domestic peace. To obtain leisure, the worker must become an active force in place of a passive working tool. In his work he must be brought to find a similar interest he normally finds in his home. Interest is the analogy of success and failure, a series of expectant spasms of joy and sorrow. To gain this interest the worker must control his work so that the exercise of his ability may replace the mere exercise of his muscles. Then will his prosperity depend not so much on his work as on his skill—skill is but another name for self-distinction—and through this instinct will he regain his soul and learn that the problems of life are neither problems of quantity or numbers, but are dynamic problems common to all. Also will he find that they can only be attained by an integration of those living forces which together create freedom for the common good.

It is difficult to explain in a few words the full meaning of this spirituality, which has nothing to do with prayers and hymn singing, but everything with the free exercise of the hunting spirit in man. Sufficient, I hope, has been written to enable the reader to realize that, if society is to be freed from its present traditions, the existing political systems of all civilized nations will have to undergo a drastic change.

Before the steam epoch, government was mainly concerned in correlating man and the external world. To-day the political outlook is pseudo-economic, the interests of the nation having been replaced by the prejudices of the ruling party. Socialization is not only no cure but an actual accentuation of disease, as it must lead to a purely mechanical political outlook. Nationalization is the worst of all forms of government, because economics express the hunting spirit and are, consequently, the domain of the individual. The rights which underlie them, the canalization of the human instincts and the economical utilization of their recoil, as well as the general security of the nation, these and these only are the true purposes of politics.

The Reformation of War

How this system of politics should be organized is too extensive a subject to discuss here. All I can say is that the model to follow is the body of man. Man's object is to live; in other words, his object is economic and ethical in nature. The hidden forces which impel man to maintain it are his instincts, to protect it his cunning and strength, and when man meets man in peaceful competition from their common purposes are rights evolved. So also with the body social. In peace its forces must be canalized so that they may produce contentment, and organized so that they may be secured against extinction.

Until the present political quantity idea is replaced by an idea which expresses a true relativity between the human energies, it will be most difficult to evolve from the traditional theory of warfare the theory which in this book I have called the moral attack. We dare not stand still. It is sheer folly to sit down monk-like and copy out, however carefully, past systems, for if the world is ever to be delivered from the horrors of war then the road which must be followed is the track which leads towards the angel and not towards the ape. I believe that wars are inevitable, but I also believe that to copy the last war is criminal, and that salvation from destruction is to be found in searching; then, quite possibly, a day will dawn when wars will be decided upon a chess-board. Finally I would ask the reader to ponder these last words. The goal of humanity is far distant; in a thousand years this present age of ours will be looked upon as a barbarous epoch, our politics will be considered fantastic, our military art brutal and our social troubles rather petty if not comic affairs. The road towards this goal runs along an upward rise. The way is dark and infested with phantoms: the devils of the past, the angels of the future. Directly angels are compelled to our will they shrivel into demoniacal forms and beckon us to halt and in our hearts whisper strange and enticing words. Heed them not, for righteousness is attainable only by the strong, the fearless and the virile—there is no short cut to Paradise.

EPILOGUE

PEACE

IT may be thought, after reading this book, or even after having merely glanced through it, that I, its writer, intoxicated on strong ale, have wished to cry with Pistol: "Why, then the world's mine oyster, which I with sword will open;" and the reader, if in disposition he be contrary to war, may perhaps answer with Falstaff: "Reason, you rogue, reason: thinkest thou, I'll endanger my soul gratis? At a word hang no more about me; I am no gibbet for you." Consequently, I must now rest my pen, but, before doing so, will, in this epilogue, once again inform the reader that my object has been not to hasten the advent of the next great war but to examine its nature. To show that without understanding the causes of war we can never hope for stability of peace; to show that, as long as peacefulness is not healthy and clean, war, in one form or another, is a very necessary cleanser and social tonic, and ultimately that peace and war are, in fact, the halves of one diameter, the circumference of which is the circle of existence.

We may or may not love war, or even a remembrance of war or a suggestion of its recurrence, and, whether we human beings be of divine origin or but a squared stone in the evolutionary temple of the Great Architect, all our instincts so far go to prove that we are animals; some of us gentle, others ferocious, and that those of carnivorous taste live on those who browse the tender herbs of life. We are slaves of a hunting spirit, which we may quell but cannot slay.

Not understanding this, and not understanding what peace and war really mean, we are subject to innumerable phantasies, hallucinations which lead us astray, and never more so than after some great awakening, when the nerves are yet on edge, as they are to-day, since the world is still suffering from " shell shock " It yearns for peace, but it is too irritable to understand that peace requires quietude.

The great danger is that this irritability may consolidate into a chronic social disease—crowd rule ; a rule without objective, or perhaps with a mixture of incompatible objectives, such as—liberty, equality and fraternity, all blurred into a hideous contradiction. Nationality has become self-determination. To determine what ? Has the crowd ever determined anything save chaos and anarchy ? Determine their material existence, say you ? But surely determination cannot be guaranteed merely by stuffing slips of paper into a ballot-box, for it requires strength and right to enforce and maintain its limits. The desire of the populace, be it well remembered, is similar to the love of Proteus · " Which, like a waxen image 'gainst a fire, bears no impression of the thing it was." The slightest friction melts and disfigures it, it is amorphous and unstable.

Peace built on mob rule and desire is but a cloud castle which is brought low in showers of blood on the first rumble of war. The crowd, the oldest of gatherings, is still incomprehensible to itself, it cannot learn. The first crowd was Adam and Eve, and the fall was not the result of some stupendous crime, some fearful cataclysm, but of a thing good to eat—an apple. Nearly every social fall since has found its origin in a similar quest—the obtaining of food. The next two members of human society were—a rather weak-charactered agriculturist and a blood-thirsty huntsman, the eternal opposites ; and the squabble was once again over food—the allegory is, therefore, correct to life.

Like Abel, the normal citizen rightly desires peace, and though for the sake of personal distinction, the soldier, during peace time, proclaims his love for war, most soldiers when it comes to ·

> " The groan, the roll in dust, the all-white eye
> Turned back within its socket . . ."

Epilogue

have learnt to sympathize with the boy in King Henry V. who exclaimed: "Would I were in an ale-house in London! I would give all my fame for a pot of ale, and safety." So also does the soldier love peace, and never more so than when the wrack and ruin of war surround him, for peace is his normal state of healthy and unhealthy life, and, being normal, neither he nor his black-coated brother understands the curative properties of war. Instead they seek balsams from mad chemists who, while searching for strange herbs, in their progress scatter the thistledown of war in their fields, and returning, wonder why the seeds of war have destroyed their money-making crops.

HONOUR

There is only one balsam which can make peace worth living —honour, which is righteousness. There are sublimer ideals than mere peacefulness, and honour is one of these. Peace without honour is degradation, and as a noble woman safeguards her honour, and will even sacrifice her life to maintain it in order to keep the family clean, and as a man will give his life to protect her and her children, so will an upright nation, because of its honour, not only protect but sacrifice itself for a righteous cause. All may be lost save honour, for without honour mankind ceases to be human.

It is the family spirit which is the predominant instinct in peace and war; and when the nation is engulfed in woe, in discord and unrighteousness, when righteous men can with Gonzalo, that honest old counsellor, say: "All torment, trouble, wonder and amazement inhabits here," then it is honour which is the "heavenly power" which will guide us "out of this fearful country!" Honour is the essence of that fellowship which Henry V. acclaims when he cries:

> "That he which hath no stomach to this fight,
> Let him depart, his passport shall be made,
> And crowns of convoy put into his purse:
> We would not die in that man's company
> That fears his fellowship to die with us."

Honour includes esteem, respect, integrity and scorn of meanness, and in a free and honourable nation every member of it, however poor, has a citizen's right to be treated as an honourable man. To despise a man because his calling does not coincide with our own is a dishonourable act not only to the individual but to the State itself.

The nation which depends for the security of its honour on some international police force has become but a kept-woman among nations. There is only one guardian of honour—a virile arm backed by a virile brain. Again, a State which is not prepared to defend its honour by a righteous war, and depends on the benevolence of others to guarantee its existence when its life is threatened, is but a paralytic living in an almshouse; it has scarcely the right to live, for it lacks the might to thrive.

WAR

If honour be worth safeguarding, war sooner or later becomes inevitable, for, in this world, there are always to be found dishonourable men, and if war does not range a nation against these, then must vice live triumphant. It is with this uncontradictable quality in human nature set clear before him which impelled Ruskin to write in his " Crown of Wild Olives " :

> " I found that all great nations learned their truth of word, and strength of thought, in war; that they were nourished in war, and wasted by peace; taught by war, and betrayed by peace: in a word, that they were born in war, and expired in peace.
>
> " The habit of living light-heartedly, in daily presence of Death, always has had, and must have, a tendency to the making and testing of honest men.
>
> " War in which the natural instincts of self-defence are sanctified by the nobleness of the institutions, and purity of the households, which they are appointed to defend: to such war as this all men are born; in such war as this any man may happily die; and forth from such war as this have arisen, throughout the extent of past ages, all the highest sanctities and virtues of humanity."[1]

In order to protect our homes and our institutions we must not only protect our army and look upon it as our shield against adversity, but we must determine whether the shield we have is

Epilogue

worthy to protect us. In this book I have examined the possibilities of future warfare in order to lead up to this conclusion. I feel that I have written enough to enable any intelligent citizen, after he has studied what I have said, to turn to the army he is paying for in order to maintain the peace which he enjoys and to say : " Thou art, or thou art not, found wanting." If the former, then it is he who can effect the change and not the soldier, who is but an instrument directed by the policy which the civilian creates.

To-day, though we have but emerged from the greatest war in history, never has England been more in need of a reliable army, not only to defend her gates but to defend her hearths, to maintain the policy chosen by her people against the wanton desires of diseased fanatics—word-mongers, corner-boys of literature and " Trafalgar-squared " crowds. To create or change a policy is neither the right nor the duty of the soldier, for the sword is the instrument of policy and not its fashioner. Unfortunately for us, sedition gropes about the world, and as Launce said to his dog : " O ! 'tis a foul thing when a cur cannot keep himself in all companies ; " so have we, for a space, to live in evil-smelling surroundings. But only for a space, for the World Spirit is abroad, he never rests ; sometimes he moves like a shadow, sometimes with the stride of a giant—ever are his footsteps measuring the earth. To each nation he is their national spirit, and to us that spiritual voice which the greatest of Englishmen still renders audible to all and resonant, even thunderous, to many in the words of Philip the Bastard :

> " O ' let us pay the time but needful woe
> Since it hath been beforehand with our griefs.
> This England never did, nor never shall,
> Lie at the proud foot of a conqueror,
> But when it first did help to wound itself.
> Now these her princes are come home again,
> Come the three corners of the world in arms,
> And we shall shock them. Nought shall make us rue,
> If England to itself do rest but true."

Herein is the " Reveille " of the English race, and the " Last Post " over her enemies !

VALE

APPENDIX

The Procedure of the Infantry Attack. A Synthesis from a Psychological Standpoint. R.U.S.I. Journal, January, 1914.

Training Soldiers for War. Book, October, 1914.

The Tactics of Penetration. A Counterblast to German Numerical Superiority. R.U.S.I. Journal, November, 1914.

The Principles of War with Reference to the Campaigns of 1914–1915. R.U.S.I. Journal, February, 1916.

The Training of the New Army, 1803–1805. R.U.S.I. Journal, November, 1916.

Instructions for the Training of the Tank Corps in France. Pamphlet, December, 1917.

Infantry and Tank Co-operation and Training. Pamphlet, March, 1918.

The Principles of War with Reference to the Campaigns of 1914-1917. Pamphlet, March, 1918.

The Influence of Tanks on Military Operations. The Ministry of Munitions Journal, December, 1918.

Tanks in the Great War. Book, February, 1920.

The Development of Sea Warfare on Land and its Influence on Future Naval Operations. R.U.S.I. Journal, May, 1920.

The Application of Recent Developments in Mechanics and other Scientific Knowledge to Preparation and Training for Future Wars on Land. R.U.S.I. Gold Medal (Military) Prize Essay for 1919. R.U.S.I. Journal, May, 1920.

The Influence of Tanks on Cavalry Tactics. A Study in the Evolution of Mobility in War. Cavalry Journal, March, July and October, 1920.

The Foundations of the Science of War. Army Quarterly, October, 1920.

Moral, Instruction and Leadership. R.U.S.I. Journal, November, 1920.

The Introduction of Mechanical Warfare on Land and its Possibilities in the Near Future. The Royal Engineer Journal, January, 1921.

The Tank—Ten Little Pictures. Royal Military College Magazine and Record, January, 1921.

The Secrets of Napoleon. The National Review, May, 1921.

The Evolution of Mechanical Warfare. Pamphlet, July, 1921.

Tanks in Future Warfare. The Nineteenth Century and After, July, 1921.

The Purpose and Nature of a Fleet. The Nineteenth Century and After, October, 1921.

The Tank—Ten Possibilities. Royal Military College Magazine and Record, January, 1922.

Problems of Mechanical Warfare. Army Quarterly, January, 1922.

What Changes are Suggested in Naval Construction and Tactics as a Result of (a) The Experiences of the War ? (b) The Development of Submarine and Aerial Warfare in the Future ? R.U.S.I. First Naval Prize Essay for 1920. The Naval Review, February, 1922.

Economic Movement. The Civil and Military Possibilities of Roadless Traction in the Near Future. Pamphlet, September, 1922.

The Influence of Aircraft on Imperial Defence. The Naval Review, February, 1923.

Appendix

ARTICLES PRIVATELY PRINTED

Infantry and Tank Battle Formations.
Man's Place in Battle.
The Evolution of Mechanics in War.
The Influence of Petrol on Land Operations.
The Development of Gas and its Influence on Tank Warfare.
Naval Strategy and Tactics Applied to Land Warfare.
The Secret of Victory.
The Scottish War Cart and Zisca's Wagenburg.
Bloodless Means of Quelling Civil Disturbances.
Road Capacity and Cross-Country Traction.
Mechanical Warfare on Land and Sea.
Chinese Use of War Carts.
The Mechanical Policeman.
Strategical Paralysis as the Objective in the Decisive Attack.

BIBLIOLIFE

Old Books Deserve a New Life
www.bibliolife.com

Did you know that you can get most of our titles in our trademark **EasyScript**™ print format? **EasyScript**™ provides readers with a larger than average typeface, for a reading experience that's easier on the eyes.

Did you know that we have an ever-growing collection of books in many languages?

Order online:
www.bibliolife.com/store

Or to exclusively browse our **EasyScript**™ collection:
www.bibliogrande.com

At BiblioLife, we aim to make knowledge more accessible by making thousands of titles available to you – quickly and affordably.

Contact us:
BiblioLife
PO Box 21206
Charleston, SC 29413